Modern Theories of Politics

Modern Theories of Politics

Evangelia Sembou

Peter Lang Oxford

Peter Lang Ltd
International Academic Publishers
52 St Giles, Oxford, OX1 3LU
United Kingdom

www.peterlang.com

A catalogue record for this book is available from the British Library

ISBN 978-1-906165-45-1

Contents

Introduction

This book is based on a series of lectures on political theory I delivered in the Department for Continuing Education at the University of Oxford in the winter of 2003 and the autumn of 2004. Its aim is to introduce the reader to the main ideas and arguments of the major political thinkers of modernity; these are Hobbes, Locke, Bentham, J. S. Mill, Rousseau, Burke, Hegel and Marx. It starts from the assumption that the best way to acquaint oneself with the ideas of a thinker is to read the work in which they are set forth. For this reason each chapter concentrates on the main writings of a single thinker and discusses in detail the views propounded therein. The book, as indeed the lectures from which it originated, is directed towards an audience that approaches the writings of the eight political philosophers for the first time. So no previous knowledge of political philosophy is presupposed. The purpose of the book is to serve as a guide to some of the most important writings on political philosophy of modern times. There are some points that I wish to make.

Firstly, the book is *not* an *history* of political thought. Therefore, the eight thinkers are not discussed in chronological order. Jean-Jacques Rousseau lived and was writing before Jeremy Bentham and John Stuart Mill. Edmund Burke lived and wrote before John Stuart Mill. John Stuart Mill and Karl Marx were contemporaries and wrote in the same period; Mill's *Principles of Political Economy* and Marx's *Communist Manifesto* were both published in 1848. Given that the approach is not historical, I do not examine the contextual background. It is certainly the case that a political theory emerges within a definite political context; that is, it is a response to a given political situation. However, an enduring political theory makes use of concepts and develops an argument that make it relevant to other situations and contexts. For instance, J. S. Mill's arguments in *On Liberty* are as relevant today as they were in 1859. The book is about modern political *theory*. Regarding English political theory,

Hobbes and Locke are exponents of social contract theory, while Bentham and J. S. Mill are representatives of utilitarianism. Rousseau was a radical democrat; although his political philosophy rests on a social contract argument, his assumptions are different from those of Hobbes and Locke – specifically, he dismisses the individualistic and rationalistic presuppositions of Hobbes's and Locke's political philosophies, while his views are close to those of classical Greek political philosophy. Burke was a conservative thinker; he was opposed to political radicalism, favouring gradual change instead; he was critical of both rationalism and abstraction in political theorizing; and he rejected the idea of 'natural rights' – for him, rights make sense only within the context of political society. Hegel disliked the liberal idea of a minimal state, a mere arbitrator between individual interests; like ancient Greek political philosophers, he believed that the state had a more substantial role; for Hegel, the liberal conception of the state corresponds to what he sees as civil society; for him, civil society is subsumed within a more comprehensive whole, namely, the state; similarly, for Hegel, human beings are essentially social beings and, like Aristotle, he believed that humans could not exist independently of the state. Marx's thought developed from idealist Hegelianism to humanist communism and then to scientific communism.

Secondly, it is important to notice that several of the thinkers discussed in this book refer to the views of the others in their writings and develop their argument in contradistinction to that of the others. For example, Rousseau refers to Hobbes in his *Discourse on Inequality*, Hegel challenges Rousseau's idea of the 'general will' in the *Phenomenology of Spirit* and Marx criticizes Hegel's political philosophy in *Critique of Hegel's Philosophy of Right*.

Thirdly, while in some cases it has been possible to provide an exposition of a thinker's political ideas by focusing on a single text – as, for instance, in the cases of Hobbes, Locke, Burke and Hegel –, in other cases it has been necessary to look at more than one texts – as, for example, in the cases of Rousseau and Mill. Providing an introduction to the political thought of Bentham and Marx proved to be a demanding task, given the great amount of works both of the aforesaid thinkers produced; for this reason I used a single-volume collection of their writings. That said, I do not claim that my exposition of a thinker's political thought is always exhaustive; my aim has in all cases been to provide a short introduction to a thinker's political ideas, not to discuss each single work of a thinker. Thus, I do not examine Bentham's *A Fragment on Government* (1776) and Mill's *Considerations on Representative Government* (1861); I concentrate on the writings of the early Marx and do not discuss the economic theory of the more technical later Marx.

Fourthly, I recognize that there are some important modern political thinkers whose writings I do not examine. Some examples are Montesquieu's *The Spirit of the Laws* (1748), James Mill's *Essay on Government* (1820) and Alexis de Tocqueville's *Democracy in America* (1835 and 1840). The influence of Montesquieu is evident in Chapters 8 to 10 of Book II of Rousseau's *The Social Contract*; James Mill was an associate of Jeremy Bentham with whom he founded utilitarianism; while John Stuart Mill was influenced by Tocqueville's *Democracy in America* – in particular, J. S. Mill shared Tocqueville's fears of mass democracy. Moreover, there are eminent modern philosophers whose philosophy has had an impact on political theory as well. Two such examples are Immanuel Kant and Friedrich Nietzsche. Kant was a philosopher in the Enlightenment tradition; he was a great influence on Hegel, who often refers to Kant in his writings, not least in the *Philosophy of Right*; Kant developed a version of social contract argument; he has been an influence on John Rawls, whose social contract theory as expressed in *A Theory of Justice* (1971) led to a revival of political philosophy. Nietzsche's philosophy marked a break with the philosophical tradition of the Enlightenment and with Kant's critical project. However, when I was preparing the lectures and when I was editing this book I had to be selective.

Before I end this introductory note, I should like to thank the students who attended my classes at Oxford for their interest and enthusiasm.

CHAPTER 1

Thomas Hobbes

Thomas Hobbes was born in 1588 in Malmesbury, Wiltshire, and lived until 1679. He lived a long life and witnessed significant developments in both science and politics. His thought is a response to both the scientific and political revolutions of his time. His political theory is an attempt to bring political stability at the time of the Civil War between Charles I and Parliament, which led to the King's execution in 1649, and a period of political and constitutional instability until the Restoration in 1660. At the same time, Hobbes's methodology is influenced by the newly emergent natural sciences.

His most important political work, *Leviathan*, was written very quickly during 1649–1650 and published in 1651. We should bear in mind that Hobbes did not regard himself as solely a political philosopher, but rather as one among such thinkers as Bacon and Descartes, who were concerned with the nature and status of philosophical enquiry. His political theory is, therefore, a part of his philosophical system. For this reason, I shall start with the method of *Leviathan*.

The Methodology of *Leviathan*

The scientific model which underlies Hobbes's argument in *Leviathan* is mathematics and in particular geometry, from which he took the method of *deduction*; that is, a reasoning (or ratiocination, as Hobbes calls it) which starts with a definition, or definitions, on the basis of which one arrives at new definitions, and so on, until one reaches something known. Hobbes firmly believed that he could apply the same method to all fields of human knowledge, thereby providing a unitary understanding of the world; all natural science, psychology and politics – the three sections of his *Elements of Philosophy* [*Elementorum Philosophiae*][1] – were based on the same model. Hobbes's definition of philosophy is the following:

> By PHILOSOPHY, is understood *the Knowledge acquired by Reasoning, from the Manner of the Generation of any thing, to the Properties; or from the Properties, to some possible Way of Generation of the same; to the end to bee able to produce, as far as matter, and humane force permit, such Effects, as humane life requireth.* (Chapter XLVI., p. 458 [367])[2]

And he goes on:

> So the Geometrician, from the Construction of Figures, findeth out many Properties thereof; and from the Properties, new Ways of their Construction, by Reasoning; to the end to be able to measure Land, and Water; and for infinite other uses. So the Astronomer, from the Rising, Setting, and Moving of the Sun, and Starres, in divers parts of the Heavens, findeth out the Causes of Day, and Night, and of the different Seasons of the Year; whereby he keepeth an account of Time: And the like of other Sciences. (Chapter XLVI., p. 458 [367])

Influenced by Galileo, Hobbes held the view that the primary, most basic, component of existence was moving matter. It follows that reality, for Hobbes, was matter in motion and life was motion. Now how does one come to *know* reality? Hobbes's answer was through sensation. This is why *Leviathan* starts with 'sense'. Once moving matter affects our sense organs, motion is transferred to the nerves and brain, producing human perception. The body's reaction or response to moving matter is experience. According to Hobbes, the world consists of bodies – animate or inanimate –, which are self-subsistent and occupy a specific place. As he puts it:

1 *De Corpore* (1655), *De Homine* (1658) and *De Cive* (1642).

2 All quotes are from Thomas Hobbes, *Leviathan*, ed. R. Tuck (Cambridge: Cambridge University Press, 1992, c. 1991).

> The Word *Body*, in the most generall acceptation, signifieth that which filleth, or occupyeth some certain room, or imagined place; and dependeth not on the imagination, but is a reall part of that we call the *Universe*. For the *Universe*, being the Aggregate of all Bodies, there is no reall part thereof that is not also *Body*; nor any thing properly a *Body*, that is not also part of (that Aggregate of all *Bodies*) the *Universe*. The same also, because Bodies are subject to change, that is to say, to variety of apparence to the sense of living creatures, is called *Substance*, that is to say, *Subject*, to various accidents; as sometimes to be Moved, sometimes to stand Still; and to seem to our senses sometimes Hot, sometimes Cold, sometimes of one Colour, Smel, Tast, or Sound, somtimes of another. (Chapter XXXIV., pp. 269–270 [207])

In Hobbes's universe bodies are constantly in motion and come to a halt only when, having struck another body, they impart their motion to them. This conception of 'motion' is characteristic of the new sciences of the seventeenth century and challenges the Aristotelian conception of 'motion', prevalent from Antiquity and through the Middle Ages. For Aristotle, the motion of a body had a purpose (or *telos*), appropriate to the nature of the body concerned. Therefore, once the body reached its purpose, motion ceased. For example, it was in the nature of the acorn to become an oak-tree. By contrast, for Hobbes, motion was ceaseless. Moreover, Hobbes conceived of matter as constitutive of reality; that is, matter is all there is:

> The World, (I mean not the Earth onely [...] but the *Universe*, that is, the whole masse of all things that are) is Corporeall, that is to say, Body; and hath the dimensions of Magnitude, namely, Length, Bredth, and Depth: also every part of Body, is likewise Body, and hath the like dimensions; and consequently every part of the Universe, is Body; and that which is not Body, is no part of the Universe: And because the Universe is All, that which is no part of it, is *Nothing*; and consequently *no where*. (Chapter XLVI., p. 463 [371])

In Hobbes's view, matter is undifferentiated. What differentiates one body from another is the space each occupies, yet he does not seem to believe that bodies or objects exist in the world as known by humans; rather he seems to think that the faculties of bodies (their 'accidents', as he calls them) elicit in humans a certain perception of them. He says that God 'instructed *Adam* how to name such creatures as he presented to his sight [...] this was sufficient to direct him to adde more names, as the experience and use of the creatures should give him occasion' (Chapter IV., p. 24 [12]).

> But all this language gotten, and augmented by *Adam* and his posterity, was again lost at the tower of *Babel* [...] And being hereby forced to disperse themselves into severall parts of the world, it must needs be, that the diversity of Tongues that now is, proceeded by degrees from them, in such manner, as need (the mother of all inventions) taught them [...] (Chapter IV., p. 25 [12])

As regards Hobbes's epistemology, although Hobbes would seem to subscribe to empiricism – i.e. the view that knowledge of reality is possible through sensation –, he also thought that empiricism was not enough. True science was concerned with the explanation of causes and consequences; it was not the mere registration of facts. And to the explanation of causal links reason was necessary (Chapter V., pp. 35–36 [21]).

Hobbes's Human Beings

In accordance with his conception of the universe, Hobbes regards human beings as moving bodies or matter in motion. His understanding of human nature is crucial to his political philosophy. This is why he devotes the first chapters of *Leviathan* to an examination of humans. Thus Chapters I–V deal with the cognitive powers of humans, while from Chapter VI onward Hobbes is concerned with humans' passions, drives and motives. It is important to notice that Hobbes's description of human nature is completely *a*moral; that is, it is not based on any moral assumptions. Initially, Hobbes treats humans in isolation from one another. It is from Chapter VIII onward that he starts to consider a plurality of human beings. As bodies in motion, humans seek to secure the continuation of their movement; for motion is life. There are two kinds of motion in humans: firstly, what Hobbes calls '*Vitall*', such as 'the *course* of the *Bloud*, the *Pulse*, the *Breathing*, the *Concoction*, *Nutrition*, *Excretion*, &c', and, secondly, '*Animall Motion*' or '*Voluntary Motion*', 'as to *go*, to *speak*, to *move* any of our limbes, in such manner as is first fancied in our minds' (Chapter VI., pp. 37–38 [23]). Humans move in space in two ways, determined by their passions:

they move either towards objects that bring them pleasure (this is the passion of 'appetite' or 'desire') or away from objects that cause them pain or distress (this is the passion of 'aversion'). In Hobbes's words:

> That which men Desire, they are also sayd to LOVE: and to HATE those things, for which they have Aversion. So that Desire, and Love, are the same thing: save that by Desire, we always signifie the Absence of the Object; by Love, most commonly the Presence of the same. So also by Aversion, we signifie the Absence; and by Hate, the Presence of the Object. (Chapter VI., p. 38 [24])

The extent to which Hobbes's account of human nature lacks any moral presuppositions is evident in his conception of 'good' and 'evil'; 'good' is the object that humans desire, whereas 'evil' is what they dislike or hate. As we shall see, it is crucial that the desires and aversions of different individuals are rarely the same, not to mention that the passions of a single human being change over time. As a body in constant motion, the human being has by nature power, which Hobbes defines as 'his present means, to obtain some future apparent Good'. This power is either 'Originall' (Hobbes also calls it 'Naturall') – such faculties of the body or mind as strength, prudence and eloquence – or 'Instrumental' – means to acquire more, e.g. wealth, reputation and friends (Chapter X., p. 62 [41]). Therefore, 'a general inclination of all mankind', as moving bodies, is 'a perpetuall and restless desire of Power after power, that ceaseth onely in Death' (Chapter XI., p. 70 [47]). Continuous success in obtaining the objects of his or her desire is 'felicity' (Chapter VI., p. 46 [29]). Surely, often humans are faced with a number of different objects of desire. However, humans are capable of 'deliberation' – that is, the weighing of the pros and cons as well as the strength of the different appetites (or, as the case might be, aversions) and acting accordingly. The 'last Appetite, or Aversion' in this process of deliberation – and usually the strongest – is the 'Will' (Chapter VI., p. 44 [28]).

The Natural Condition of Humankind

Given that this is human nature, what is the natural condition of humankind? This Hobbes discusses in Chapter XIII and is known as the 'state of nature'. Here we have a depiction of the interaction of humans, as this is *deduced* from the physical make-up of human beings, described earlier on in the book. In the 'state of nature' all human beings are equal in the faculties of both body and mind. It may well be that an individual is stronger physically, but then another has greater intellectual powers, so that, in total, the one is equal to the other. Given this equality, they all seek to attain their goals and, should one's goal coincide with another's (for example, if two or more desire the same object), there arises conflict. Given his conception of the world as moving matter, Hobbes considers this conflict to be inevitable. It arises from the equality of the human bodies in motion as well as from their equal concern to remain in motion; that is, to remain alive. In other words, they all seek their self-preservation. In order to attain this goal, they are prepared to do anything and will 'endeavour to destroy, or subdue one an other' in the process (Chapter XIII., p. 87 [61]). Due to their 'diffidence of one another', the only way to secure themselves is 'anticipation'; that is, by controlling (by either force or deceit) the movements or person of others. In the natural human being there are three causes of conflict or quarrel with others of his/her kind: a) competition, b) diffidence and c) glory (Chapter XIII., p. 88 [61]). Competition makes humans quarrel for gain, diffidence for safety and glory for reputation. Competition makes humans use violence 'to make themselves Masters of other mens persons, wives, children, and cattell'; diffidence makes them use violence to defend themselves and their family; reputation leads them to violence 'for trifles, as a word, a smile, a different opinion, and any other signe of undervalue' (Chapter XIII., p. 88 [62]).

In consequence, if, and as long as, there is no power to restrain them, humans are in a condition of war – a war of all against all. Hobbes makes clear that war does not consist only in battle, but for as long as humans are prepared or willing to fight against each other. At all other times there is peace. Notice the significance of time. What is this war like? For Hobbes, whatsoever attends a time of war, also attends the time when humans live without security – i.e. the time when, owing to the diffidence of one another, they attempt to gain dominance over their peers. In this state of affairs there is no industry and no cultivation of the land, as the produce would be plundered immediately by the strongest, fastest or most cunning; there is no navigation or imports, no buildings; there is no sense of time, no science, no arts or letters; nor is there any society. There is not what we would call civilization. Worst of all, there is continuous fear of death; 'And the life of man, solitary, poore, nasty, brutish, and short' (Chapter XIII., p. 89 [62]). Moreover, in this war of all against all there is no place for justice or injustice. For 'Where there is no common Power, there is no Law; where no Law, no Injustice' (Chapter XIII., p. 90 [63]). The 'state of nature' is, therefore, *a*moral but *not im*moral. 'Justice' and 'injustice' are notions which pertain to a political society; where no such society exists, they do not make sense (viz. they are irrelevant). Hobbes deduces the interaction of humans in their natural condition from his conception of human nature. An interesting point regarding his methodology should be made here. Having described the 'state of nature' on the basis of deduction, he uses empirical evidence in order to establish the validity of deduction. Thus he says:

> It may seem strange to some man, that has not well weighed these things; that Nature should thus dissociate, and render men apt to invade, and destroy one another: and he may therefore, not trusting to this Inference, made from the Passions, desire perhaps to have the same confirmed by Experience. Let him therefore consider with himselfe, when taking a journey, he armes himselfe, and seeks to go well accompanied; when going to sleep, he locks his dores; when even in his house he locks his chests; and this when he knows there bee Lawes, and publike Officers, armed, to revenge all injuries shall bee done him; what opinion he has of his fellow subjects, when he rides armed; of his fellow Citizens, when he lockes his dores; and of his children, and servants, when he locks his chests. Does he not there as much accuse mankind by his actions, as I do by my words? (Chapter XIII., p. 89 [62])

One issue which arises at this point concerns the status of this 'State of Nature'. Did this condition ever really exist? And, if yes, when? As Hobbes says:

> It may peradventure be thought, there was never such a time, nor condition of warre as this; and I believe it was never generally so, over all the world: but there are many places, where they live so now. (Chapter XIII., p. 89 [63])

A few lines below Hobbes adds:

> But though there had never been any time, wherein particular men were in a condition of warre one against another; yet in all times, Kings, and Persons of Soveraigne authority, because of their Independency, are in continuall jealousies, and in the state and posture of Gladiators; [...] But because they uphold thereby, the Industry of their Subjects; there does not follow from it, that misery, which accompanies the Liberty of particular men. (Chapter XIII., p. 90 [63])

What does this mean? Firstly, one should bear in mind that the 'state of nature' is not meant to be an historical epoch. According to Hobbes, science was based on mathematical deduction; that is, a reasoning which started with a definition, or definitions, on the basis of which one arrived at new definitions, and so on, until one reached something known. Accordingly, the 'state of nature' was, as Hobbes puts it, an 'Inference, made from the Passions' (Chapter XIII., p. 89 [62]). In other words, the 'state of nature' is purely hypothetical, *deduced* from Hobbes's conception of human nature. It is a logical postulate that accords with Hobbes's methodology.

Some scholars have attempted to explicate the 'state of nature' by reference to the social and economic developments of the seventeenth century. Most famously Macpherson but also Strauss have advanced the thesis that Hobbes's human beings are not humans in their natural (i.e. uncivilized) condition, but the individuals of an emergent market society.[3]

3 C. B. Macpherson, *The Political Theory of Possessive Individualism: Hobbes to Locke* (Oxford & New York: Oxford University Press, 1962); L. Strauss, *The Political Philosophy of Hobbes: Its Basis and Its Genesis* (Chicago: University of Chicago Press, 1963).

Accordingly, the Hobbesian human beings are the members of the burgeoning 'bourgeois' class. This interpretation has been challenged by other writers. For example, I. Hampsher-Monk has argued that, although Hobbes 'emphasizes the egoistic calculating aspect of human beings', a lot of the characteristics of humans in the 'state of nature' (e.g. pride) are those of an aristocratic order, while Hobbes's account is in many particulars 'scornful of the opportunism and calculation required of the new commercial and upwardly mobile groups, and of those aristocrats who had joined them'.[4]

Another view has it that the 'state of nature' is to be understood in religious terms. The Augustinian tradition and Lutheran Protestantism considered humans' evil nature (displaying many of the characteristics of Hobbes's humans in the 'state of nature') to be the result of the original Sin or Fall.[5] However, as I. Hampsher-Monk has argued, 'although Hobbes shared an Augustinian view of man's fallen nature, he is much more optimistic than Augustine about the ability of political science to contribute some measure of real security and happiness'.[6]

The Laws of Nature

What is the significance of Hobbes's portrayal of the 'state of nature'? And what is the use of 'this Inference, made from the Passions', as Hobbes puts it? It allows Hobbes to make another deduction, on the basis of which he will eventually construct his political edifice. Humans, these bodies in constant motion, are motivated by a desire to keep going, that is, to stay alive. Fear of death, therefore, leads them to seek peace. More particularly:

4 I. Hampsher-Monk, *A History of Modern Political Thought: Major Political Thinkers from Hobbes to Marx* (Oxford & Cambridge, Massachusetts: Blackwell, 1992), p. 27.

5 For this see ibid., pp. 28–29.

6 Ibid., p. 29.

> The Passions that encline men to Peace, are Feare of Death; Desire of such things as are necessary to commodious living; and a Hope by their Industry to obtain them. (Chapter XIII., p. 90 [63])

Their experience of the 'state of nature', in which each comes into conflict with others in pursuance of his or her aims (we can easily draw the analogy with Hobbes's physical mechanics here, where two or more bodies moving in space, when attracted by the same object, come to collide), awakens in humans their capacity to reason. And *reason* prescribes to humans what Hobbes calls 'the Lawes of Nature', which are 'Articles of Peace' (Chapter XIII, p. 90 [63]). Therefore, the 'laws of nature' are *deduced* from the 'state of nature' and are described in Chapters XIV and XV of *Leviathan*.

Before laying out the 'laws of nature', Hobbes gives us a definition of the 'right of nature'. This is the liberty of each human being to use his power, as he wills, for the purpose of self-preservation; that is, in order to sustain his life. To this end, he has the right or liberty to do anything that he reasons to be necessary (Chapter XIV., p. 91 [64], paraphrased). Where 'By LIBERTY is understood [...] the absence of externall Impediments' (Chapter XIV., p. 91 [64]). This is a '*negative*' conception of liberty – that is, the area within which a human being can act unobstructed.[7] It should be noted that 'The right of nature [...] legitimized the state of nature', as 'it gave each person a right of war against all others ...'.[8]

Now what are the 'laws of nature'? Hobbes's definition is as follows:

> A LAW OF NATURE [...] is a Precept, or generall Rule, found out by Reason, by which a man is forbidden to do, that, which is destructive of his life, or taketh away the means of preserving the same; and to omit, that, by which he thinketh it may be best preserved. (Chapter XIV., p. 91 [64])

7 On 'negative' freedom see Isaiah Berlin's famous essay 'Two Concepts of Liberty' in I. Berlin, *Four Essays on Liberty* (Oxford: Oxford University Press, 1992, c. 1969), pp. 122–131.

8 M. Forsyth, 'Thomas Hobbes: *Leviathan*', in M. Forsyth and M. Keens-Soper (eds), *The Political Classics: A Guide to the Essential Texts from Plato to Rousseau* (Oxford & New York: Oxford University Press, 1992), p. 138.

Crucially, a 'law of nature' does *not* forbid one to do something, but is a rule based on reason *by which* one is forbidden to do something. This means that the 'laws of nature' are *not* imposed from without (by some external authority or power), but lie *within* human reason; hence their *natural* status (as 'laws of *nature*'). It is also important to distinguish between 'right' and 'law'; 'RIGHT', Hobbes says, 'consisteth in liberty to do, or to forbeare', whereas 'LAW, determineth, and bindeth to one of them' (Chapter XIV., p. 91 [64]). So what do the 'laws of nature' prescribe? First and foremost, to seek peace and follow it – this is the 'fundamental law of nature', discovered by reason (Chapter XIV., p. 92 [64]); otherwise humans would be led to their self-destruction. The second 'law of nature' rules that one should be willing, when others are too, to lay down one's right to everything (a right he/she has in the 'state of nature') and to contract to make peace (Chapter XIV., p. 92 [64–65]). Note that reason demands that one should be prepared to give up one's right to everything, *provided*, or *when* and *only* when, others are prepared to do likewise. This is presupposed by the equality of humans in the 'state of nature', in accordance with which no human could possibly be willing to do what others are not prepared to do, thereby putting him- or herself at an obvious disadvantage. A right can be laid down in one of two ways: a) by renouncing it or b) by transferring it; in the former case, he or she who renounces the right, does not care who will benefit from this renunciation, while in the latter, he or she intends someone to reap the benefit(s) (Chapter XIV., p. 92 [65]). Once someone lays down a right in one of the abovementioned ways – a voluntary act –, he or she is 'OBLIGED or BOUND, not to hinder those, to whom such Right is granted, or abandoned, from the benefit of it' (Chapter XIV., pp. 92–93 [65]). Therefore, from a renunciation or transference of a right, there follows *obligation* and *duty*, which means that it becomes an act of *injustice* – it is an *injury* – to make void a renunciation or transference, which is one's own voluntary act. Obviously, since the renunciation or transference of a right is a voluntary act, there are certain rights which no human can possibly renounce or transfer – such as the right of resistance in case of assault of one's person or imprisonment, for example. These are *inalienable rights*, as they have to do with one's self-preservation (one's right to life). What is crucial to Hobbes's political theory is that the *mutual* transference of right is a *contract* (Chapter XIV., p. 94 [66]), which may well be considered as a promise made by the contracting parties. In some cases, one of the parties may promise to fulfill his or her part of the agreement at some time in the future; then the contract is a 'pact' or 'covenant' (Chapter XIV., p. 94 [66]). The first two 'laws of nature' are also the most significant in Hobbes's political philosophy. The remaining 'laws of nature' – seventeen 'laws of nature' are listed in Chapter XV and one more in the concluding chapter of *Leviathan* – enjoin the kind of behaviour that is essential on reasonable grounds for the maintenance of peace and safe co-existence of humans – e.g. justice, gratitude, compleasance, willingness to pardon, the need for punishment only when it serves some future good, respect (no contumely), no pride, modesty, equity, and so forth. The 'natural laws' may be summed up in the general rule '*Do not that to another, which thou wouldest not have done to thy selfe*' (Chapter XV., p. 109 [79]). Of these one in particular, the third 'law of nature', deserves our attention; it enjoins humans to observe the covenants made. It is in this law that lies 'the Fountain and Originall of JUSTICE'. For, as long as there is no covenant, everyone has a right to everything. However, once a covenant has been made, 'to break it is *Unjust*'; 'And the definition of INJUSTICE', claims Hobbes, 'is no other than *the not Performance of Covenant*' (Chapter XV., p. 100 [71]). It is now that arises the issue of morality.

The Commonwealth

The 'laws of nature' may well restrain or contain evil in the 'state of nature', but this is not enough. This is because their observation and implementation is dependent on each one of Hobbes's self-seeking individuals. There is nothing to *guarantee* that all humans will behave and act in accordance with reason at all times, however. Moreover, the right to determine one's goals and act accordingly ultimately rests with each human being him- or herself. So how far can one trust the other? There is a need of a greater power underpinning the contracts made, so that the consequences of breaking them would be greater than the advantages reaped. This is how Hobbes *deduces* the state – or, as he calls it, the 'Common-wealth' – whose purpose is to provide security (Chapter XVII., p. 117 [85]). Hobbes considers the question why some creatures such as bees and ants live sociably with one another, despite the fact that they lack the faculties of reason and of speech (Chapter XVII., pp. 119–120 [86–87]). His answer is that, contrary to the aforesaid insects, human beings are constantly in competition for honour and dignity; they distinguish the private from the common good; because they have reason, there are many among humans who think they are wiser than their peers and thereby more capable of governing others; due to their capacity for speech, humans can use words to make what is good pass for evil and what is evil pass for what is good; human beings are easily offended and concerned with self-aggrandizement; finally, as opposed to the agreement of insects which is 'natural', the agreement of humans is 'artificial' and, as such, a 'Common Power' is necessary 'to keep them in awe, and to direct their actions to the Common Benefit'. The only way to set up 'such a Common Power' is to confer all their power and rights on one person or assembly of persons, in such a manner that they are all united in one (Chapter XVII., p. 120 [87]). Hobbes names he (or they) who has (have) that capacity 'SOVERAIGNE', enjoying '*Soveraigne Power*', and everyone else 'SUBJECT' (Chapter XVII., p. 121 [88]).

According to Hobbes, there are two ways whereby a commonwealth may be introduced: either by institution or by acquisition; in the former case, a commonwealth is established when humans agree voluntarily to surrender their rights 'to some Man, or Assembly of men' who will be responsible for their protection against external threats, while in the case of the generation of a commonwealth by acquisition, humans surrender to a conqueror following defeat in battle for fear of their lives – here Hobbes also includes the submission of children to the authority of their parents (Chapter XVII., p. 121 [88]). We are interested in the commonwealth by institution, which Hobbes also calls 'a Politicall Common-wealth' (Chapter XVII., p. 212 [88]).

Hobbes sets out his theory of representation or authorization as follows:

> A *Common-wealth* is said to be *Instituted*, when a *Multitude* of men do Agree, and *Covenant, every one, with every one*, that to whatsoever *Man*, or *Assembly of Men*, shall be given by the major part, the *Right* to *Present* the Person of them all, (that is to say, to be their *Representative*;) every one, as well he that *Voted for it*, as he that *Voted against it*, shall *Authorise* all the Actions and Judgements, of that Man, or Assembly of men, in the same manner, as if they were his own, to the end, to live peaceably amongst themselves, and be protected against other men. (Chapter XVIII., p. 121 [88])

Hobbes's theory of authorization implies that henceforth the subjects are the authors of all actions of the sovereign. Let us remember that the sovereign is a *deduction* from the insecurity regarding the observance of the 'laws of nature'. As such, it is not meant to be taken literally, that is, as having taken place at some point in history. Rather it is intended to show that the possibility of community or peaceful co-existence breaks down, once political authority collapses. In putting forth this argument, Hobbes is obviously influenced by the political instability and insecurity which resulted from the Civil War and lasted at least until the Restoration. He was concerned to show people the disastrous consequences of civil disobedience and rebellion. The social contract is, therefore, an analytical device in Hobbes's political theory; its purpose is to show that political authority is based on the *consent* of the subjects. Yet this is where one significant issue arises. If the social contract is not taken literally, Hobbes's theory of authorization loses its force. This is a problem in Hobbes's theory of political obligation.

What are the rights of the sovereign?[9] These are extensive and are described in Chapter XVIII of *Leviathan*. Here I shall focus on the two rights which I consider to be most important. One is what Hobbes lists as the second right, namely, that the sovereign cannot lose his power on the grounds that he has breached his contract with his subjects. For the sovereign has *not* contracted with his subjects; rather it is the subjects who have contracted among themselves to institute a sovereign. The second sovereign right which I consider to be important is the sixth in Hobbes's list. This is that the sovereign is to decide which doctrines or opinions are to

9 I mean the sovereign by institution.

be disseminated to the public (i.e. his subjects). This censorship may sound outrageous nowadays, but we have to bear in mind the historical juncture in which *Leviathan* was produced; this was a period of Civil War. In fact, Hobbes makes explicit his motivation for granting the sovereign the right of censorship: 'It belongeth [...] to him that hath the Soveraign Power, to be Judge, or constitute all Judges of Opinions and Doctrines, as a thing necessary to Peace; therby to prevent Discord and Civill Warre' (Chapter XVIII., p. 125 [91]). Some of these doctrines – or perhaps most of them – were bound to be religious. But Hobbes was convinced that there should be no separation of Church and State if peace were to be preserved. Thus in a later chapter of the book he says:

> [...] the Kingdom of God is a Civil Common-wealth [...] the Kingdom of God is to be on Earth [...] But because this doctrine [...] will appear to most men a novelty; I doe but propound it; maintaining nothing in this, or any other paradox of Religion; but attending the end of that dispute of the sword, concerning the Authority, (not yet amongst my Country-men decided,) by which all sorts of doctrine are to bee approved, or rejected; and whose commands, both in speech, and writing, (whatsoever be the opinions of private men) must by all men, that mean to be protected by their Laws, be obeyed. For the points of doctrine concerning the Kingdome of God, have so great influence on the Kingdome of Man, as to be determined, but by them, that under God have the Soveraign Power. (Chapter XXXVIII., p. 311 [241–242])

Note the phrase 'whatsoever be the opinions of private men' (in parenthesis). It seems that, for Hobbes, if (and in this he is influenced by the teachings of Protestantism) the believer's relationship to God was a private experience, then the believer could just as well outwardly profess the doctrines that the sovereign instructed him, without believing them deeply in his heart. Hobbes's argument is politically motivated. As he says, '*a Kingdome divided in it selfe cannot stand*'; and, if power had not been divided between the King, the House of Lords and the House of Commons, the people would not have been divided and led to Civil War – 'first between those that disagreed in Politiques; and after between the Dissenters about the liberty of Religion' (Chapter XVIII., p. 127 [93]). For this reason, he insisted that the sovereign's rights be indivisible (Chapter XVIII., p. 127 [93–94]). In Chapter XXXIX he will say more emphatically:

> *Temporall* and *Spirituall* Government, are but two words brought into the world, to make men see double, and mistake their *Lawfull Soveraign* [...] There is therefore no other Government in this life, neither of State, nor Religion, but Temporall; nor teaching of any doctrine, lawfull to any Subject, which the Governour both of the State, and of the Religion, forbiddeth to be taught: And that Governor must be one; or else there must needs follow Faction, and Civill war in the Common-wealth, between the *Church* and *State*; between *Spiritualists*, and *Temporalists*; between the *Sword of Justice*, and the *Shield of Faith*; and (which is more) in every Christian mans own brest, between the *Christian*, and the *Man*. (Chapter XXXIX., p. 322 [248])

It is important to make clear that the indivisibility of sovereign power does *not* necessarily imply the institution of a monarchy. Hobbes also envisaged the possibility of an assembly, which could be either 'an Assembly of All that will come together', namely, a democracy, or 'an Assembly of a Part onely', that is, an aristocracy (Chapter XIX., p. 129 [94]). He did, however, believe that a monarchy was likely to be more stable, as in a monarchy the private interest is more easily united with the public, there is a wider circle of counsellors, less inconstancy, no disagreement and possibly less corruption.

Despite the fact that the sovereign enjoys extensive rights, Hobbes also assigns to him (or them if it is an assembly) certain obligations. This is often not taken into consideration. In particular, the sovereign is expected to uphold the rule of law (Chapter XXX., p. 231 [175]),[10] not to punish arbitrarily (Chapter XXVIII., pp. 214–216, 219 [162–163, 165]), to promote equity – e.g. the equal administration of justice, equal imposition of taxes (Chapter XXX., pp. 237 [180] & 238–239 [181], respectively) and to concern himself with more than the mere preservation of his (or their) subjects, that is, 'all other Contentments of life' (Chapter XXX., p. 231 [175]).

10 'The OFFICE of the Soveraign (be it a Monarch, or an Assembly,) consisteth in the end, for which he was trusted with the Soveraign Power, namely the procuration of *the safety of the people*; to which he is obliged by the Law of Nature, and to render an account thereof to God, the Author of that Law, and to none but him [...] And this is intended should be done [...] by a generall Providence, contained in publique Instruction, both of Doctrine, and Example; and in the making, and executing of good Lawes' (Chapter XXX., p. 231 [175]).

The Liberty of Subjects

Given the extensive rights of the sovereign, what is the position of the subjects? Are the free in any sense? Hobbes repeats the definition of liberty he has already given in an earlier chapter of *Leviathan* (Chapter XIV., p. 91 [64]: 'LIBERTY, or FREEDOME, signifieth (properly) the absence of Opposition; (by Opposition, I mean externall Impediments of motion;)' (Chapter XXI., p. 145 [107]). Accordingly, 'A FREE-MAN, *is he, that in those things, which by his strength and wit he is able to do, is not hindred to doe what he has a will to*' (Chapter XXI., p. 146 [108]). To this definition he adds that the terms '*Free*' and '*Liberty*' are properly applicable to '*Bodies*' and that, in all other cases they are abused; for what does not move, cannot be externally constrained. It follows that 'liberty' cannot refer to the will of a human being, but only to the human conceived as a moving body or matter in motion. This implies that fear and liberty are not incompatible, as many of us would think. According to Hobbes's understanding of liberty, all human actions undertaken for fear of the law are actions that the doers had liberty not to do. Similarly, liberty is compatible with necessity. Sure enough, all human actions are motivated by some cause and, in this sense, they are determined by necessity. Yet there cannot be unmotivated actions – there will always be some cause; so liberty cannot be understood in terms of the absence of any causes whatsoever. What is important is for someone to be free from external constraints. Hobbes argues that in the same way as humans have created 'an Artificiall Man' (viz. the Commonwealth), they have also created 'Artificiall Chains', which are no other than 'Civill Lawes' (Chapter XXI., p. 147 [108]). However, he insists that the liberty of the subjects is consistent with the absolute power of the sovereign and that the sovereign cannot do an injustice to a subject, since in the final analysis it is the subject who has authorized – and continues to authorize – the sovereign's acts (Chapter XXI., p. 148 [109]). For Hobbes, in the act of submission to a sovereign lies both humans' *obligation* and *liberty*; there can be no obligation on anyone which does not derive from some act of his own, since everyone is by nature equally free. Therefore, obligation and liberty stem either from such words as '*I Authorise all his Actions*' or from the purpose of the sovereign – that is, internal peace and defence against external threats (Chapter XXI., p. 150 [111]).

For most liberties the subjects 'depend on the Silence of the Law', which means that, where there is no law to prescribe or forbid a course of action, the subject may do as he or she pleases (Chapter XXI., p. 152 [113]). Hobbes even allows that in cases of dispute a subject can sue the sovereign for his or her right in accordance with the precedence of the law (Chapter XXI., pp. 152–153 [113]). Otherwise, the only right of the subjects is that of self-preservation (Chapter XXI., p. 153 [114]).

CHAPTER 2

John Locke

John Locke lived from 1632 to 1704. He was born to a well-off, landed, Puritan family in Wrington, Somerset. His family supported the parliamentarians during the Civil War. He was educated first at Westminster School and then at Christ Church, Oxford. Although – at least initially – not particularly noteworthy as a scholar, Locke was to remain in Oxford for around thirty years. He did not study philosophy in Oxford at all; rather he received a bachelor's degree in medicine. Politics had been one of his interests however – his major concerns being the separation of political from religious matters, as well as Natural Law. In those early days his politics was rather authoritarian, although even then he was against arbitrary authority. Locke was always a constitutionalist, concerned with legal authority. But, it seems, Peter Laslett has got a point in arguing that

> The uneasy, anarchical months between the death of Oliver Cromwell and the Stuart Restoration had made this slightly sceptical, unselfconfident Oxford don into the determined defender of authority, a man prepared to go to great lengths to secure quiet.[1]

While at Oxford he wrote the *Essays on the Law of Nature* (1660) and *An Essay on Toleration* (1667), but his mature political theory was the result of his long association with the First Earl of Shaftesbury, a famous Whig politician. Lord Ashley, later first earl of Shaftesbury was of ill health however. He had a chronic affection of the liver and after one of his attacks he went to Oxford in order to try the waters of Astrop. This was in July 1666 and it was then that he met Locke. The affection of the liver had caused a

1 Peter Laslett, Introduction to his edition of John Locke's *Two Treatises of Government* (Cambridge: Cambridge University Press, 1992, c. 1988), p. 20.

malign abscess that had to be removed. A doctor in his early thirties, Locke supervised a successful operation and thereafter became Shaftesbury's best friend and confidant. Locke was invited to live in Shaftesbury's household and it was there that he developed both his philosophical and political thinking. In fact, his job was to analyze social and political problems to his patron, as well as giving him advice. There is historical evidence to suggest that Locke had written *Two Treatises of Government* many years – indeed a decade – before he sent it to press in 1689; it was published anonymously in 1690. This means that the work precedes the 'Glorious Revolution' of 1688.[2] It is worth bearing this in mind when we come to the role of revolution in his political theory. For it becomes evident that, in recognizing that there might be legitimate grounds for revolution, he was not trying to legitimize or justify a revolution that had already taken place, but was voicing the need for revolution. Given the tumultuous historical period and the radicalism of his views – he was expelled from the University of Oxford by Royal order in 1684 –, Locke had been very anxious to conceal the fact that he was the author of the *Two Treatises*, acknowledging authorship in a codicil to his will a few weeks before his death.[3] Let us now turn to *Two Treatises of Government*.

The *Two Treatises of Government*

Here we shall be concerned with Locke's *Second Treatise of Government*. The *First Treatise* is a critique of Sir Robert Filmer's patriarchalism, as put forth in his work *Patriarcha*. In *Patriarcha* Filmer had attempted to legitimize royal absolutism by making a case for a version of the divine right of kings. For Filmer, God had given Adam authority over the earth. It follows that the world was a grant by God to Adam and his heirs. Filmer goes on

2 Ibid., III, pp. 45–66.

3 Ibid., p. 4.

to argue that political authority is analogous to paternal authority, which is absolute. In the *First Treatise* Locke is, therefore, concerned to show that God has not chosen anyone to rule others. That said, Locke does not always treat Filmer fairly and on some occasions he refutes a more general version of patriarchalism.

It is against this background that the *Second Treatise* is to be read, although it has been argued that Locke wrote the *Second Treatise* first, adding to it the *First Treatise* a year later.[4] Accordingly, the first chapter of the *Second Treatise* is meant to be a link between the two treatises.

The State of Nature

Although Locke criticizes Filmer's reading of the Old Testament, he does not reject the Bible as such. Rather he constructs his political theory on the basis of it. Therefore, references to the Bible abound in the *Second Treatise*. For him, humans are all creatures of God, brought to earth to enjoy its products in common. It follows that Locke's conception of the 'state of nature' is very different from that of Hobbes; it is not *a*moral but moral. In the 'state of nature' humans are in 'a *State of perfect Freedom*' to act as they please but 'within the bounds of the Law of Nature' (para. 4, p. 269).[5] This 'Law of Nature' is the Law of God. As well as free, humans are also equal, no one enjoying more power than others. We can, therefore, see how Locke uses the biblical account of the Creation in order to refute the interpretation of Filmer. Although not directly attacking Filmer in the *Second Treatise*, this constitutes Locke's positive answer to him. As Locke puts it:

4 Ibid., pp. 61–62, 65.

5 All references are to John Locke, *Two Treatises of Government*, ed. P. Laslett (Cambridge: Cambridge University Press, 1992, c. 1988).

> there being nothing more evident, than that Creatures of the same species and rank promiscuously born to all the same advantages of Nature, and the use of the same faculties, should also be equal one amongst another without Subordination or Subjection, unless the Lord and Master of them all, should by any manifest Declaration of his Will set one above another, and confer on him by an evident and clear appointment an undoubted Right to Dominion and Sovereignty. (para. 4, p. 269)

This equality of humans before the eyes of God no doubt derives from Protestantism. However, albeit 'a *State of Liberty*', Locke's 'state of nature' is unlike Hobbes's in that 'it is *not a State of Licence*' (para. 6, p. 270). Again echoing a Protestant belief, Locke says that, although each human is free to act and make use of his possessions as he wishes, 'yet he has not Liberty to destroy himself, or so much as any Creature in his Possession' (para. 6, pp. 270–271). He adds: 'The *State of Nature* has a Law of Nature to govern it, which obliges every one' (para. 6, p. 271); that is, the 'law of nature' *obliges* everyone to its Author, namely, God. And this moral law enjoins that 'being all equal and independent, no on ought to harm another in his Life, Health, Liberty, or Possessions' (para. 6, p. 271). The 'law of nature' is known to humans by reason; in fact, Locke says that it *is* reason (para. 6, p. 271). So the relationship between God, nature, law and reason is the following: God created nature and gave the world a law after His own rational mind; and humans, being creatures of God, have a god-like nature in them. But they are also His property. As a result, each one of them has a responsibility to God to preserve as much him- or herself as his or her fellow humans; for they all share in 'one Community of Nature' (para. 6, p. 271). For this reason Locke regards slavery as morally wrong; 'For a Man, not having the Power of his own Life, *cannot*, by Compact, or his own Consent, *enslave himself* to any one, nor put himself under the Absolute, Arbitrary Power of another, to take away his Life, when he pleases' (para. 23, p. 284).

Given that the 'law of nature' enjoins peace and the preservation of all humankind, everyone is responsible (to God) for its execution, which means that everyone has the right to punish the transgressor(s) to the degree that is necessary for the prevention of future crimes (para. 7, p. 271). And it is in this way that 'in the State of Nature, *one Man comes by a Power over another*' (para. 8, p. 272). Yet, significantly, this is 'no Absolute or Arbitrary Power' to do to the transgressor whatever one pleases, but '*only* to retribute to him', in accordance with reason, 'what is proportionate to his Transgression' (para. 8, p. 272). Thus retribution or punishment serves only the purposes of '*Reparation*' and '*Restraint*' (para. 8, p. 272). For, as well as being a breach of the 'law of nature', the transgression is usually also an injury to some other party. It is Locke's argument that the latter can seek reparation and that others may join him or her to this end (para. 10, p. 273). In the 'state of nature' everyone can act as judge with respect to the 'law of nature', because, as Locke says, 'having renounced Reason, the common Rule and Measure, God hath given to Mankind', the transgressor 'hath by the unjust Violence and Slaughter he hath committed upon one, *declared War against all Mankind*' (para. 11, p. 274).[6] Note that Locke does *not* describe the 'state of nature' as a 'war of all against all' as Hobbes does; rather there ensues a war of *one* human being against the whole of humanity, once he or she violates the 'law of nature', which ensures humans' peaceable co-existence. Locke also considers a reply to the argument that it is unfair for humans to be judges in matters that affect them, since they are likely to be partial or biased and that therefore a civil government (a monarchy in particular) is better suited to act as arbitrator, arguing instead that absolute monarchs are humans themselves, while it always depends on the form of government – on its nature – whether it is a better judge than humans in the 'state of nature' (para. 13, pp. 275–276). Moreover, Locke insists,

> Much better it is in the State of Nature wherein Men are not bound to submit to the unjust will of another: And if he that judges, judges amiss in his own, or any other Case, he is answerable for it to the rest of Mankind. (para. 13, p. 276)

And one might also say that he is accountable for his judgement to God.

Let us pause to consider the status of Locke's 'state of nature' and to compare it with that of Hobbes. In Hobbes the 'state of nature' is *hypothetical*, an inference made from human nature. Is that so in Locke? The short answer is 'no'. What is it then? Paragraph 15 suggests that it is the

6 My italics for emphasis.

condition of humankind before they contract to establish a political society (para. 15, p. 278). *Yet*, and this is important, unlike Hobbes, Locke asserts that other compacts and promises *are* made within the 'state of nature' (para. 14, pp. 276–277). Moreover, since the compact which 'puts an end to the State of Nature between Men' is 'only this one of agreeing together mutually to enter into *one* Community, and make *one* Body Politick' (para. 14, pp. 276–277),[7] in the field of international relations, where there are '*Independent* Governments', prevails a 'State of Nature' (para. 14, p. 276). In Locke the 'state of nature' would seem, therefore, to describe a specific historical period. This does not mean that the 'state of nature' is historical, but perhaps one can agree with the view that 'Locke can treat the state of nature as a kind of historical fiction with descriptive content'.[8] Thus, 'although not primarily historical in conception, the state of nature provides a point from which a speculative history of man's political and economic development might be started'.[9]

In Chapter III of the *Second Treatise* we have a description of the 'State of War'. In Locke war is not a necessary and permanent aspect of human life in the 'state of nature' but may happen – it is a possibility. It occurs when someone has 'a sedate setled Design' on the life of someone else (para. 16, p. 278), while it is he or she who threatens to subjugate another that is responsible for the beginning of war (para. 17, p. 279). In paragraph 19 Locke differentiates between '*the State of Nature*' and '*the State of War*', which he says 'some Men have confounded' (para. 19, p. 280) – this is a clear reference to Hobbes. The possibility of war (though not its inevitability) makes the 'state of nature' inconvenient, though not a condition of constant fear and mutual mistrust as it is for Hobbes. And avoidance of war is one major reason why humans are led to abandon the 'state of nature' (para. 21, p. 282).

7 My italics.

8 I. Hampsher-Monk, *A History of Modern Political Thought: Major Political Thinkers from Hobbes to Marx* (Oxford & Cambridge, Massachusetts: Blackwell, 1992), p. 85.

9 Ibid.

The Theory of Property

Not the only reason, however. Chapter V of the *Second Treatise* introduces another concept, that of property. Most – if not all – commentators would agree that this chapter is impressive. As one author has remarked, were it not for property, 'some would say that the *Second Treatise* could be consigned to the same oblivion as the *First*'.[10] As Locke was to say a year before he died: 'Property I have nowhere found more clearly explained, than in a book, entitled Two Treatises of Government'.[11]

According to Locke, God gave the entire world to all humans in common. Attacking Sir Robert Filmer once again, he says:

> it is impossible that any Man, but one universal Monarch, should have any *Property*, upon a supposition, that God gave the world to *Adam*, and his Heirs in Succession, exclusive of all the rest of Posterity. (para. 25, p. 286)

It should be born in mind, therefore, that Locke is not the individualist that he is often claimed to be. At least, he is not only an individualist, as there are frequent references to commonality in the *Second Treatise*.[12] As well as giving the world to all humanity in common, God has also given human beings 'reason' to use the earth and its products to 'the best advantage of Life, and convenience' (para. 26, p. 286). This means that, although the fruits of the earth and the members of the animal kingdom are common to all humans, each one of them has a right '*to appropriate*' them if they are to be of use to him or her at all (para. 26, pp. 286–287). Crucially, Locke does not regard as property only the animals or the fruits that one may come to appropriate. He uses 'property' in another sense too – to designate

10 C. Hughes, 'John Locke: *The Second Treatise of Government*', in M. Forsyth and M. Keens-Soper (eds), *The Political Classics: A Guide to the Essential Texts from Plato to Rousseau* (Oxford & New York: Oxford University Press, 1992), p. 156.

11 Quoted in P. Laslett's Introduction to Locke, *Two Treatises of Government*, p. 3.

12 See Laslett, ibid., p. 101 and Hughes, 'John Locke: *The Second Treatise of Government*', p. 156.

one's body. For Locke, I own my body and personality; my person is my property (para. 27, p. 287). In this double sense, one owns both what is within and without oneself. Concerning the latter sense, one may own – or come to appropriate – both goods or land and one's labour. For labour is the process whereby something is removed from the natural state in which it exists, while through labour an individual mixes the natural thing with 'something that is his or her own'. In this way, it becomes his or her '*Property*' (para. 27, p. 288).

Locke's definition of labour in paragraphs 27–30 has been a great source of inspiration – the seed of classical liberal political economy as well as Marx's theory of value. But it is not only my *own* labour that makes a thing my property. Locke says that 'the Grass my Horse has bit; the Turfs my Servant has cut' also 'become my *Property*, without the assignation or consent of any body' (para. 28, p. 289). Consequently, as Macpherson has noted, an individual's right 'is equally established by the labour he has purchased'.[13] Therefore, Locke would seem to be assuming the existence of wage-labour.[14] Locke's views on property have often made him vulnerable to Marxist criticism, which sees him as an apologist for the emergent bourgeois class.

It is worth stressing, however, that Locke does not allow continuous accumulation of the land and its products. For him, God has given us the earth and its fruits '*To enjoy*'. This means that one can appropriate only as much as he or she can use before it goes to waste; 'Nothing was made by God for Man to spoil or destroy' (para. 31, p. 290). In consequence, it is wrong, for example, for one to collect more apples than one can eat or to appropriate more land than one can cultivate. Furthermore, Locke argues that God did not give the world to the lazy, greedy and quarrelsome but 'to the use of the Industrious and Rational' (para. 34, p. 291). These two restrictions to the accumulation of land and its products – i.e. moderation in appropriation and industry – seem to Locke to be sufficient to

13 C. B. Macpherson, *The Political Theory of Possessive Individualism: Hobbes to Locke* (Oxford & New York: Oxford University Press, 1964), p. 215.

14 Ibid., p. 216.

ensure that there is enough land and goods left for the others (para. 34, p. 291; para. 36, pp. 292–293). To be sure, common land in a given country cannot be appropriated, as it is regulated by the laws of the country in question, but this is different from the situation that prevailed in the beginning (para. 35, p. 292). Locke comes to legitimate the private possession of land by saying that its cultivation makes it ten or one hundred times more productive (cultivated land yields more crops) and thereby more beneficial to the rest of humanity (para. 37, p. 294) on condition that the fruits of the land are not left to rot or the land itself does not lie waste (para. 37, pp. 294–295; para. 38, p. 295). Drawing on the Bible, Locke explains how, as private possessions enlarged, families settled together and built cities, demarcating 'the *bounds of their distinct Territories*', and, when there was no more land available in the same place, they emigrated to another place (para. 39, pp. 295–296). But common land is bound to be exhausted sometime; Locke seems to imply that, when this happens, the landless will have the opportunity to work on the land of others: 'the *Property of labour* should be able to over-balance the Community of Land' (para. 40, p. 296). This will increase productivity even more; 'For 'tis *Labour* indeed that *puts the difference of value* on every thing' (para. 40, p. 296).[15] The extent to which this is true, claims Locke, is exemplified by a comparison of the Indians in America with the working-class in England. The former 'are rich in Land', but, because most of the land lies waste, 'poor in all the Comforts of Life'; 'And a King of a large and fruitful Territory there feeds, lodges, and is clad worse than a day Labourer in *England*' (para. 41, pp. 296–297).

According to Locke, gradually money was invented (para. 36, p. 293). This allowed greater private accumulation. Since land and most of its products do not last long (para. 46, pp. 299–300), money offered humans the possibility to enlarge their possessions (para. 46, p. 300; para. 48, p. 301) without violating what Locke has called the '*Rule of Propriety*' – that is, 'that every Man should have as much as he could make use of' (para. 36, p. 293). In point of fact, says Locke, 'Gold, Silver, and Diamonds, are things, that

15 Cf. para. 42, pp. 297–298; para. 43, p. 298.

Fancy or Agreement hath put the value on, more then real Use, and the necessary Support of Life' (para. 46, p. 300). It is in this way that money came 'by mutual consent' to be exchanged for 'the truly useful, but perishable Supports of Life' (para. 47, pp. 300–301). 'Thus in the beginning all the World was *America*', Locke says (para. 49, p. 301), by which he means that the whole world belonged to everyone – land and its produce seemed to be inexhaustible, available to anyone to consume and to appropriate in accordance with his or her needs. But, following the invention of money, whose value derives from the *consent* of humans, it is evident that humans 'have agreed to disproportionate and unequal Possession of the Earth'. It is crucial to Locke's argument that this 'inequality of private possessions' has taken place outside society, 'without compact' and 'only by putting a value on gold and silver and tacitly agreeing in the use of Money'. For governments regulate by laws 'the right of property' (which private property already exists), while 'the possession of land is determined by positive constitutions' (para. 50, pp. 301–302). As the editor of Locke's *Two Treatises of Government* has commented with respect to Locke's theory of property, 'The whole argument is intended to show that individual property did not arise from the common consent of all mankind, though in the end the *actual distribution* of it is held to be due to money, which is a matter of consent, perhaps even worldwide consent'.[16] Locke's justification of inequality can be read in both a liberal and Marxist way.

Civil Society

We have seen that Locke uses the term 'property' to refer to both land and goods and one's body or personality. In paragraph 87 'property' comes to be defined as one's 'Life, Liberty and Estate' (para. 87, p. 323). It is in this

16 P. Laslett in his Introduction to Locke, *Two Treatises of Government*, pp. 101–102 (my emphasis), referring to paras 45, 50 etc.

general sense that 'property' is meant in the *Second Treatise* from now on. And it is 'property' which induces humans to form a political society, as 'property' cannot be sufficiently secure in the 'state of nature'. So political society comes into being when all individuals give up their natural right to protect their own property and to punish the transgressors of the 'law of nature'. Political society is thenceforth 'Umpire' or judge for all members of the community, 'indifferent, and the same to all Parties' (para. 87, p. 324).

In Chapter VII Locke, rather confusingly, uses 'civil' and 'political' society interchangeably. In fact, Locke was the first thinker to distinguish between 'civil' and 'political' society, the sphere of economic relations and that of government or the state respectively. But, at times, he appears to 'forget' this distinction himself.[17] 'Civil society', the sphere of the market, was just beginning to emerge in Locke's lifetime. For a market economy to be fully established, the following precondition had to be fulfilled: Individuals should have the right to own property and dispose of it as they please. Thus, 'civil society' can exist independently of the state and in Locke's political theory it precedes the establishment of the state. The state or political society is established in order to protect property and hence the stability of 'civil society'. To be sure, 'The doubt is', as Christopher Hughes has put it, 'whether the distinction of civil or political society was actually fully present in his [Locke's] mind, or is contained in the text of the *Second Treatise* [...] To say it is not there in express words, taking into account repetitions and denials, is defensible'.[18] Nevertheless, as the aforesaid commentator has gone on to say:

> There is also a good reason why it is not consistently there on the page of Locke. Civil society develops into government, and creates government by an act of will, but having created it, is changed and perfected. It needs government.[19]

17 See Hughes, 'John Locke: *The Second Treatise of Government*', p. 159.
18 Ibid., p. 160 (my square brackets).
19 Ibid.

Here I shall use the term 'commonwealth' – which Locke also uses on several occasions – to refer to political society proper and to avoid the confusion that may result from using 'civil' and 'political society' interchangeably. The commonwealth consists of two branches – 'the *power of making Laws*' and 'the *power of War and Peace*', the legislative and executive powers respectively (para. 88, pp. 324–325). It is established by a social contract; that is:

> where-ever any number of Men, in the state of Nature, enter into Society to make *one* People, *one* Body Politick under *one* Supreme Government, or else when any one joyns himself to, and incorporates with any Government already made. (para. 89, p. 325)[20]

Through this act individuals *authorize* the commonwealth to make laws for them as well as to see that these laws are implemented; in fact, Locke maintains that individuals ought to assist the executive to implement those laws (para. 89, p. 325).

But, as opposed to Hobbes, Locke does not think that absolute monarchy is the best form of government. Far from it – Locke claims that it is '*inconsistent with Civil Society*, and so can be no Form of Civil Government at all' (para. 90, p. 326). For 'the *end of Civil Society*' is 'to avoid, and remedy those inconveniencies of the State of Nature, which necessarily follow from every Man's being Judge in his own Case, by setting up a known Authority', while the '*Absolute Prince*' concentrating 'both Legislative and Executive Power in himself alone, there is no Judge to be found, no Appeal lies open to any one' and, therefore, any injury 'that may be suffered from the Prince or by his Order' cannot be redressed (paras 90–91, p. 326). Being an absolute judge unto himself, 'such a Man', Locke argues, 'however entitled, *Czar*, or *Grand Signior*, or how you please, is as much *in the state of Nature*, with all under his Dominion, as he is with the rest of Mankind' (para. 91, p. 326). In fact, according to Locke, an absolute monarchy is even worse than the 'state of nature'. For, 'whereas, in the ordinary State of Nature' each individual 'has the liberty to judge of his Right, and according to the best of his Power, to maintain it', in an absolute monarchy

20 My italics.

> whenever his Property is invaded by the Will and Order of his Monarch, he has not only no Appeal, as those in Society ought to have, but as if he were degraded from the common state of Rational Creatures, is denied a liberty to judge of, or to defend his Right, and so is exposed to all the Misery and Inconveniencies that a Man can fear from one, who being in the unrestrained state of Nature, is yet corrupted with Flattery, and armed with Power. (para. 91, p. 327)

This is a criticism of Hobbes's *Leviathan*. Certainly, Locke recognized that those who opposed monarchical rule in his days were considered to be 'the Voice of Faction and Rebellion'. He points to the absurdity of Hobbes's monarchical and absolutist solution as follows:

> As if when Men quitting the State of Nature entered into Society, they agreed that all of them but one, should be under the restraint of Laws, but that he should still retain all the Liberty of the State of Nature, increased with Power, and made licentious by Impunity. (para. 93, p. 328)[21]

Adding with a tone of mockery:

> This is to think that Men are so foolish that they take care to avoid what Mischiefs may be done them by *Pole-Cats*, or *Foxes*, but are content, nay think it Safety, to be devoured by *Lions*. (para. 93, p. 328)

By contrast, Locke emphasizes the necessity of everyone's subjection to – what we would call – the rule of law: '*No Man in Civil Society can be exempted from the Laws of it*' (para. 94, p. 330). If a human being is above law, then he or she is still in the 'state of nature' and thus cannot be a member of the commonwealth or civil society; 'unless any one will say, the State of Nature and Civil Society are one and the same thing', an anarchical state of affairs, which, says Locke, he has 'never yet found any one so great a Patron of Anarchy as to affirm' (para. 94, p. 330).

21 Still, Hobbes allowed for the possibility of there being an assembly.

Consent

'Consent', as well as 'property', are the two most important ideas in Locke's political theory. For Locke, humans being 'by Nature, all free, equal and independent, no one can be put out of this Estate, and subjected to the Political Power of another, without his own *Consent*' (para. 95, p. 330). Locke's social contract explicitly requires that humans have '*consented to make one Community* or Government'. Following this express consent, they 'make *one Body Politick*, wherein the *Majority* have a Right to act and conclude the rest'. Locke is clear that 'any number of' individuals can give their consent to become members of political society and that those who do not do so may, and do, remain in the 'state of nature' (para. 95, p. 331). Paragraph 95 of Chapter VIII, when read in conjunction with paragraphs 87–89 of the previous chapter, suggest two phases of the social contract: first, human beings in the 'state of nature' come together and agree to form a community; and, subsequently, they, as a community, set up a government.[22] But, once more, Locke's terminology is confusing; the full sentence, of which I have already quoted parts, reads, for instance:

> When any number of Men have so *consented to make one Community* or Government, they are thereby presently incorporated, and make *one Body Politick*, wherein the *Majority* have a Right to act and conclude the rest. (para. 95, p. 331)

The later part of the above sentence – 'wherein the *Majority* have a Right to act and conclude the rest' – makes matters worse. Majoritarianism is not the same as unanimity, which consent would seem to imply, so how does Locke move from the latter to the former? In other words, what is important, how does he justify majority rule? In the next paragraph Locke suggests that unanimity – i.e. 'the consent of every individual' – is necessary in order to make 'a *Community*', thenceforth this community being 'one Body, with a Power to Act as one Body', it cannot do so unless it is 'by the will and determination of the *majority*' (para. 96, p. 331). For the

22 Cf. Hampsher-Monk, *A History of Modern Political Thought*, p. 98.

community being made up of individuals who have given their consent thereto, while the community being conceived as *one* body, action would be impossible, were it not based on 'the *consent of the majority*' (para. 96, pp. 331–332; see also para. 98, pp. 332–333).[23] Locke anticipates a problem which is inherent in Rousseau's social contract theory. According to Locke, action requires that 'the *act of the Majority* passes for the act of the whole' (para. 96, p. 332). Arguably, this makes Locke the theoretical founder of contemporary liberal democracies, which are based on majority rule.

With the social contract there arises *obligation* – obligation of everyone to everybody else in the commonwealth 'to submit to the determination of the *majority*, and to be concluded by it' (para. 97, p. 332).

Locke considers two objections to his theory of government. Briefly they are the following: The first objection is that there are not any examples of a group of independent and equal human beings who came together in order to establish a government (para. 100, p. 333) – to which Locke replies that we have very few historical examples of this, because the 'state of nature' is so inconvenient that, no sooner had humans come together than they formed a political society; in fact, the formation of government always precedes all records available, while people do not concern themselves with letters until they have lived together in society for a long time and have satisfied their primary needs (para. 101, p. 334). Besides, there is evidence to suggest that 'in many parts of *America*' there was initially 'no Government at all', while there are parts of southern and northern America that do not have a government to this day (that is, to Locke's days) (para. 102, p. 335). Moreover, although history would seem to teach us that the most usual form of government was monarchical, Locke argues, this is due to the fact that monarchy was the simplest and most understandable form of government to humans, since they had been accustomed to paternal authority when growing up. Yet, as with the passage of time humans came to understand the nature of political rule better and to assess monarchy, they limited the power of the monarch and found ways to prevent his abuse of power. In this sense, they gave their consent to a restricted monarchical

23 Cf. Hughes, 'John Locke: *The Second Treatise of Government*', p. 164.

rule (paras 103–112, pp. 335–344). The second objection is that it cannot be that humans come together to form a government, since everybody is born under one government and is thereby subject to it (para. 100, p. 334) – to which Locke retorts: 'If this Argument be good; I ask, how came so many lawful Monarchies into the World?' If this argument were correct, 'either all Men, however *born*, are *free*, or else there is but one lawful Prince, one lawful Government in the World' (para. 113, p. 344). To which it can be added that there are many instances in history of people withdrawing their allegiance from the government in which they were born and lived their lives until then or from the family into which they were brought up (para. 115, p. 345). Locke emphasizes that 'whatever Engagements or Promises any one has made for himself, he is under the Obligation of them, but *cannot* by any *Compact* whatsoever, bind *his Children* or Posterity'. Once grown up, the child as an adult is 'as Free as the Father' to make what promises he pleases (para. 116, p. 346). This means that '*a Child is born a Subject of no Country or Government*'. He is under paternal authority when young and when he comes of age he is free to choose 'what Government he will put himself under' (para. 118, p. 347). The father can oblige his son to be a member of the political community into which he was born and of which he (the father) is also a member *only if* the son wishes to 'enjoy those Possessions which were his Fathers' (para. 116, p. 346).

This brings us to another issue in Locke's political philosophy – that of 'express' and 'tacit' consent, a distinction which is not always clear. The difficulty is not so much with 'express' as with 'tacit consent'. Regarding 'tacit consent', Locke says:

> [...] every Man, that hath any Possession, or Enjoyment, of any part of the Dominions of any Government, doth thereby give his *tacit Consent*, and is as far forth obliged to Obedience to the Laws of the Government, during such Enjoyment, as any one under it [...] (para. 119, p. 348)

Therefore, according to Locke, one gives his or her *tacit* consent to a government when one owns land in the territory over which the government concerned has jurisdiction, whenever one stays in a lodging if only for a week, or whenever one travels on the highway of that country (para. 119,

p. 348). Significantly, however, 'submitting to the Laws of any Country [...] and enjoying Privileges and Protection under them, *makes not a Man a Member of that Society*'. Only *express* consent can make someone a member of a commonwealth (para. 122, p. 349) – a naturalized subject, as it were. But there is confusion in respect of inheritance: On the one hand, in paragraph 117 Locke says that 'the Son cannot ordinarily enjoy the Possessions of his Father, but under the same terms his Father did; by becoming a Member of the Society: whereby he puts himself presently under the Government, he finds there established, as much as any other Subject of that Commonwealth'. Thus it would seem that an 'express consent' is necessary in order for someone to inherit property – this being due to the fact that commonwealths do not permit 'any part of their Dominions to be dismembred' (para. 117 p. 346). On the other, in paragraph 120 Locke says that, given that the government reaches the owner of the land 'only as he dwells upon, and enjoys that', its jurisdiction over the owner '*begins and ends with the Enjoyment*' (para. 121, p. 349).[24] This would seem to imply only a 'tacit consent'.

Yet a problem remains. Locke's argument of consent could lead to a situation where a significant part of the population are not members of the commonwealth, since in the seventeenth century they did not have the right to vote. How else could they give their *express* consent to the government? There are different answers to this question. John Dunn has argued that there were many instances when in seventeenth-century England people could give their express consent to the government – for example, prayers for the king while attending Mass in Church, oaths of allegiance often required of citizens, and so forth.[25] Another explanation is given by Iain Hampsher-Monk who says that one should bear in mind 'what it was in Filmer that Locke wanted to deny'.[26] Specifically, Locke wished to refute Filmer's argument that people have political obligations by

24 Cf. para. 120, p. 348.

25 J. Dunn, *The Political Thought of John Locke: An Historical Account of the Argument of the 'Two Treatises of Government'* (Cambridge: Cambridge University Press, 1969), pp. 137–141; cited in Hampsher-Monk, *A History of Modern Political Thought*, p. 100.

26 Hampsher-Monk, *A History of Modern Political Thought*, p. 100.

virtue of their birth, which meant two things: 'Firstly, that because political obligations are fixed by birth they are absolute and cannot be revoked; and secondly that the location of those obligations is determined by birth'; that is, 'being born in England or of English parents determines that it is the English king (and not the French) to whom we owe obligation'.[27] Concerning the first of Filmer's points, Locke is interested in showing that 'because we are morally responsible for our own obligations they are ultimately limited and consensual'; consequently 'we can withdraw that consent when the limits are transgressed'.[28] We shall come to the issue of the withdrawal of consent in a while. What is important for our present purposes is that 'consent functions here only to *justify* (when necessary) the withdrawal of allegiance, *not* as a positive sign or creator of it', so the issue of 'express consent' does not emerge.[29] Regarding the second point of Filmer, Hampsher-Monk notes that Locke 'did not bother to clear up the confusion' as 'he made the perfectly commonplace (although patriarchal) assumption, that the Englishness of English children could be assumed from their birth even though the absolute nature of their obligations to an English monarch could not'. Therefore, one could 'presume, in the case of English children that they *wished* to join their native commonwealth'. Obviously, 'they were at liberty not to', but 'this would require an act of withdrawal'.[30] This leads us to the following conclusion – in the words of the afore-mentioned commentator:

> [...] the main thrust of Locke's arguing that government is based on consent is to establish that consent can be withdrawn if need be, *not* that it has to be shown to have been given in the first place. The consensual nature of government in the end seems to be an assertion about its *moral status*, rather than a claim about what precise sort of actions must have accompanied its creation or continuance.[31]

27 Ibid., pp. 100–101.
28 Ibid., p. 101.
29 Ibid. (my emphasis)
30 Ibid. (my italics for emphasis)
31 Ibid. (my italics). Cf. J. Dunn, 'Consent in the Political Theory of John Locke', *Historical Journal*, Vol. 10, No. 2 (1967).

Political Society

Property being insecure in the 'state of nature', the end of political society is the preservation of property, generally defined as the 'Lives, Liberties and Estates' of individuals (para. 123, p. 350). Although, for Locke, the 'state of nature' is not awful, as it is for Hobbes, yet it is inconvenient. This inconvenience stems from the lack of an established law (other than the unwritten Law of Nature) as the standard of right and wrong, an impartial judge and a power to impose punishment to transgressors of the law (paras 124–126, pp. 350–351).

> Thus Mankind, notwithstanding all the Priviledges of the state of Nature, being but in an ill condition, while they remain in it, are quickly driven into Society [...] The inconveniencies, that they are therein exposed to, by the irregular and uncertain exercise of the Power every Man has of punishing the transgressions of others, make them take Sanctuary under the establish'd Laws of Government, and therein seek *the preservation of their Property* [...] And in this we have the original *right and rise* of both *the Legislative and Executive Power* [...] (para. 127, p. 352)

We have discussed the three stages from the 'state of nature' to 'civil' and then to 'political society' before. We have also referred to the two phases of the social contract in Locke – first, the formation of a community and then the establishment of a lawful state. If this procedure is not hypothetical nor historical in the strict sense, then what is it? I have cited Hampsher-Monk who suggests that the 'state of nature' is a point from which a *speculative* history of human economic and political development can start. Even if we accept that the transition from the state of nature to civil society and thence to political society is a speculative history of humanity, we still have to say a little more about Locke's method. In other words, how did Locke construct this history? And why did he proceed in the way in which he did? I think Christopher Hughes has given a clear answer to these questions. Locke's account is '"generative" in method', by which is meant that Locke is interested in demonstrating that 'the nature of a thing is how it comes about'. Accordingly, 'There is, first, natural society [...] then civil society, and then political society'.[32] Moreover, Hughes identifies three stages in 'natural society' (the state of nature) – the second stage being introduced with the appointment of third-party judges and the third with the discussion of property in Chapter V. You will sometimes come across two or three stages in the 'state of nature' in the literature, but what is important for our purposes here is that 'the *Second Treatise* is built on a theory of *successive* stages of society'.[33]

So individuals give up the powers of doing whatever they judge to be necessary for the preservation of themselves as well as their fellows and of punishing the transgressors of the 'law of nature'. These powers they *entrust* to the government (paras 129–130, pp. 352–353). The notion of *trust* plays a significant role in Locke's political theory.[34] Given that the end of political society is the preservation of property in Locke's wide sense, its power '*can never be suppos'd to extend farther than the common good*'. It follows that, 'whoever has the Legislative or Supream Power of any Common-wealth, is bound to govern by establish'd *standing Laws*, promulgated and known to the People, and not by Extemporary Decrees; by *indifferent* and upright *Judges*' and to execute the law at home as well as defending the commonwealth against external threat (para. 131, p. 353). We see here expressed what is *the* most fundamental principle of western liberal democracies, namely, the separation of legislative, executive and judicial powers. Bear in mind that the doctrine of the separation between the legislative, executive and judicial functions of government is closely associated with the idea of the 'rule of law', according to which there has to be at least a separation of the executive and the judiciary.[35] However, Locke does not elaborate the doctrine of the separation of powers further in the *Second Treatise*; here he

32 C. Hughes, 'John Locke: *The Second Treatise of Government*', p. 149.

33 Ibid.

34 Cf. para. 134, p. 356; para. 136, p. 359; para. 139, p. 361; para. 142, p. 363; para. 149, p. 367; para. 155, p. 370; para. 156, p. 371; para. 164, p. 377 ; para. 171, p. 381; para. 210, p. 405; paras 221–222, p. 412; paras 226–227, pp. 415–416; para. 231, p. 419; para. 239, p. 424; para. 240, p. 427; para. 242, p. 427.

35 D. Robertson, *The Penguin Dictionary of Politics* (Harmondsworth: Penguin, 1986), pp. 300–301.

develops mostly the relations and distinct functions of the legislative and the executive branches of government.

For Locke, the commonwealth may have one of three forms of government – a democracy, an oligarchy or a monarchy (Chapter X, paras 132–133, pp. 354–355). What is crucial and what really interests Locke is the extent of the power that the government has over its subjects. We are told that 'the *first and fundamental positive Law* of all Commonwealths' is the establishment of the legislature and 'the *first and fundamental natural Law*, which is to govern even the Legislative it self' is the preservation of political society and of every individual in it. The legislative is the supreme power of the commonwealth; no edict or other (subordinate) power has the authority to make a law without the sanction of the legislature (para. 134, pp. 355–356). However, Locke is anxious to emphasize that, despite the supremacy of the legislative branch of government, its power is not unlimited or unchecked. Firstly, it cannot exercise power arbitrarily, for it is subject to the 'Law of Nature', which 'stands as an Eternal Rule to all Men', legislators and others alike (para. 135, p. 358). Secondly, it cannot rule 'by extemporary Arbitrary Decrees' but only on the basis of '*promulgated standing Laws, and known Authoris'd Judges*' (para. 136, p. 358). Thirdly, it cannot take from anyone any part of his or her property without his or her consent (paras 138–140, pp. 360–362). In fact, Locke claims that taxation must be based on consent and that where no such consent exists, there is a breach of 'the Fundamental Law of Property'; but the problem we noted earlier concerning unanimity and majoritarianism props up yet again, for in the very same paragraph – actually, in a single sentence – Locke refers to both consent and majority rule, as if the two were exactly the same thing. He says that taxation 'must be with his own Consent, i.e. the Consent of the Majority' (para. 140, p. 362). Fourthly, 'The *Legislative cannot transfer the Power of Making Laws* to any other hands', for 'it being but a delegated Power from the People, they who have it, cannot pass it over to others' (para. 141, p. 362).

According to Locke, the legislative power should rest with an assembly, which, after making the laws of the commonwealth, should dissolve (para. 143, p. 364). By contrast, the executive power should always remain in existence, as there will constantly be a need for the implementation of the laws (para. 144, pp. 364–365). Yet, once dissolved and having entrusted 'the *Execution* of the Laws' to the executive, the legislative has the power to assemble anew when it is necessary; that is, in order to address any maladministration against the laws (para. 153, p. 369). Otherwise, when the legislative is not in existence, it rests with the executive to convene a new legislature in one of two ways in accordance with the constitution: either when the constitution requires the assembling and acting of the legislative at specific periods of time or when the amendment of old, or the making of new, laws is necessary (para. 154, p. 370). Locke insists, however, that, although the executive has the power to convene and dismiss the legislative, it is not superior to it; rather the convoking and dissolving of the legislative is a power with which the executive has been *entrusted* (para. 156, pp. 371–372). There is also a third power in the commonwealth which Locke calls '*Federative*' and is the branch of government which is charged with the international relations of the commonwealth (para. 146, p. 365); in reality, the federative and executive powers are 'almost united' however (para. 147, p. 365) and, therefore, ought to be placed in the same hands (para. 148, p. 366). It is best to think of the federative power as that part of the executive which deals with international relations, as opposed to domestic affairs. I think the reason why Locke insists on the distinction between the executive and federative powers is in order to make clear that, when considered in relation to other political societies, each commonwealth is 'in the State of Nature, in respect of all other States or Persons out of its Community' (para. 145, p. 365). Finally, Locke discusses 'prerogative power'. This is not another branch of government, but the power of the executive to act according to its discretion in cases when there is no provision in the law, always *with the proviso* that this action serves the common good (para. 158, pp. 373–374 & Chapter XIV, paras 159–168, pp. 374–380).

Revolution

Locke is the first political theorist to legitimize recourse to revolution when the government does not perform the tasks for which it was appointed. The possibility of rebellion appears for the first time at the beginning of Chapter XIII, where it is said:

> [...] the Legislative being only a Fiduciary Power to act for certain ends, there remains still *in the People a Supream Power* to remove or *alter the Legislative*, when they find the *Legislative* act contrary to the trust reposed in them. For all *Power given with trust* for the attaining an *end*, being limited by that end, whenever that *end* is manifestly neglected, or opposed, the *trust* must necessarily be *forfeited*, and the Power devolve into the hands of those that gave it, who may place it anew where they shall think best for their safety and security. (para. 149, p. 367)

Revolution is, therefore, justified on the grounds of trust. Hence the crucial role of trust in Locke's political philosophy. Since the people have *entrusted* the legislative with the protection of their property, they can take their trust back if the legislative does not accomplish its task or abuses its power. It is in this sense that 'the *Community* may be said [...] to be *always the Supream Power*' (para. 149, p. 367). We have already noted the two phases of the formation of political society as implied in Locke's social contract theory – that is, the formation of a community and then the establishment of government. It follows that, unlike Hobbes, Locke does not think that the overthrow of government will lead to a return to an anarchic state of nature. This is why the gradual establishment of the commonwealth in Locke's political theory is so important. As Locke puts it, one should 'distinguish between the *Dissolution of the Society*, and the *Dissolution of the Government*' (para. 211, p. 406).

Before discussing the dissolution of government, Locke considers some governments which are based on illegitimate grounds – these being, briefly, despotic power (Chapter XV), political power following conquest (Chapter XVI), usurpation (Chapter XVII) and tyranny (Chapter XVIII). It should be emphasized that Locke does not think that revolution or popular revolt is justified whenever the people disapprove of a policy or are not satisfied with a course of action. Such disapproval or dissatisfaction cannot be a criterion for the legitimacy of revolution. A revolution can be justified only when the government exercises arbitrary power on a day-to-day basis (para. 210, p. 405).

In the final chapter, entitled 'Of the Dissolution of Government', Locke argues that a government can be dissolved either from without – that is, from external threat – or from within, but here he is mostly concerned with internal dissolution, which results from an abuse of power by the government. So there is abuse when 'the *Legislative* is *altered*' (para. 212, p. 407), which can happen in one of four ways: first, when a 'Prince sets up his own Arbitrary Will in place of the Laws' which the legislative has enacted (para. 214, p. 408); second, when the legislature is hindered from holding sessions (para. 215, p. 409); third, when elections are gerrymandered (para. 216, p. 409); fourth, when the government delivers its subjects to another power (para. 217, p. 409). The government also dissolves when the executive abandons it, so that there is no one to implement the laws (para. 219, pp. 410–411). All the above were practices of the Stuart monarchs in Locke's days.[36] When the government dissolves in one of the ways just mentioned, claims Locke, the people are free 'to provide for themselves' by setting up a new legislative (para. 220, p. 411). However, Locke goes on to say:

> [...] the state of Mankind is not so miserable that they are not capable of using this Remedy [i.e. the establishment of a new legislative], till it be too late to look for any. To tell *People* they *may provide for themselves*, by erecting a new Legislative, when by Oppression, Artifice, or being delivered over to a Foreign Power, their old one is gone, is only to tell them they may expect Relief, when it is too late, and the evil is past Cure. This is in effect no more than to bid them first be Slaves, and then to take care of their Liberty; and when their Chains are on, tell them, they may act like Freemen [...] And therefore it is, that they have not only a Right to get out of it but to prevent it. (para. 220, p. 411)

It follows that a government also dissolves when it acts contrary to the people's trust (para. 221, p. 412). In both the abovementioned circumstances, says Locke, when the legislative is changed or the legislature betrays the

36 Hampsher-Monk, *A History of Modern Political Thought*, p. 113.

trust of the people, 'those who are guilty are *guilty of Rebellion*' because they have waged a war against the people (para. 227, p. 416). And 'the Appeal then lies no where but to Heaven' (para. 242, p. 427) – that is, to God or the law of nature –, which means that people have the right to rebel.

In conclusion, there is one point I should like to stress. This concerns the meaning of revolution in Locke's political theory. We have become accustomed to the idea of revolution as involving radical social and political change – that is, a change in the structure of society as well as the form of government. This is the modern sense of revolution – a sense which emerged in the eighteenth century with the French Revolution. Understood in this way, revolutions are class conflicts.[37] But this is not what Locke means by revolution. For him, a revolution does not result in social and political change but in the restoration of the rule of law; it is a return to an earlier ordered state of affairs. Therefore, Locke's understanding of revolution is the same as Plato's and as that which prevailed from antiquity to Locke's time; it is part of a cyclical understanding of history and comes to pass whenever a diversion from the rule threatens human societies.[38]

37 Robertson, *The Penguin Dictionary of Politics*, p. 291.

38 Cf. Hampsher-Monk, *A History of Modern Political Thought*, p. 114.

CHAPTER 3

Jeremy Bentham

Jeremy Bentham was born in London in 1748. His talents were recognized early on by his father, who entertained high ambitions for young Jeremy. He went to Westminster School at the age of seven and to Queen's College, Oxford at twelve. He graduated from Oxford in 1763 at the age of fifteen. His father wanted his son to pursue a legal career and hoped that Jeremy would become Lord Chancellor. In this sense, Jeremy disappointed his father when, having been admitted to the Bar in 1769, he did not practise the legal profession. We know that Jeremy was withdrawn by character and so the social obligations of a legal career would have been a great burden to him.

Jeremy Bentham devoted his life to theoretical studies. He wrote on law, government, social administration, economics and philosophy, his writings influencing a variety of writers and having an impact on a wide range of fields. So far as method is concerned, he introduced a rigorous method of analysis and minuteness – not employed since Aristotle – and changed the way in which the above-mentioned subjects were studied.[1] What is important, however, is that Bentham was not just a person of theory but of practice as well; he wanted to see his theories implemented in practice and his theoretical studies were directed to this effect. His views formed the basis of 'philosophic radicalism'[2] – a doctrine combining utilitarianism, classical political economy, a jurisprudence whose object was to rationalize the law and a justification of democracy.[3]

One of the difficulties in studying Bentham is that there is no single work representative of Bentham's political thought. Bentham wrote a lot,

1 D. Miller et al. (eds), *The Blackwell Encyclopedia of Political Thought* (Oxford: Blackwell, 1991), p. 37.

2 Ibid.

3 Ibid., p. 369.

while he had the habit of rewriting or revising his writings very often; what is more, his concern with detail and precision – almost an anxiety, one could say – had as a result that many of his writings were left unfinished. But, to make matters even worse, it seems that his editor had felt in liberty to re-organize and polish up Bentham's writings, so that there is often uncertainty as to whether this was really what Bentham said or meant. Werner Stark has demonstrated that 'at times Bowring seems to have reshuffled the manuscript as if it were a pack of cards', while it has also been shown that 'Bowring was incapable of leaving a single sentence in the form in which Bentham wrote it when he produced his nineteenth-century edition'.[4] In fact, Bentham's manuscripts are unreadable – he had a terrible handwriting, which makes their decipherment a great pain.[5] A group of scholars at University College London are involved in the publication of Bentham's works from his manuscripts; this is known as the 'Bentham Project'.

Bentham's political theory is based on the 'utility principle', expounded in his best-known work, *An Introduction to the Principles of Morals and Legislation*, printed in 1780 and eventually published nine years later. This is a study of penal law to which Bentham applies his principle of utility. We shall not be concerned with Bentham's examination of offences and punishments; we shall concentrate on the 'utility principle'. So what is this principle?

The Principle of Utility

Bentham once said:

> I dreamt the other night that I was a founder of a sect; of course, a personage of great sanctity and importance. It was the sect of the utilitarians.[6]

4 R. Harrison, *Bentham* (London: Routledge & Kegan Paul, 1983), p. x.
5 I. Hampsher-Monk, *A History of Modern Political Thought: Major Political Thinkers from Hobbes to Marx* (Oxford & Cambridge, Massachusetts: Blackwell, 1992), p. 305.
6 Quoted by B. Parekh, *Bentham's Political Thought*, p. 13.

He had this dream in 1870, the year *An Introduction to the Principles of Morals and Legislation* was printed. At the very beginning of this work Bentham says:

> Nature has placed mankind under the governance of two sovereign masters, *pain* and *pleasure* [...] The *principle of utility* recognises this subjection, and assumes it for the foundation of that system, the object of which is to rear the fabric of felicity by the hands of reason and law.[7]

Therefore, for Bentham, humans are motivated by pleasure and pain. These are, as he puts it elsewhere, 'the main pillars or foundations' of the other 'psychological entities' (e.g. emotions, passions, inclinations),[8] the only real ones, all others being fictitious.[9] This implies that no human act can ever be disinterested.[10] It is evident that there is no place for God in Bentham's psychological and moral theory; psychology and morality are absolutely secular. Equally, Bentham's is a materialistic theory. Driven by pleasure and pain as they are, his individuals are affected by their immediate environment – physical or natural. The 'principle of utility' is 'that principle which approves or disapproves of every action whatsoever, according to the tendency which it appears to have to augment or diminish the happiness of the party whose interest is in question'.[11] In fact, as Bentham is eager to make clear, the 'principle of utility' is a standard by means of which not only the actions of individuals but also measures of government are to be judged.[12] Moreover, 'utility' has a general meaning in Bentham and refers to all benefit, advantage, pleasure, happiness, good, or simply the avoidance

7 J. Bentham, *An Introduction to the Principles of Morals and Legislation*, edited by J. H. Burns and H. L. A. Hart, with a new introduction by F. Rosen (New York: Oxford University Press, 1996), p. 11.

8 *Bentham's Political Thought*, ed. B. Parekh, p. 62 (from *A Table of the Springs of Action*).

9 Ibid., pp. 62–63.

10 Ibid., pp. 63–65.

11 Bentham, *An Introduction to the Principles of Morals and Legislation*, p. 12.

12 Ibid.

of pain.[13] According to Bentham, the community is merely 'a fictitious *body*', consisting of the individuals who are regarded as 'its *members*'. It follows that the 'interest of the community' is 'the sum of the interests of the several members who compose it',[14] while a measure of government is informed by the 'principle of utility' when 'the tendency which it has to augment the happiness of the community is greater than any which it has to diminish it'.[15]

Bentham's morality rests on his psychology. What ought or ought not to be done, right and wrong all depend on the extent to which they tend to maximize happiness and minimize pain. In point of fact, for Bentham, it is only when understood in this way that moral notions have any meaning at all.[16] At the same time, he recognizes that there is not any direct proof of the principle's validity. As he puts it: 'for that which is used to prove every thing else, cannot itself be proved'.[17] Yet the utility principle underlies all human action – even if unknowingly or inconsistently. For this reason it is not only impossible to prove it, but such a proof is also unnecessary.[18] For Bentham, it would seem, it sufficed that all attempts at challenging the utility principle relied on it all the same, so that what they suggested – if anything – was that the principle was often '*misapplied*'.[19] So long as no other principle which accounted for human behaviour could be found, the validity of the utility principle counted as proven and the critic argued on the basis of 'his own unfounded sentiments' or – what one might also call – '*caprice*'.[20] While if he argued that he judged actions with no regard to their consequences, one could then ask this critic whether he considered his sentiment to be the standard of right and wrong with regard to all human beings or thought that every individual's sentiments could have the

13 Ibid.
14 Ibid.
15 Ibid., p. 13.
16 Ibid.
17 Ibid.
18 Ibid.
19 Ibid., pp. 14–15.
20 Ibid., p. 15.

same weight in determining what was a right or wrong course of action.[21] In the former case, his principle would be 'despotical', while in the latter 'anarchical', for would there then not be 'as many different standards of right and wrong as there are men?'[22] And, if he were to say that his proposed sentiment was based on reflection, he would still have to spell out its particulars. Further, if he were to combine the principle of utility with some other principle, he would still have to specify to what extent he adopted the utility principle and to what extent not; while if he were to subscribe to some other principle he would have to say what, according this newly propounded principle, was the motive of human action.[23]

For Bentham, the happiness of the members of a political community 'is the end and the sole end which the legislator ought to have in view'.[24] To be able to accomplish this task, the legislator should know the nature of pleasure and pain, as well as their causes. Bentham identifies four sources of pleasure and pain – namely, the physical, the political, the moral and the religious. These he calls '*sanctions*', as they have 'a binding force'.[25] The physical sanction consists in any natural or physical causes – that is, ways in which the natural environment at large as well as natural

21 Ibid., pp. 15–16.

22 Ibid., p. 16.

23 Ibid. For Bentham, if the utility principle were right, which he was sure it was, all other principles had to be wrong (ibid.). There were two ways in which other principles differed from that of utility and were thereby wrong. First, by defining themselves in opposition to the principle of utility, this being the case of 'the principle of *asceticism*'; second, by being opposed to it or not, depending on the circumstances, this being the case of 'the principle of *sympathy* and *antipathy*' (ibid., p. 17). On the 'principle of asceticism' see ibid., pp. 17–21; on the 'principle of sympathy and antipathy' see ibid., pp. 21–31. On the '*theological* principle' see ibid., p. 31. Ultimately, the 'theological principle' is one of the other three principles – namely, the principles of utility, asceticism, sympathy and antipathy – in disguise, as it were (ibid., pp. 31–32; footnote g). Bentham also considers the possibility that antipathy should lead to a perfectly right action. Yet it 'can never be a right ground of action'. The 'only right ground of action' is utility (ibid., p. 32).

24 Ibid., p. 34.

25 Ibid.

events (may) affect the behaviour of human beings. The political sanction consists in the expectation or fear of the action(s) that may be taken by the rulers or other magistrates of the state in favour of or against an individual or individuals. The moral sanction – which Bentham, perhaps more appropriately, also calls the popular sanction – is not what one might expect (that is, some moral rule of behaviour or moral obligation); it is rather what we would more commonly call the influence of public opinion. Finally, by religious sanction is meant the idea of God when it acts on humans as a motive for action. Although all physical, political and moral sanctions refer to the present life, the religious sanction can refer to a future life as well as to the present.[26] Bentham makes clear that the pleasures or pains which relate to any one of the above-mentioned sanctions do not differ 'in kind' from those which relate to the others – the only difference being 'the circumstances that accompany their production'.[27] Accordingly, the same sort of pain may be suffered by an individual as a result of a natural cause (namely, physical sanction) – in which case it will be 'a *calamity*' –, of the political sanction – in which case it will be 'a *punishment*' –, of the moral sanction – in which case it will be a punishment imposed on him or her by the other members of the community – and of the religious sanction – in which case it will be a punishment imposed by God.[28]

To be sure, Bentham says, humans cannot possibly know the pleasures and pains which belong to the religious sanction and which relate to a future life.[29] What is crucial, however, is that the physical sanction is the basis of the political, moral and religious sanctions – of the religious in so far as it relates to the present life.[30] In his words:

26 Ibid., p. 35.
27 Ibid., p. 36.
28 Ibid.
29 Ibid., pp. 36–37.
30 Ibid., p. 37.

> [...] the powers of nature may operate of themselves; but neither the magistrate, nor men at large, *can* operate, nor is God in the case in question *supposed* to operate, but through the powers of nature.[31]

As well as knowing the sources of pleasure and pain, the legislator, Bentham maintains, should also understand their '*value*', since they 'are the *instruments* he has to work with'.[32] Accordingly, so far as an individual '*by himself*' is concerned, 'the value of a pleasure or pain considered *by itself*, will be greater or less', depending on its intensity, duration, certainty or uncertainty, propinquity or remoteness.[33] As regards the tendency of a specific pleasure or pain to bring about a further pleasure or pain, its value will also depend on its '*fecundity*' – that is, the possibility of it leading to 'sensation of the *same* kind' ('pleasures, if it be a pleasure: pains, if it be a pain') – and its '*purity*' – to wit, its tendency to cause 'sensations of the *opposite* kind' ('pains, if it be a pleasure: pleasures, if it be a pain').[34] Nevertheless, Bentham qualifies this claim by saying that the latter two are, strictly speaking, not 'properties of the pleasure or pain itself' but 'properties only of the act, or other event, by which such pleasure or pain has been produced'. It follows that 'in strictness' they should not be considered when calculating the value of a given pleasure or pain itself.[35] So far as 'a *number* of persons' is concerned, the value of a specific pleasure or pain will depend on all the aforesaid factors *as well as* on its extent, by which is meant 'the number of persons to whom it *extends*; or (in other words) who are affected by it'.[36]

Bentham proceeds to an explanation of the procedure whereby the calculation of the value of a pleasure or pain can be effected. Briefly, the procedure consists in this: the value of each pleasure *and* pain experienced or likely to be experienced by an individual is to be estimated. Next *all* the values of *all* the pleasures as well as *all* the values of *all* the

31 Ibid.

32 Ibid., p. 38.

33 Ibid.

34 Ibid., pp. 38–39.

35 Ibid., p. 39.

36 Ibid.

pains experienced by the individual in question are to be summed up. Depending on where the balance tilts, it will be determined whether the act is beneficial to his or her interests or not. The same procedure is to be repeated by estimating the value of all the pleasures and pains of each individual concerned. These individual pleasures and pains are then to be summed up and the balance taken – which (balance), 'if on the side of *pleasure* will give the general *good tendency* of the act, with respect to the total number or community of individuals concerned; if on the side of pain, the general *evil tendency*, with respect to the same community'.[37] But, as Bentham concedes:

> It is not to be expected that this process should be strictly pursued previously to every moral judgment, or to every legislative or judicial operation. It may, however, be always kept in view: and as near as the process actually pursued on these occasions approaches to it, so near will such process approach to the character of an exact one.[38]

For Bentham, the same procedure applied to pleasure and pain, whatever form they took – whether they be called good, profit, convenience, advantage, benefit, emolument, happiness and suchlike, on the one hand, evil, mischief, inconvenience, disadvantage, loss, unhappiness, etc. on the other.[39] And he was convinced that this is what humans did in fact do in practice[40] – what we would call today a cost-benefit analysis.

It should be noted that, although pleasure and pain derived from external causes, Bentham did not believe that there was a clear-cut correspondence between a specific cause and the pleasure or pain it produced.[41] Individuals experience pleasure and pain in different degrees, depending on such circumstances as their health, strength, hardiness, bodily imperfection, quantity and quality of knowledge, strength of intellectual powers, firmness of mind, steadiness, bent of inclinations, moral sensibility, moral biases, religious sensibility, religious biases, sympathetic sensibility, sympathetic

37 Ibid., pp. 39–40; quotation p. 40.
38 Ibid., p. 40.
39 Ibid.
40 Ibid.
41 Ibid., p. 51.

biases, antipathetic sensibility, antipathetic biases, insanity, habitual occupations, pecuniary circumstances, connexions in the way of sympathy, connexions in the way of antipathy, radical frame of body, radical frame of mind, sex, age, rank, education, climate, lineage, government, religious profession.[42] So Bentham believed that the legislator should take account of all the above factors (or circumstances) in determining the right punishment, which will always be tailored to specific individuals.

To summarize: For Bentham, human behaviour is determined by pleasure and pain. These are real entities, not fictions. The principle of utility is an objective standard by means of which pleasures and pains are assessed. Therefore, utilitarianism is a materialistic and consequentialist moral theory.

The Political Theory

I.

Bentham's political theory is based on his psychology. Given than humans are motivated by pleasure and pain, the purpose of political society should be to maximize pleasure and minimize pain. As we have seen, in the first few paragraphs of the *Introduction to the Principles of Morals and Legislation* Bentham already says that 'The community is a fictitious *body*, composed of the individual persons who are considered as constituting as it were its *members*.' And to the question 'The interest of the community then is, what?', he answers 'the sum of the interests of the several members who compose it'.[43] When he comes to define political society Bentham says:

42 Ibid., p. 52 (enumerated), pp. 53–69 (analyzed).
43 Ibid., p. 12.

> When a number of persons (whom we may style subjects) are supposed to be in the habit of paying obedience to a person, or an assemblage of persons, of a known and certain description (whom we may call governor or governors) such persons altogether (subjects and governors) are said to be in a state of political society.[44]

He distinguishes the 'idea of a political society', which is 'a positive one', from the 'idea of a natural society', which is 'a negative one'.[45] For Bentham, the criterion of this distinction is 'the presence or absence of an habit of obedience'.[46] Thus in a 'natural society' – which he also calls 'state of nature'[47] – humans are associated without having a common ruler; they are merely 'in the habit of conversing with each other'.[48] However, he explains that both a perfect state of nature and a perfect political society are impossible.[49] He believes that, in reality, societies are somewhere in between; they 'in proportion as the habit of obedience is more perfect, recede from; in proportion as it is less perfect, approach to, a state of nature'.[50]

Obviously, one and the same person may be both in a state of authority and a state of submission at the same time *with reference to* other persons.[51] Moreover, authority and submission alternate, so one person may be ruler at one time and subject at another.[52] Equally, the same people, 'considered among themselves', may at one time be in a state of nature and at another in a state of political society (or, as Bentham also terms it, 'a state of government').[53]

Considering that there can never be a perfect natural society nor a perfect political society, the question is when it can be said that a society is of the former and when of the latter type. In other words, is there a

44 *Bentham's Political Thought*, p. 128.
45 Ibid.
46 Ibid.
47 Ibid., pp. 130, 131, 132.
48 Ibid., p. 128.
49 Ibid., pp. 130–131.
50 Ibid., p. 129.
51 Ibid., p. 132.
52 Ibid., p. 133.
53 Ibid.

distinguishing mark able to determine when a society is natural or political? Bentham confesses that the only such mark he can find is 'the establishment of names of office'.[54] This leads to the issue of disobedience and revolt.[55] The real question here is whether 'every act of disobedience' constitutes a revolt.[56] Bentham considers that this cannot be the case, for then no government could ever exist.[57] He believes that it is important to distinguish between conscious and unconscious disobedience, in respect of both law and fact. It then appears that, when disobedience is unconscious with regard to both law and fact, it is not a revolt. Regarding conscious disobedience with respect to both law and fact, it matters whether it is 'secret' or 'open'; or – what amounts to the same thing – 'fraudulent' or 'forcible'. And he concludes that only when disobedience is 'forcible' (that is, violent or armed) it constitutes a revolt.[58] In that case, all the number of persons involved, their acts and their intentions should be taken into account.[59]

Let us make a few observations now. Note that, for Bentham, political society is *not* the result of some plan or a collective decision, as social contract theorists would argue. Rather he saw the habit of obedience to a superior as somehow inherent in human affairs. From the beginning of human history the talented and more powerful seem to have exercised power over the less able and weak. But, so long as this has been the case in all human societies, it has also been possible this ruler-ruled relationship to assume a moral character. As a writer has put it:

> Within the framework of human relationships there lies not only the likelihood of any gifted man grasping and exercising power to his own advantage, there also lies the possibility of this man finding his actions beneficial to others, and the subject of their approval. The moral authority thereby conferred on him depends upon his being able to behave consistently in this fashion.[60]

54 Ibid., p. 134.
55 Ibid., pp. 134–135.
56 Ibid., p. 135.
57 Ibid., pp. 135–136.
58 Ibid., p. 136.
59 Ibid.
60 D. J. Manning, *The Mind of Jeremy Bentham* (London: Longmans, 1968), p. 47.

So, although Bentham did not see a common identity or history as being the basis upon which a political society is founded, he nonetheless seemed to believe that 'The more men live in public the more amenable they are to the moral sanction'[61] – namely, to public opinion acting upon the members of a political community as a motive. Elie Halévy explains the importance of the principle of utility to Bentham's theory of politics as follows. In applying the principle of utility,

> Bentham solves the problem in favour of authority [...] Speak of utility, and you convince the individual that he must submit to constraints in order that the interest of each should be artificially identified with the interest of all. Speak of natural right, of the law of nature, and you invite everyone, strong in his conscience and given up to the promptings of the principle of sympathy and antipathy, to take up arms against every law which happens to displease him.[62]

II.

I shall now proceed to discuss Bentham's conception of law and how it bears on his political theory. For Bentham, 'A law is a command.'[63] It is distinguished from 'custom', which is the regular or habitual way of doing things.[64] It is also different from 'utility'; 'For utility is but a quality [...] a property an act has of increasing happiness' or 'of averting pains'. Therefore, 'Utility is a quality of many kinds of acts', whereas 'a command is one particular kind of act itself'.[65] Nor is a 'dictate of utility' a law; 'For a dictate of utility is but someone's opinion that there is utility in a certain mode of conduct'[66] – 'that the mode of conduct in question is likely upon the

61 Quoted in ibid., p. 48 (MSS UCL, Box 15, Folder 19, p. 199).
62 E. Halévy, *The Growth of Philosophic Radicalism*, translated by M. Morris, with a preface by A. D. Lindsay (London: Faber & Faber Ltd., 1928), p. 144.
63 *Bentham's Political Thought*, p. 149.
64 Ibid., p. 150.
65 Ibid., p. 151.
66 Ibid., pp. 151–152.

whole to be productive of more pleasure (good) than it is of pain (evil).'[67] And an opinion is 'an act of the understanding', whereas 'a *command* is an *act* of the *will*.'[68] Bentham also distinguishes law from resolution,[69] from a promise,[70] from a compact[71] and from a command in general.[72] Regarding the latter, it is a *specific type* of command which is a law – 'on account of one or other of three particulars', namely, 'its source, its substance, and (or) its formalities'.[73] Accordingly, a command is a law only when it derives from 'a sovereign', that is, 'any person or assemblage of persons to whose will a whole political community are (no matter on what account) supposed to be in a disposition to pay obedience: and that in preference to the will of any other person'.[74] Bentham distinguishes different sorts of mandate and this is where he becomes legalistic.[75] What is important is that, for Bentham, so long as law is made by the sovereign, it is legitimate. There are no *moral* grounds on which a particular law can be criticized. This means that 'The right to make law [...] is not a moral right. It is a legal one.' Accordingly, 'Political obedience is also a legal obligation.'[76] So Bentham's conception of legitimacy is very different from that to which we are used. Whenever a sovereign – or government, for that matter – is obeyed, it is regarded as legitimate. Illegitimate is only the sovereign who has failed to win support. For this reason Bentham did not consider an oppressive government to be a usurpation, *provided* it enjoyed the obedience of the people. To be sure,

67 Ibid., pp. 152–153.
68 Ibid., p. 153.
69 Ibid., p. 153.
70 Ibid., p. 154.
71 Ibid.
72 Ibid.
73 Ibid., p. 155.
74 Ibid., p. 157.
75 Eg. a mandate of conception or one of adoption (ibid., p. 160); in respect of time, one by 'suspension' or by 'pre-adoption' (ibid., p. 161); with regard to the persons whose mandates are adopted – former sovereigns or subordinate power-holders (ibid.); with respect to the degree in which the mandate is adopted (ibid.); and, in respect of the form of expression – i.e. 'primordial' or 'superventitious' (ibid., pp. 165–166).
76 Manning, *The Mind of Jeremy Bentham*, p. 56.

a sovereign was more likely to have popular support if it promoted the 'greatest happiness of the greatest number'.[77] If it did not, it ran the risk of losing popular support and thereby being toppled.[78] It is in the light of this legal framework that Bentham's notions of legality, illegality, offence and punishment have to be understood. Thus a mandate is illegal when it does not express the will of the sovereign,[79] for the will of the law must always be 'the will of the sovereign in a state'.[80] Bentham acknowledged the existence of subordinate powers in a state. Yet, at the same time, he believed that all subordinate mandates were 'the mandates of the sovereign'; in his words,

> [...] every mandate that is issued within the limits of sovereignty and that is not illegal, is in one sense or the other the mandate of the sovereign.[81]

It follows that an 'offence' is 'a mode of conduct contrary to the mode of conduct commanded by a law', which may either be 'a forbearance, when the mode of conduct commanded by the law is action' or 'an action, when the mode of conduct commanded by the law [...] is forbearance'.[82] As for punishment, it 'is nothing but pain inflicted by or by command of a superior for or, in other words, on account of an act done'.[83]

III.

Until about 1809–1810 Bentham supported a form of enlightened despotism, with the legislator(s) being responsible for the happiness of the people. During 1809–1810, however, Bentham was converted to radicalism. Having lost faith in the possibility of reforming the rulers, he came

77 *Bentham's Political Thought*, pp. 195, 309.
78 Cf. Manning, *The Mind of Jeremy Bentham*, p. 56.
79 *Bentham's Political Thought*, p. 159.
80 Ibid., p. 157.
81 Ibid., p. 162.
82 Ibid., p. 156.
83 Ibid.

to believe that only the people could prevent the governors from abusing their power. Thereafter he became a supporter of representative government. The publication of the *Plan of Parliamentary Reform* in 1817 attests to this fundamental change in his political thinking. In the 1820s he was preoccupied with the writing of the *Constitutional Code*, a voluminous, yet unfinished, work. Albeit of a legal character, the *Constitutional Code* contains Bentham's mature political thought – his thoughts on the institutions of a representative democracy, as well as on the structure of the legislative, executive and judicial branches of government.

Let us look at the legislature first. Bentham thought it was of utmost importance that a member of parliament should identify with the interest of his constituency.[84] Therefore, if the 'particular aggregate interest' of his constituents is different from the 'national interest', it would be his duty to vote in favour of his constituents' interest.[85] In this way, votes in parliament would represent the particular interests of the different constituencies in the country. To ensure that members of parliament are serious about their task and their responsibility to their constituents, Bentham suggested that all aspiring MPs should deposit one hundred and twenty pounds before they could stand for elections. Moreover, they would be allowed to be MPs only one year in every three.[86] Once elected, the parliament's task would be to promote 'the national felicity' or 'the happiness of the greatest number';[87] each MP would *directly* represent the interest(s) of his constituents. This *direct* representation implies that the MP would not be allowed to speak in parliament on behalf of his constituents – that is, by saying what he thought was the interest of his constituency. Rather he would be communicating to the legislature what his constituents – more precisely, the majority of them – had told him was their interests. Put simply, he would be their mouthpiece. For this reason Bentham deemed it important that the constituents were well-informed of matters of common concern.[88] The

84 Ibid., pp. 216–218.
85 Ibid., p. 217.
86 Manning, *The Mind of Jeremy Bentham*, p. 67.
87 *Bentham's Political Thought*, p. 218.
88 Manning, *The Mind of Jeremy Bentham*, p. 67.

legislature would sit six days a week, while in an emergency there would be no vacations.[89] To ensure attendance, Bentham proposed that every MP should deposit four hundred pounds with the Clerk of the House at the beginning of each session.[90] Each time an MP attended a debate he would be paid out of this money; so no attendance, no money back. Indeed, one is surprised when one reads Bentham's detailed account of attendance and remuneration. He says:

> Each day, on entrance into the assembly chamber, each member receives that day's pay at the hands of the doorkeeper. In his view, and in that of the company in the assembly chamber, is a clock. On delivery of the pay, the doorkeeper stamps, in the *Entrance and Departure Book*, on the page of that day, the member's name, adding an hour and minute.[91]

In addition, no MP may leave without the permission of the president. The only excuse for not attending a debate would be illness, but again even in that case a medical certificate would be required.[92] Interesting is Bentham's proposal of a 'continuation committee', whose members will have the task of making sure that 'the designs and proceedings' of the preceding legislature are carried on by the next parliament.[93] The continuation committee would be composed of all MPs of the outgoing legislature as well as 'every member of the continuation committee, serving in that same legislature'.[94] The continuation committee members would be able to stand on the committee 'for any number of consecutive years', but, owing to the fact that they would not be elected by the people, they would have no vote; nonetheless, they would have a 'right of argumentation' or 'speech' and 'initiation' or 'motion'.[95] In addition to the continuation committee, Bentham recommended that some MPs with the assistance of civil servants would

89 *Bentham's Political Thought*, p. 218.
90 Manning, *The Mind of Jeremy Bentham*, pp. 67–68.
91 *Bentham's Political Thought*, p. 219.
92 Ibid.
93 Ibid., pp. 219–220.
94 Ibid., p. 220.
95 Ibid.

be responsible for collecting information about impending legislation – this would come close to a modern select committee. Lastly, he suggested that a standing committee be established to give advice to the House with regard to the drafting of bills and to elucidate existing laws.[96]

One should bear in mind, of course, that the electorate would be limited. Initially, Bentham would support only a middle-class suffrage. In the *Plan for Parliamentary Reform* he came to propound one man one vote.[97] Even this did not seem to be enough for a utilitarian, however, for 'why a person of the one sex should have less happiness than a person of the other sex'?[98]

Turning to the executive now, I am not going to get into the details of the functions of the prime minister and the number of ministers. The importance of Bentham's contribution lies in his attempt to abolish patronage and corruption within the executive branch of government. To avoid a system of favours, he recommended that all offices be filled on the basis of competitive examinations. Furthermore, posts would be distributed to people who would be prepared to accept the minimum salary 'for the honour of serving the public'.[99] For Bentham, ministers had to be very well qualified. The qualifications he proposed for some ministers, for example, are: The Foreign Relation Minister had to master languages, international law, history, geography, political economy and statistics, while the Health Minister should know medicine, chemistry, natural history and geography.[100] To prevent negligence and mismanagement, he describes, for instance, how official papers would be sent from office to office in locked boxes to prevent their loss or their being stolen, something which, Bentham says bitterly, has happened several times: 'The offices being, many of them, out of sight of one another, and situated at indefinite distance – the bearers

96 Manning, *The Mind of Jeremy Bentham*, p. 68.
97 Ibid., p. 66.
98 Quoted in ibid.
99 Ibid., p. 68.
100 Ibid.

of these boxes have been way-laid, and for some sinister political purpose robbed of them.'[101]

Regarding the judiciary, Bentham made it clear that it was to be separate from the executive. In fact, the Minister of Justice was to enjoy as much power as the Prime Minister, each in their respective fields, so that they would check one another.[102] Bentham supported a system of checks and balances. It should be remarked that Bentham did not favour a separation of governmental powers on the grounds that it secured the liberty of the people. Surely, he thought that 'the functions of the executive, the judiciary and the legislative were different [...] but by political liberty he understood the freedom of the people to intimidate their government'.[103] In general, Bentham was a trenchant critic of the judiciary of his own day.

It has been argued that Bentham understood politics to be mere administration.[104] He was thus unable to grasp the complexity and richness of political activity, believing that it could organized in accordance with fixed rules.[105] For example:

> In Bentham's reformed parliament it would be futile to try to persuade the members to vote according to their conscience simply because they have none – they merely represent interest. The business of the House is not persuasive oratory and argument so much as the registering and counting of votes, votes which have already been determined by constituency opinion. The House is a calculating machine rather than a debating chamber [...][106]

Moreover, in seeking unanimity on political issues, Bentham did not allow for the possibility of a diversity of opinion or belief.[107] Further, what he was concerned with was the adoption of a 'master plan' and 'a technique' for putting it into action in specific circumstances; this precluded the existence

101 *Bentham's Political Thought*, p. 223.
102 Manning, *The Mind of Jeremy Bentham*, p. 69.
103 Ibid.
104 Ibid., p. 72.
105 Ibid., p. 73.
106 Ibid.
107 Ibid., pp. 73–74.

of different legal and political systems.[108] What we perhaps should think about is whether this is what politics is or should be like.

I shall finish with the *Leading Principles of a Constitutional Code for any State*, published in *The Pamphleteer* in 1823 (No. 44). There Bentham discusses the tasks of government. Apart from the general utilitarian claim that the constitution 'has for its general end in view, the greatest happiness of the greatest number',[109] Bentham sets out four 'specific' ends of government – namely, subsistence, abundance, security and equality, each to be 'maximized, in so far as is compatible with the maximization of the rest'.[110] In respect of these ends, two points deserve our attention. The first is Bentham's claim that one of the dangers against which the constitution should guard the people is the 'internal evil-doers',[111] especially the 'official', that is, those 'whose means of evil-doing are derived from the share they respectively possess, in the aggregate of the powers of government';[112] in other words, the politicians. This – if anything – shows his distrust of politicians. The second is his concern with inequality; 'in proportion as inequality has place, evil has place', he says.[113] He considered inequality to be both a 'domestic or civil' and a 'national or constitutional' evil.[114] The former pertains to material wealth and consists in the following:

> The more remote from equality are the shares possessed by the individuals in question, in the mass of the instruments of felicity, the less is the sum of felicity, produced by the sum of those same shares.[115]

The latter relates to power. With regard to this, Bentham says:

108 Ibid., pp. 74–75.
109 *Bentham's Political Thought*, p. 195.
110 Ibid., p. 196 (analyzed pp. 196–202).
111 Ibid., pp. 198–199.
112 Ibid., p. 199.
113 Ibid., p. 200.
114 Ibid.
115 Ibid.

> The greater the quantity of power possessed, the greater the facility and the incitement to the abuse of it. In a direct way, this position applies only to power. But, between power and wealth such is the connexion, that each is an instrument for the acquisition of the other: in this way, therefore, the position applies to wealth likewise.[116]

Bentham was, therefore, particularly wary of the interrelation between wealth and power – power produced wealth and vice versa – and thought that the most notorious example of this was the institution of monarchy, followed by aristocracy (both considered in their pure forms).[117] In consequence:

> [...] throughout the whole population of a state, the less the inequality is, between individual and individual, in respect of the share, possessed by them, in the aggregate mass or stock, of the instruments of felicity, the greater is the aggregate mass of felicity itself [...][118]

This is yet another evidence of Bentham's distrust of – if not disgust with – politicians, based on his own experience. For this reason he turned to representative democracy after years of advocating enlightened rule.

How are the above-mentioned ends of government to be achieved? Bentham says by 'maximization of appropriate official aptitude, on the part of rulers.'[119] It was the inaptitude of the politicians, civil servants, judges and other public figures of his day that he detested most and his programme for legal and political reform was directed to combating this. In a nutshell, he considered official aptitude to be consisting of three skills – namely, an appropriate moral aptitude, an appropriate intellectual aptitude (which in turn consisted of both an appropriate knowledge and an appropriate judgement) and an appropriate active aptitude.[120] For Bentham, every other branch of law depends on the constitutional branch of law:

116 Ibid.
117 Ibid., p. 201.
118 Ibid., pp. 201–202.
119 Ibid., p. 202.
120 Ibid., p. 202 (analyzed pp. 202–204).

> For, on this branch of law, depends, in all its branches, the relative and appropriate aptitude, of those functionaries, on whose will depends at all times, the texture of every other branch of law. If, in the framing of this branch of law, the greatest happiness of the greatest number is taken for the end in view, and that object pursued with corresponding success, so will it be in the framing of those other branches: if not, not.[121]

Bentham regarded 'the constitution of the Anglo-American United States' as the best example of a good constitution available.[122]

121 Ibid., p. 200.
122 Ibid., pp. 204–205.

CHAPTER 4

John Stuart Mill

John Stuart Mill lived from 1806 to 1873. He was the first of six children. His father was responsible for his education. With this task James Mill was often assisted by Jeremy Bentham. His father and Bentham designed a rigorous education for the junior Mill, the purpose being to make him a perfect utilitarian, as they wanted him to take over the leadership of the philosophic radicals. John Stuart Mill started to learn ancient Greek when he was three. As he says in his *Autobiography*:

> My earliest recollection on the subject, is that of committing to memory what my father termed vocables, being lists of common Greek words, with their signification in English, which he wrote out for me on cards. Of grammar, until some years later, I learnt no more than the inflexions of the nouns and verbs, but after a course of vocables, proceeded at once to translation.[1]

Thus by seven John Stuart Mill had read an impressive – considering his age – amount of ancient Greek literature – Aesop's Fables, most of Herodotus's works, Xenophon's *Cyropsedia*, the account of the lives of some philosophers by Diogenes Laertius, part of Lucian and Isocrates, as well as the six earliest Platonic dialogues.[2] In this early part of his education Mill was also taught arithmetic.[3] And at the age of eight he started Latin.[4] At about the same time he started mathematics and science, and by twelve he had learnt

1 J. S. Mill, 'Autobiography', in J. S. Mill and T. Carlyle, *Autobiography etc. Essays and Address*, ed. C. W. Eliot, The Harvard Classics (Norwalk, Connecticut: The Easton Press, 1993), p. 9.

2 Ibid., pp. 9–10.

3 Ibid., p. 10.

4 Ibid., pp. 9 & 12.

'elementary geometry and algebra thoroughly'.[5] At twelve the young Mill was instructed in logic.[6] What his mental education lacked altogether, however, was – as John Stuart Mill himself only later realized – an emotional development. His education had been based on the 'doctrine of association'. In Mill's words:

> My course of study had led me to believe, that all mental and moral feeling and qualities, whether of a good or of a bad kind, were the results of association; that we love one thing, and hate another, take pleasure in one sort of action or contemplation, and pain in another sort, through the clinging of pleasurable or painful ideas to those things, from the effect of education or of experience. As a corollary of this, I had always heard it maintained by my father, and was myself convinced, that the object of education should be to form the strongest possible associations of the salutary class; associations of pleasure with all things beneficial to the great whole, and of pain with all things hurtful to it.[7]

Although initially successful, this exacting (analytical) educational programme eventually resulted in Mill's mental crisis in the autumn of 1826 – Mill was then twenty-six years old.[8] It has been suggested that by 'mental crisis' Mill did not mean what nowadays we call mental breakdown.[9] Perhaps it was not so serious. What Mill meant by 'mental crisis' was 'a dull state of nerves, such as everybody is occasionally liable to; unsusceptible to enjoyment or pleasurable excitement; one of those moods when what is pleasure at other times, becomes insipid or indifferent'.[10] It was as if he had 'awakened' from his previous educational experience and conception of life 'as from a dream'.[11] He suddenly realized that, even if all his 'objects in life were realized' and 'all the changes in institutions and opinions' which he had been 'looking forward to' took place, this would not be 'a great joy

5 Ibid., p. 13 (natural science p. 17).
6 Ibid., p. 17.
7 Ibid., p. 90.
8 Ibid., pp. 88–89.
9 W. Thomas, *The Philosophic Radicals: Nine Studies in Theory and Practice, 1817–1841* (Oxford: Clarendon Press, 1979), pp. 151ff.
10 Mill, 'Autobiography', p. 89.
11 Ibid., p. 88.

and happiness' to him.[12] So it seemed as if the utilitarianism of Bentham did not mean to him anything any more and, as he says:

> At this my heart sank with me: the whole foundation on which my life was constructed fell down.[13]

This disillusionment did not prevent Mill from pursuing his 'usual occupations', but he 'went on with them mechanically, by the mere force of habit'.[14] That said, his 'mental crisis' was 'one stage onward', as he himself puts it.[15] It made him open to new influences – Coleridge, Carlyle, the Saint-Simonians and Auguste Comte –[16] and led him to an appreciation of 'the internal culture of the individual'.[17] More importantly, it led him to revise utilitarianism, turning what was a strict doctrine into a more humanitarian one.

Mill's Refinement of Utilitarianism

It is in an essay published in 1861, 'Utilitarianism', that Mill puts forth his version of a revised utilitarianism. Mill recognizes that the question as to what is the highest good for humans, which is the foundation of morality, has caused much controversy among philosophers, who have divided themselves into different schools. Although there is a similar controversy regarding the first principles of all sciences, this does not affect the other sciences as much as ethics, for 'the detailed doctrines of a science are not

12 Ibid., p. 89.
13 Ibid.
14 Ibid., p. 92.
15 Ibid., p. 88.
16 Ibid.. Coleridge, pp. 89 & 93; Saint-Simonians & Comte pp. 107ff; Carlyle pp. 94 & 114ff.
17 Ibid., p. 94.

usually deduced from, nor depend for their evidence upon, what are called its first principles'.[18] This is not the case with ethics; being 'a practical art', all action is for the purpose of some end or goal, while rules of action are derived from that end.[19] It is for this reason that first principles are so important in moral philosophy. However, despite the fact that there is no agreement among different schools of thought concerning the first principle or foundation of ethics, Mill argues, it is true that humans' 'sentiments, both of favour and aversion, are greatly influenced by what they suppose to be the effects of things upon their happiness'. Therefore, 'the principle of utility, or as Bentham latterly called it, the greatest-happiness principle' has informed 'the moral doctrines even of those who most scornfully reject its authority' – Mill cites Kant's moral theory as an example.[20] As Mill says, in this essay he attempts to contribute 'towards the understanding and appreciation of the Utilitarian or Happiness theory, and towards such proof as it is susceptible of'.[21] He stresses, however, that 'ultimate ends' cannot be proven. The only way to prove that something is good is by demonstrating that it is 'a means to something admitted to be good without proof'.[22] One can explore whether the intellect supports the utilitarian principle and this, for Mill, amounts to the same thing as proof.[23] Having set out his objective in this essay, Mill goes on to explain what utilitarianism is.

For all utilitarians from Epicurus to Bentham, 'utility' has meant pleasure or exemption from pain.[24] Accordingly, utilitarianism propounds that 'actions are right in proportion as they tend to promote happiness, wrong as they tend to produce the reverse of happiness', where happiness means 'pleasure, and the absence of pain' and unhappiness 'pain, and the privation

18 J. S. Mill, 'Utilitarianism', in *On Liberty and Other Essays*, ed. J. Gray (Oxford & New York: Oxford University Press, 1991), p. 131.

19 Ibid., p. 132.

20 Ibid., pp. 133–134.

21 Ibid., p. 134.

22 Ibid.

23 Ibid., p. 135.

24 Ibid., p. 136.

of pleasure'.[25] For Mill, utilitarianism is not simply a theory of morality but – importantly – a theory of life, according to which pleasure and avoidance of pain 'are the only things desirable as ends'.[26] But he comes to differ from Bentham by arguing that there are 'some *kinds* of pleasure' which 'are more desirable and more valuable than others'.[27] *Contra* Bentham, he emphasizes the *quality* of pleasures, rather than their quantity, while he believes that one can know which of two pleasures is higher, once one has had experience of both.[28] Likewise:

> Of two pleasures, if there be one to which all or almost all who have experience of both give a decided preference, irrespective of any feeling of moral obligation to prefer it, that is the more desirable pleasure.[29]

Higher pleasures are the cultivation of the higher faculties – for example, through art, science or letters – whereas lower pleasures are bodily pleasures. Although one who has cultivated the higher faculties requires more to be happy and is, correspondingly, more likely to feel pain oftener, John Stuart Mill believed that no human being would want to be degraded to a lower standing, since humans have 'a sense of dignity'.[30] As he famously put it: 'It is better to be a human being dissatisfied than a pig satisfied; better to be Socrates dissatisfied than a fool satisfied.'[31] So, 'if the fool, or the pig, is of a different opinion, it is because they only know their own side of the question'[32] – that is, they have not experienced the higher pleasures.

Mill concedes that sometimes people who know the 'higher pleasures' prefer or give in to the lower. But, claims Mill, this does not mean that the 'higher pleasures' are not inherently superior; rather all that it means is that human character is often weak or unstable, so that one may

25 Ibid., p. 137.
26 Ibid.
27 Ibid., p. 138.
28 Ibid., pp. 138–139; cf. ibid., p. 141.
29 Ibid., p. 139.
30 Ibid., pp. 139–140 ('sense of dignity' on p. 140).
31 Ibid., p. 140.
32 Ibid.

knowingly indulge in a base pleasure because it is more easily accessible. He also admits that it often happens that people who in their youth desired what was 'noble', cease to do so as they grow older. This is due to incapacity, Mill says.[33]

> Capacity for the nobler feelings is in most natures a very tender plant, easily killed, not only by hostile influences, but by mere want of sustenance; and in the majority of young persons it speedily dies away if the occupations to which their position in life has devoted them, and the society into which it has thrown them, are not favourable to keeping that higher capacity in exercise.[34]

Therefore, if one does not have any time to devote to study, one loses the 'intellectual tastes' one used to have and turns to lower pleasures instead.[35] Mill's distinction of higher and lower pleasures gives an historical dimension to utilitarianism, which now acknowledges the development of humanity. Thus Mill entertains the belief that 'most of the great positive evils of the world are in themselves removable, and will, if human affairs continue to improve, be in the end reduced within narrow limits'.[36] And again: 'All the grand sources [...] of human suffering are in a great degree, many of them entirely, conquerable by human care and effort ...'.[37]

It is crucial that 'the utilitarian standard [...] is not the agent's own greatest happiness, but the greatest amount of happiness altogether', which means, Mill argues, that, even if a noble person is not happier than others, still his or her nobleness leads to the happiness of the generality of people.[38] This then, the 'Greatest Happiness Principle', is the 'standard of morality'.[39] Distancing himself from the more egoistic tendencies of Bentham's utilitarianism, Mill maintains that 'As between his own happiness and that of others, utilitarianism requires' every individual 'to be as strictly impartial

33 Ibid., pp. 140–141.
34 Ibid., p. 141.
35 Ibid.
36 Ibid., p. 146.
37 Ibid.
38 Ibid., p. 142.
39 Ibid., pp. 142–143.

as a disinterested and benevolent spectator'.[40] So altruism, self-sacrifice and impartiality *do* have a place in Mill's utilitarianism. It follows that, for Mill, utilitarianism can, and does, unite individual with social happiness. This can be accomplished in two ways: first, by means of laws and social institutions which put into harmony as far as possible the happiness or interest of each individual with the happiness or interest of society at large; and, second, by inculcating in the mind of each individual through education and opinion 'an indissoluble association' between his or her own happiness and that of society.[41]

John Stuart Mill considers a number of objections to utilitarianism, to which he sets forth his own counter-arguments. I shall not go into these here. Some of the answers he gives to such criticisms are, however, important, since they elucidate his utilitarianism further.

Regarding the applicability of the utility principle, says Mill, it is wrong to suppose that it implies that people should always have the good or happiness of society (even of the whole world) in mind before proceeding to action. In real life humans have to consider the happiness of the individuals with whom they come into contact at a particular place and time. Therefore, at any one time a person is not required to take into account the general good of society but only that of 'the particular persons concerned', provided that 'in benefiting them he is not violating the rights – that is, the legitimate and authorized expectations – of any one else'.[42] It is only in exceptional cases that an individual can be 'a public benefactor'; and only then 'is he called on to consider public utility; in every other case, private utility, the interest or happiness of some few persons, is all he has to attend to'. Alone those persons whose actions have an impact on society at large need to consider the public good in all circumstances.[43] Again, one should bear in mind that, although an action might seem 'beneficial' in a particular case, one should rather avoid engaging in it if it is 'of a class'

40 Ibid., p. 148.
41 Ibid.
42 Ibid., p. 150.
43 Ibid., p. 151.

which would in general – that is, in most other cases – be injurious.[44] In addition, Mill suggests that moral rules consist in humans' experience, accumulated through the ages, regarding the effects of actions on their happiness. Thus moral rules derive from utility. This does not mean that all these rules of conduct are fixed; far from it, 'The corollaries from the principle of utility, like the precepts of every practical art, admit of indefinite improvement, and, in a progressive state of human mind, their improvement is perpetually going on'.[45] With increasing experience, humans come to adapt moral rules to changing circumstances. That said, Mill is eager to avoid a misunderstanding:

> [...] to consider the rules of morality as improvable, is one thing; to pass over the intermediate generalizations entirely, and endeavour to test each individual action directly by the first principle is another.[46]

Therefore, the utility principle is a standard of moral *rules* and not of specific actions; as such, it is the ultimate foundation of morality.

To recapitulate, Mill's revisions to classical utilitarianism are the following: Firstly, he refined utilitarianism in moral terms, by distinguishing higher from lower pleasures. This allowed him to develop a theory of progress and human development. Secondly, he refined it psychologically, by acknowledging the altruistic feelings of human beings. Thirdly, he specified the applicability of the utility principle – to particular circumstances and as a criterion of moral rules.

So, this being Mill's refinement of utilitarianism, what is the 'sanction' of the utility principle? Mill uses Bentham's term 'sanction' to refer to 'the motives to obey' the utility principle, to 'the source of its obligation' or of 'its binding force'.[47] This question emerges whenever someone is to adopt a moral standard or has to account for the basis of morality.[48] Mill's answer

44 Ibid.
45 Ibid., p. 156.
46 Ibid.
47 Ibid., p. 159.
48 Ibid.

is that the sanction of the utility principle is 'moral sense', which is the result of moral education. As he says, 'by the improvement of education', the feeling of unity with our fellow humans will become 'deeply rooted in our character', while in our consciousness it will be 'a part of our nature'.[49] Like all other moral systems, the principle of utility has 'external' and 'internal' sanctions – the former being hope of favour, fear and suchlike, the latter coming from one's inner self.[50] To be sure, the 'ultimate sanction' of all morality is 'conscience' or 'the conscientious feelings of mankind'.[51] In saying this, Mill shows the humane (as well as social) face of utilitarianism. It is evident that he has come a long way from Bentham's crude utilitarianism. Mill also stresses that, albeit not innate – 'but acquired' – 'the moral feelings' are not 'for that reason the less natural'.[52] Rather, 'the moral faculty' is 'susceptible of being brought by cultivation to a high degree of development', in the same way as it is unfortunately possible to direct it through cultivation to 'almost any direction'.[53] However, Mill admits, if there were no some natural sentiment with which the moral feelings would harmonize, these feelings might just as easily fade away as they were laboriously acquired.[54] Yet there is such a natural sentiment, which constitutes the solid foundation of utilitarian morality and that is 'the social feelings of mankind', which tend to become stronger with the advance of civilization. In fact, says Mill, the 'social state' is 'at once so natural, so necessary, and so habitual' to human beings that none of them can imagine living 'otherwise than as a member of a body'.[55]

> Any condition, therefore, which is essential to a state of society, becomes more and more an inseparable part of every person's conception of the state of things which he is born into, and which is the destiny of a human being.[56]

49 Ibid., pp. 159–160.
50 Ibid., pp. 160–161.
51 Ibid., p. 161.
52 Ibid., p. 163.
53 Ibid.
54 Ibid., p. 164.
55 Ibid.
56 Ibid.

Consequently, personal interest comes all the more to be identified with the interest(s) of others, so that each individual 'comes, as though instinctively, to be conscious of himself as a being who *of course* pays regard to others'.[57] Note how education (which in Mill is more importantly moral education) is interrelated with the advance of civilization and political improvement.

How does Mill justify utilitarianism? A few words have already been said on this. As Mill says at the very beginning of the essay, 'ultimate ends' cannot be proven. The only way to prove that something is good is by demonstrating that it is 'a means to something admitted to be good without proof'.[58] In a later chapter he returns to this issue. If human beings, he says, desire nothing but happiness (specifically, something which is 'either a part of happiness or a means of happiness'), there is no need of another proof; 'happiness is the sole end of human action, and the promotion of it the test by which to judge of all human conduct'. In consequence, happiness 'must be the criterion of morality'.[59] This can be ascertained by self-observation as well as observation of others.[60] The only objection which may arise is that all moral action is the result of 'will' and 'will' is not the same as 'desire'. And the virtuous person acts without regard to pleasure. Although Mill concedes that 'will' is indeed different from 'desire', he argues that the 'will' is a result of habit.[61] Therefore, what humans initially do from desire, they come in time to do from habit. So far as the virtuous individual is concerned, he or she wills from habit what he or she would desire – that is, a higher pleasure. This means 'we may will from habit what we no longer desire for itself, or desire only because we will it'. The implications of Mill's argument here are far-reaching. For, by 'bringing home' to someone the connection between the right act and pleasure or the wrong act and pain, the person concerned can be taught to will what is virtuous, acting 'without thought of either pleasure or pain' any more.[62] Mill adds

57 Ibid., p. 165.
58 Ibid., p. 134.
59 Ibid., p. 172.
60 Ibid.
61 Ibid., p. 173.
62 Ibid., p. 174.

that it is important that virtue dissociates itself from pleasure and pain, as otherwise individual behaviour remains unpredictable and cannot be counted on. In Mill's words, 'it is because of the importance to others of being able to rely absolutely on one's feelings and conduct, and to oneself of being able to rely on one's own, that the will to do right ought to be cultivated into this habitual independence.'[63] What this means, Mill argues, is that the 'will' is 'a means to a good' and does not challenge the utility principle, according to which humans desire happiness or what is pleasurable. If this is so, then 'the principle of utility is proved'.[64]

Let us now turn to Mill's *On Liberty*, which is by common consent the most important of Mill's political works.

On Liberty

Right at the beginning of the essay Mill makes clear that his subject-matter is not the 'Liberty of the Will' as opposed to necessity, but 'Civil, or Social Liberty' – in particular, the limits of the legitimate power of society over the individual.[65] The civil or social liberty with which he is concerned is not that of subjects from authority. Whereas at earlier historical periods there was often a struggle between subjects – or certain groups among them – and the government, in modern democratic societies, claims Mill, the problem is 'the tyranny of the majority', as philosophers and political theorists have come increasingly to recognize.[66] Although in the essay by 'society' Mill sometimes refers to the government, his primary interest – and by far what makes the essay's originality – is public opinion. Mill

63 Ibid., pp. 174–175.

64 Ibid., p. 175.

65 J. S. Mill, 'On Liberty', in *On Liberty and Other Writings*, ed. S. Collini (Cambridge: Cambridge University Press, 1989), p. 5.

66 Ibid., pp. 5–8 ('tyranny of the majority', p. 8).

argues that when society in the latter sense 'is itself the tyrant – society collectively, over the separate individuals who compose it – its means of tyrannizing are not restricted to the acts which it may do by the hands of its political functionaries'. Rather, as Mill puts it:

> [...] it practices a social tyranny more formidable than many kinds of political oppression, since [...] it leaves fewer means of escape, penetrating much more deeply into the details of life, and enslaving the soul itself.[67]

So there is a social tyranny exercised by 'prevailing opinion and feeling' or set of 'rules of conduct'.[68] And, although most would agree that 'There is a limit to the legitimate interference of collective opinion with individual independence',[69] the crucial question, to which an answer can be given only with difficulty, is 'where to place the limit'.[70] For Mill, custom can be oppressive, especially as it is often mistaken for our first (i.e. true) nature.[71] In fact, society's likings and dislikings, sympathies and antipathies influence individual behaviour. The only example of difference of opinion is in the field of religion, as there is in modern times religious freedom or freedom of conscience.[72] Mill had a good reason for writing the essay *On Liberty*; for in England the tyranny of opinion was greater than the force of law, which was the case in most Europeans countries.[73] Accordingly, he sees the 'object of this Essay' to be 'to assert one very simple principle'.

> That principle is, that the sole end for which mankind are warranted, individually or collectively, in interfering with the liberty of action of any of their number, is self-protection. That the only purpose for which power can be rightfully exercised over any member of a civilized community, against his will, is to prevent harm to others.[74]

67 Ibid., p. 8.
68 Ibid.
69 Ibid., pp. 8–9.
70 Ibid., p. 9.
71 Ibid.
72 Ibid., pp. 9–12.
73 Ibid., p. 12.
74 Ibid., p. 13.

A problem that arises is how one interprets 'harm'; harm may be physical (i.e. an injury) but it may also be taken to mean inconvenience, annoyance or displeasure. A few lines below Mill says: 'The only part of the conduct of any one, for which he is amenable to society, is that which concerns others.' Otherwise, in matters which concern oneself, over one's 'own body and mind, the individual is sovereign'.[75] Individual sovereignty is the most fundamental principle of liberalism and perhaps no one would contest it today, but in the Victorian society of 1859 when *On Liberty* was published it was quite an extraordinary claim. To be sure, Mill says, the doctrine of individual sovereignty is meant to apply only to mature human beings and not to children, for whom their parents are responsible until they come of age. What is important is that Mill did not propound the doctrine of individual sovereignty as an 'abstract right' but as one that utility itself requires. Why this is so will become apparent in due course. Mill stresses that he considers 'utility' to be 'the ultimate appeal on all ethical questions' – a claim which points to the essay on utilitarianism, began at the same time as *On Liberty* but published two years later; what is more, 'it must be utility in the largest sense, grounded on the permanent interests of man as a progressive being'.[76]

John Stuart Mill's contribution to social and political theory is his definition of liberty as 'a sphere of action' with which society should not interfere.[77] This domain comprises, first, 'the inward domain of consciousness' or freedom of conscience, second, the liberty of individuals to pursue their own interests or goals and to plan their lives according to their preferences, provided they do not harm others, and, third, the liberty of combination, with the proviso that their association does no harm to others and that the persons combining are mature and are not compelled or misled.[78] Mill discusses liberty of thought and discussion, the value of individuality and the limits to the authority of society over individuals in turn.

75 Ibid.
76 Ibid., p. 14.
77 Ibid., p. 15.
78 Ibid., pp. 15–16.

I.

Regarding liberty of thought and discussion, Mill argues that it is always wrong, indeed 'evil', to prevent the expression of opinion. His argument is a utilitarian one; 'silencing the expression of an opinion' amounts, Mill claims, to 'robbing the human race; posterity as well as the existing generation; those who dissent from the opinion, still more than those who hold it'.[79] This is the case no matter whether the opinion in question is true or false. If it be true, the consequences are more obvious. And the desire to suppress it assumes infallibility.[80] However, there is a great difference, says Mill, between assuming an opinion to be true because, having been open to criticism, it has not as yet been refuted, and assuming an opinion to be true in order to prevent its refutation.[81] This latter is what opponents to freedom of expression commonly do; at the same time, they hold their supposedly infallible view, without allowing it to be subjected to criticism. More importantly, assuming the certainty of their view, while there is someone or some others who would question it if allowed, but who are not allowed, implies that they are 'the judges of certainty', what is more, 'judges without hearing the other side'.[82] Mill concedes that in modern times people do not so much insist on the validity of conventional views because they think they are true, but because they are beneficial to society. Yet even the 'usefulness of an opinion' cannot be certain, since different people have different understandings of what is useful and when. In any case, the usefulness of an opinion cannot be separated from its truth, as 'The truth of an opinion is part of its utility'.[83] In order to substantiate his argument, Mill mentions a number of examples in history when in the eyes of posterity serious mistakes were committed in the name of truth – namely, the condemnation of Socrates, the crucifixion of Christ and the persecution of Christianity by Emperor Marcus Aurelius, who was in all

79 Ibid., p. 20.
80 Ibid., pp. 20–21.
81 Ibid., p. 22.
82 Ibid., p. 25.
83 Ibid.

other respects 'the best and most enlightened among his cotemporaries'.[84] And, although in the nineteenth century there were not any overt persecution of people with non-conventional views, all the same there was legal persecution (especially in England) which led to these views being held in private – the damage to society thus being greater than that suffered by the individuals who hold such views.[85] Mill's claim that it is 'utility in the largest sense, grounded on the permanent interests of man as a progressive being'[86] with which utilitarian ethics is concerned becomes clearer now. So does the interrelationship between the principle of utility and the principle of liberty. Specifically, the conception and expression of novel views contributes to human development – at both individual and social levels. Those who avoid listening to others' views have, as a result, narrow minds and do not allow their intellectual as well as moral faculties to develop. Put more crudely, they stifle their development. But they also stifle the intellectual and moral development of those who, not being heretics, yet are afraid to express nonconformist views, lest they be characterized so.[87] In fact:

> Among them we may occasionally see some man of deep conscientiousness, and subtle and refined understanding, who spends a life in sophisticating with an intellect which he cannot silence, and exhausts the resources of ingenuity in attempting to reconcile the promptings of his conscience and reason with orthodoxy, which yet he does not, perhaps, to the end succeed in doing. No one can be a great thinker who does not recognize, that as a thinker it is his first duty to follow his intellect to whatever conclusions it may lead.[88]

With respect to the social consequences of silencing the expression of opinion, under such circumstances 'we cannot hope to find that generally high scale of mental activity which has made some periods of history so remarkable'.[89] There is another argument, connected to the above and

84 Ibid., pp. 27–28 (Marcus Aurelius p. 28).
85 Ibid., pp. 31–35.
86 Ibid., p. 14.
87 Ibid., p. 35.
88 Ibid., pp. 35–36.
89 Ibid., p. 36.

which Mill associates with Dr Johnson: this is that, far from harming truth, persecution may in fact serve it, because, if the view propounded survives the trial, this will be evidence of its validity. Not only does Mill disagree with the maltreatment of people who should rather be regarded as benefactors, he does not think that this is a serious argument at all:

> People who defend this mode of treating benefactors, cannot be supposed to set much value on the benefit; and [...] this view of the subject is mostly confined to the sort of persons who think that new truths may have been desirable once, but that we have had enough of them now.[90]

After all, there have been many examples in history of truth suppressed by persecution.[91]

We have seen how Mill justified on utilitarian grounds that quashing a true view when it does not accord with the conventions of society is 'evil'. But Mill insisted that, even if a newly propounded view is false, its suppression is again 'evil'. Once more, the explanation is utilitarian. Although conventional views may indeed be true, if they are not contested, they will be nothing but 'dead dogmas' or superstitions. Humans cannot claim to *know* the truth, unless they fully understand *why* a view, belief or statement is true.[92] As Mill puts it:

> If the cultivation of the understanding consists in one thing more than in another, it is surely in learning the grounds of one's opinions.[93]

And individuals can come to comprehend the grounds of their opinions only by listening carefully to opposing views and responding to criticism; otherwise, they cannot know those parts of their opinions which refute the arguments of their opponents. Again, we can see how the principle of liberty promotes human development and cultivation. More importantly, people not only forget the grounds of their opinions in the absence of discussion

90 Ibid., p. 30.
91 Ibid., p. 31.
92 Ibid., p. 37.
93 Ibid.

or debate, but the meaning of these opinions as well.[94] For Mill, therein lies the significance of 'negative criticism' – historical or philosophical examples of which are the Socratic dialectics and the school disputations of the Middles Ages.[95]

Finally, claims Mill, the truth often lies between two competing views. In such cases 'the nonconforming opinion is needed to supply the remainder of the truth, of which the received doctrine embodies only a part'.[96] This is most common in religious, moral, social and political matters. So, for instance, in order to be healthy, political life requires both a party of order or stability and a party of progress or reform; moreover, the positions of those supporting democracy or oligarchy, equality or property, co-operation or competition, sociality or individuality, discipline or liberty, abstinence or luxury must all be heard.[97] For in practical matters truth consists in the reconciliation and combination of opposites.[98]

Mill winds up his argument by claiming that the liberty of expression should adhere to a morality of public discussion, in accordance with which it is wrong to conceal facts, misstate relevant data, misrepresent others' views, use sophistical arguments or 'stigmatise' opponents 'as bad and immoral men'.[99]

II.

Mill turns next to a discussion of the value of individuality. For him, it is important that individuality be expressed, provided it does no harm to others.[100] The assertion of individuality is crucial, for it contributes to social progress as well as individual development. For this reason Mill associates

94 Ibid., p. 41.
95 Ibid., pp. 45–46.
96 Ibid., p. 47.
97 Ibid., pp. 48–49.
98 Ibid., p. 49.
99 Ibid., pp. 54–55.
100 Ibid., pp. 56–57.

the free expression of individuality with civilization, instruction, education and culture; in point of fact, it 'is itself a necessary part and condition of all those things'.[101] By the expression of individuality Mill means 'individual spontaneity', which he considers to have 'intrinsic worth'.[102] There is a problem with this, however. For one thing, it has been noted that if individuality is intrinsically valuable, then it would seem that the principle of utility cannot be a justification for it – as Mill, no doubt, intended. For another, as Cowling has suggested, among others, if utilitarianism *does* provide a justification for it, then the value of the expression of individuality seems to be only a means to an end (i.e. happiness).[103] An answer to this issue is provided in the essay on utilitarianism, where Mill argues that '[t]he ingredients of happiness are very various, and each of them is desirable in itself, and not merely when considered as swelling an aggregate'.[104] In *Utilitarianism* Mill discusses virtue in response to a criticism.[105] Concerning virtue, Mill says:

> Those who desire virtue for its own sake, desire it either because the consciousness of it is pleasure, or because the consciousness of being without it is a pain, or for both reasons united; as in truth the pleasure and pain seldom exist separately, but almost always together, the same person feeling pleasure in the degree of virtue attained, and pain in not having attained more.[106]

This, it appears, is, for Mill, the case with individuality too. Therefore:

> [...] there is in reality nothing desired except happiness. Whatever is desired otherwise than as a means to some end beyond itself, and ultimately to happiness, is desired as itself a part of happiness, and is not desired for itself until it has become so.[107]

101 Ibid., p. 57.
102 Ibid.
103 See I. Hampsher-Monk, *A History of Modern Political Thought: Major Political Thinkers from Hobbes to Marx* (Oxford & Cambridge, Massachusetts: Blackwell, 1992), pp. 373–374 (Cowling cited on p. 374, note 130). See also M. Cowling, *Mill and Liberalism* (Cambridge: Cambridge University Press, 1963).
104 Mill, 'Utilitarianism', p. 170.
105 Ibid., pp. 169–172.
106 Ibid., p. 172.
107 Ibid.

Mill clearly believes that individuality is consistent with his principle of utility 'in the largest sense, grounded on the permanent interests of man as a progressive being'.[108] For, as he says:

> The human faculties of perception, judgment, discriminative feeling, mental activity, and even moral preference, are exercised only in making a choice [...] The mental and moral, like the muscular powers, are improved only by being used.[109]

This is all the more true as:

> Human nature is not a machine to be built after a model, and set to do exactly the work prescribed for it, but a tree, which requires to grow and develope itself on all sides, according to the tendency of the inward forces which make it a living thing.[110]

For this reason, claims Mill, desires and impulses are as important 'a part of a perfect human being' as understanding and beliefs. In fact, 'Strong impulses are but another name for energy', while only the 'person whose desires and impulses are his own' has 'a character';[111] the person whose impulses are strong is, accordingly, 'an energetic character'.[112] Mill holds Calvinism responsible for the suppression of individuality, for, regarding human nature as essentially corrupt, it preached 'that man needs no capacity, but that of surrendering himself to the will of God'.[113]

For Mill, who in the essay on utilitarianism wrote that 'the utilitarian standard [...] is not the agent's own greatest happiness, but the greatest amount of happiness altogether',[114] the significance of the expression of individuality lies not solely in the fact that it contributes to personal development, but also, and more importantly, in that, having become

108 Mill, 'On Liberty', p. 14.
109 Ibid., p. 59.
110 Ibid., p. 60.
111 Ibid.
112 Ibid., p. 61.
113 Ibid., p. 62.
114 Mill, 'Utilitarianism', p. 142. Cf. 'the happiness which forms the utilitarian standard of what is right in conduct, is not the agent's own happiness, but that of all concerned'. Ibid., p. 148.

'more valuable to himself', the individual 'is therefore capable of being more valuable to others'.[115] In other words, there is an intimate connection between individual and social development. Social progress is largely the result of a rich, diversified life, which can exist only when the expression of individuality is allowed. Mill's explanation of the value of individuality is as much aesthetic as utilitarian. In this Mill was influenced by the work of Wilhelm von Humboldt, a German intellectual whom he cites on a number of occasions.[116]

Having extolled the value of individuality, Mill proceeds 'to point out to those who do not desire liberty' that they may benefit from 'allowing other people to make use of it without hindrance'.[117] Firstly, they may learn something useful from those who wish to (and do) develop their faculties freely.[118] He recognizes that not everybody is capable of contributing to the general improvement of humankind. Yet there are certain individuals inspired by originality, 'persons of genius', as he calls them;[119] 'but in order to have them, it is necessary to preserve the soil in which they grow' – 'Genius can only breathe freely in an *atmosphere* of freedom.'[120] In antiquity, the Middle Ages and – to a lesser extent – the historical period from feudalism to modernity, Mill argues, the talented individual was a real power. By contrast, in modern times 'individuals are lost in the crowd'. So much so that 'In politics it is almost a triviality to say that public opinion now rules the world'.[121] This public opinion is a 'mediocrity' and leads to social conformism.[122] It is *precisely because of this reason* that 'eccentricity' becomes all the more important. For, when and where 'eccentricity' abounds, there is a great 'amount of genius' in society. 'That so few now dare to be eccentric, marks the chief danger of the time' – is a matter of

115 Mill, 'On Liberty', p. 63.
116 E.g. ibid., pp. 58, 72, 103–104, 108.
117 Ibid., p. 64.
118 Ibid.
119 Ibid., pp. 64–65 ('persons of genius' p. 65).
120 Ibid., p. 65.
121 Ibid., p. 66.
122 Ibid. ('mediocrity')

utmost concern.[123] Secondly, Mill argues, human beings are so different in terms of desires, aversions, tastes and so forth, 'that unless there is a corresponding diversity in their modes of life, they neither obtain their fair share of happiness, nor grow up to the mental, moral, and aesthetic stature of which their nature is capable'.[124] Why then should this diversity not be recognized?[125] 'Human beings are not like sheep; and even sheep are not undistinguishably alike.'[126] Mill's argument rests on the opposition between the 'despotism of custom' and human advancement or progress.[127] When and where individuality is suppressed, progress is halted – and Mill draws to his readers' attention the example of China.[128] If Europe has not had the fate of Eastern societies – China in particular – as yet, Mill claims, this is due to the 'remarkable diversity of character and culture' of its nations. But, there follows Mill's warning, 'it already begins to possess this benefit in a considerably less degree. It is decidedly advancing towards the Chinese ideal of making all people alike.'[129] So, if individuality is ever to be asserted, it has to happen before complete assimilation has taken place.[130] Mill's second point to the opponents of individuality is, therefore, that, although they do not desire individuality, they are bound to benefit, in the long run, from the improvement of the human species.

III.

Having discussed the importance of individuality, Mill considers two interrelated questions: First, are there any limits to the sovereignty of the individual over him- or herself – and, if yes, what are these limits? Secondly, when

123 Ibid., p. 67.
124 Ibid., p. 68.
125 Ibid.
126 Ibid., p. 67.
127 Ibid., pp. 70–72 ('despotism of custom' p. 70).
128 Ibid., pp. 71–72.
129 Ibid., p. 72.
130 Ibid., p. 74.

can society intervene and what are the limits to the authority of society over the individual? In other words, what are the boundaries between the individual and society?[131] These are difficult questions and Mill's answer poses more problems than it offers solutions. His answer is the following:

> To individuality should belong the part of life in which it is chiefly the individual that is interested; to society, the part which chiefly interests society.[132]

Although as a utilitarian John Stuart Mill does not subscribe to a social contract theory – indeed, he is critical of such explanations of the basis of political authority and obligation –, he nonetheless concedes that 'every one who receives the protection of society owes a return for the benefit' and, therefore, should observe the 'rules' (in the loose sense) of social conduct.[133] These 'rules' enjoin, first, that each should respect (that is, not injure) the 'interests' of others and, secondly, that each should contribute to the defence of society and its members against 'injury and molestation'.[134] A couple of points are worth our attention here. Albeit a utilitarian, Mill says that others' 'interests' 'either by express legal provision or by tacit understanding, ought to be considered as rights'.[135] So Mill seems to acknowledge that individuals have certain *rights*. We may well wonder how this is consistent with his utilitarianism, but, once again, the essay on utilitarianism gives us the answer. There Mill says:

> When we call anything a person's right, we mean that he has a valid claim on society to protect him in the possession of it, either by the force of law, or by that of education and opinion.[136]

And, if it be asked, why should society protect individuals' rights, the answer is for the purpose of 'general utility'.[137] What then is this 'general

131 Ibid., p. 75.
132 Ibid.
133 Ibid.
134 Ibid.
135 Ibid.
136 Mill, 'Utilitarianism', p. 189.
137 Ibid.

utility'? It is 'security', which, as Mill explains, is the fundamental interest of humankind.[138] In this way Mill reconciles the idea of 'right' with utilitarianism. The other point which deserves our attention is that both in *On Liberty* and *Utilitarianism* Mill says that individuals' rights are protected either by law or by public opinion. It is in discussing the legitimate authority of society over individuals that Mill distinguishes more clearly between society as the government or state and society as public opinion.

In fact, Mill thinks that public opinion has a significant role. It steps in in all matters not regulated by law, praising or criticizing an individual's behaviour. Mill does not deplore this. Far from it, he believes it can do individuals a service by making them see their weaknesses or mistakes; he even says that 'It would be well, indeed, if this good office were much more freely rendered than the common notions of politeness at present permit'.[139] Although he recognizes that this is not always the case, Mill says that society's judgement on individuals should be made from good motives and be unbiased – what he calls 'disinterested benevolence'.[140] Mill insists that the judgement of others is a result of one's own behaviour. But he also suggests that every individual has 'a right' to respond to the unfavourable opinion of another person by, for instance, avoiding his or her society and even warning others, *without* however suppressing the other's individuality but only to the extent that it is necessary in order to express one's own.[141]

It is important to note the distinction Mill draws between 'self-regarding deficiencies'[142] or 'self-regarding faults'[143] and 'moral vices';[144] examples of the former are recklessness, stubbornness, self-conceit and lust, while of the latter infringement of other people's rights, unfair dealings with others or damages inflicted on them, even 'selfish abstinence from defending them

138 Ibid., p. 190.
139 Mill, 'On Liberty', p. 77.
140 Ibid., p. 76.
141 Ibid., pp. 77–78.
142 Ibid., p. 77.
143 Ibid., p. 79.
144 Ibid.

against injury';[145] whereas the former should be subjected only to the judgement of public opinion, the latter, as they affect others, should be subject to 'moral retribution' and, if necessary, punishment.[146]

Mill's argument about the proper boundaries between the individual and society is based on a distinction between 'self-regarding' and 'other-regarding' actions. Yet this distinction is problematical. As Mill himself acknowledges, according to one view, there cannot possibly be any part of a person's behaviour that does not affect others in some way or other – if only by example. If society is responsible for protecting children, who are thought to be as yet unable to look after themselves, why should it not also do so when adults are equally unable to take care of themselves? All the more so since an individual's bad habits may have consequences for others, especially any dependants. Examples of such bad habits include drunkenness, profligacy, idleness, uncleanliness and gambling, among other things.[147] Mill's answer is as follows:

> When, by conduct of this sort, a person is led to violate a distinct and assignable obligation to any other person or persons, the case is taken out of the self-regarding class, and becomes amenable to moral disapprobation in the proper sense of the term.[148]

One of the examples he gives is when an individual becomes unable to support his family any more.[149] That said, Mill believes that, if society 'lets any considerable number of its members grow up mere children', unable to act rationally, 'society has itself to blame for the consequences'.[150] The implication here is that society should be able to pre-empt such undesirable consequences through a correct (moral) education and good-natured advice to individuals who show the first signs of misbehaviour. Besides, claims Mill, too much interference on the part of society may have an opposite effect – that is, a person's bad habits may become even worse as

145 Ibid., p. 78.
146 Ibid.
147 Ibid., pp. 80–81.
148 Ibid., p. 81.
149 Ibid.
150 Ibid., p. 82.

a result of an attempt to assert one's individuality. As for the possibility of an individual's setting a bad example, Mill's view is the following:

> [...] the example, on the whole, must be more salutary than hurtful, since, if it displays the misconduct, it displays also the painful or degrading consequences which, if the conduct is justly censured, must be supposed to be in all or most cases attendant on it.[151]

For Mill:

> [...] the strongest of all the arguments against the interference of the public with purely personal conduct, is that when it does interfere, the odds are that it interferes wrongly, and in the wrong place.[152]

Surely, in such matters as social morality or duty to others public opinion, 'though often wrong, is likely to be still oftener right', as their interests are involved.[153] But, in respect of 'self-regarding conduct', public opinion 'is quite as likely to be wrong as right';[154] for in most cases public opinion only means 'at the best, some people's opinion of what is good or bad for other people' – or even 'their own preferences', so that public opinion is disguised under the name of 'moral laws'.[155]

IV.

The last chapter of the essay *On Liberty*, entitled 'Applications', is meant to clarify issues which concern the application of the principle of liberty. Sometimes, Mill says, in pursuance of his or her own interest, an individual unwittingly affects the interests of others.[156] Such clashes of

151 Ibid., p. 83.
152 Ibid.
153 Ibid.
154 Ibid., pp. 83–84.
155 Ibid., p. 84.
156 Ibid., pp. 94–95.

interests are often due to bad social institutions, but in some cases they 'would be unavoidable under any institutions'.[157] Examples of inevitable clashes of interests are competitive examinations, individual success in an overcrowded profession and economic competition in societies where the doctrine of free trade prevails. It is Mill's argument that in cases such as these a clash of interests is legitimate and society should not interfere in favour of the losers; for it is in the general interest of all the members of society that the best succeed in examinations or advance the professions and that the business of the merchant who supplies the best-quality and cheapest commodities is led to flourish.[158]

Another case which Mill considers and which is a limitation to his principle of liberty is society's action against crime. Whenever the sale and purchase of potentially injurious substance is involved – e.g. poisons –, 'pre-appointed evidence' (Mill uses Bentham's term here) should be provided. This would not prevent anyone from buying the commodity in question, but would be a 'considerable' obstacle to its 'improper use'.[159] There are occasions, Mill insists, that personal conduct, which would otherwise be 'self-regarding', has negative consequences for others. For instance, drunkenness as such should not be punishable, but when it leads to violent behaviour, it does affect others and should, therefore, be punished. In other words, society has the 'right' to intervene. A similar example is idleness, in itself not punishable, but subject to punishment when an individual from idleness ignores his or her obligations to others.[160]

Moreover, there are cases, claims Mill, that, although the state should not interfere with blameable personal behaviour, it should intervene when such behaviour is encouraged or instigated by an individual or group of individuals. Thus, though it would be illegitimate for the state to punish gambling or fornication, it would be legitimate to close down gambling-houses or punish pimps.[161]

157 Ibid.
158 Ibid., pp. 95–96.
159 Ibid., p. 97.
160 Ibid., p. 98.
161 Ibid., pp. 98–100.

Another instance of the application of the principle of liberty relates to the question whether the state can legitimately discourage behaviour which is harmful to the agent, despite the fact that it does not prohibit it altogether. Mill argues in a utilitarian manner that the answer depends on the purposes of any restriction or legislation. Accordingly, whereas the sale of stimulants cannot be discouraged – as it illegitimately intervenes with the buyer's freedom –, it would be right for the state to impose taxation on stimulants on the grounds that indirect taxation is necessary in most countries and that it is better to tax commodities which, when used immoderately, may cause harm, rather than taxing other products. However, the state cannot justifiably limit the number of pubs, since, in so doing, it would make them less accessible to certain individuals or groups of people, restricting in that way their liberty.[162]

In further considering the implications of the principle of liberty, Mill argues that it 'cannot require' that an individual 'should be free not to be free'; for 'It is not freedom, to be allowed to alienate his freedom'.[163] Yet:

> The principle [...] which demands uncontrolled freedom of action in all that concerns only the agents themselves, requires that those who have become bound to one another, in things which concern no party, should be able to release one another from the engagement [...][164]

Therefore, partners should be free to separate if they so wish. The situation becomes more complex when there are third parties (i.e. children) too. In such a case, Mill claims, a marriage cannot dissolve without taking into consideration the interests of the children, since a divorce obviously affects them as well. But Mill remains undecided on this issue. He recognizes the dilemma involved and denies that the obligations to offspring 'extend to requiring the fulfilment of the contract at all costs to the happiness of the reluctant party'.[165] All the same, these obligations 'are a necessary element

162 Ibid., pp. 100–102.
163 Ibid., p. 103.
164 Ibid., p. 103.
165 Ibid., p. 104.

in the question'; and, although they ought to make no much difference 'in the *legal* freedom of the parties to release themselves from the engagement', they nonetheless 'necessarily make a great difference in the *moral* freedom'.[166]

Mill argues that, unfortunately, 'liberty is often granted where it should be withheld, as well as withheld where it should be granted'.[167] Although it is generally agreed that the state, while respecting personal liberty in one's affairs, should oversee the power of individuals over others, it is not acknowledged that the state should do so with respect to 'family relations'.[168] The examples he concentrates on concern the liberty of parents (especially, of the father) to bring up their offspring as they like. It is generally assumed, Mill argues, that the state is not responsible for ensuring that parents fulfil their obligations towards their children. The first example cited is children's education. Mill's view is that the state should intervene here – that is, it should see that parents provide their children with a minimum of general education. At the same time, Mill insists that the state itself should not provide education.[169] His reasons are as much utilitarian as consistent with his principle of liberty. As he puts it:

> All that has been said of the importance of individuality of character, and diversity in opinions and modes of conduct, involves, as of the same unspeakable importance, diversity of education. A general State education is a mere contrivance for moulding people to be exactly like one another: and as the mould in which it casts them is that which pleases the predominant power in the government [...] it establishes a despotism over the mind, leading by natural tendency to one over the body.[170]

Mill did not think that state education should not exist at all, but he insisted that, should this be the case, it should be 'one among many competent experiments, carried on for the purpose of example and stimulus, to keep

166 Ibid.
167 Ibid.
168 Ibid., pp. 104–105.
169 Ibid., p. 105.
170 Ibid., p. 106.

the others up to a certain standard of excellence'.[171] So, for Mill, there was a difference between 'universal' and 'state' education. And he suggested that 'universal education' be enforced by means of public examinations, held once a year with increasing difficulty and range of subjects, testing a specified minimum of general knowledge; beyond that minimum, examinations should be voluntary. Finally, although certificates and degrees should be given, surprisingly for us, the competence of individuals should be judged by public opinion.[172] The second example to which Mill refers is the lack of appreciation of the fact that bringing a child to the world 'is one of the most responsible actions in the range of human life'. Consequently, 'To undertake this responsibility – to bestow a life which may be either a curse or a blessing –, without being able to provide the means of 'a desirable existence' amounts to 'a crime' against the child. Mill even suggests that in an over-populated country having many children is also an 'offence' against others, since 'the remuneration of their labour' is accordingly reduced.[173]

At the end of the essay Mill spells out three 'objections' to government intervention in individual matters, even when such intervention does not encroach on individual liberty. Mill explains that 'the question is not about restraining the actions of individuals, but about helping them [...] whether the government should do, or cause to be done, something for their benefit, instead of leaving it to be done by themselves'.[174] Firstly, he argues, individuals know their interests better and are better suited to carry out their business; thus they should be left to themselves.[175] Secondly, even though individuals may not do – or may be unable to do – something very well, it is always better to let them do it by themselves 'as a means to their own mental education'.[176] The only way in which the state can, and should, contribute is by becoming 'a central depository, and active circulator of the experiences resulting from many trials'. Therefore, its proper task 'is to enable

171 Ibid.
172 Ibid., pp. 106–108.
173 Ibid., p. 108.
174 Ibid., p. 109.
175 Ibid.
176 Ibid.

each experimentalist to benefit by the experiments of others; instead of tolerating no experiments but its own'.[177] This latter argument resembles that in favour of plurality in education. Lastly, and most crucially, an increase in government power is not only undesirable but 'evil'.[178] The danger of which Mill warns is the emergence of an all-powerful bureaucracy – a notorious example being the bureaucracy of the Russian Empire.[179] Where there is a strong bureaucratic machine, Mill claims, the governors are as 'slaves' as the governed, the only difference being that, whereas the governed are the slaves of the governors, the latter are 'the slaves of their organization and discipline'.[180] In fact, Mill believed that the more efficient and educated the bureaucracy, the greater the evil.[181] In addition, the recruitment of the more talented people of the country to the administration is bound to inhibit the mental development of the administrative body itself.[182] For, working in accordance with strict rules, administrative officials are likely to end up in a mechanical routine or may be led to execute the orders of their superiors without thought. All this can be prevented by an equally enlightened criticism from without, yet this external criticism is lacking. It is precisely for this reason, Mill maintains, that there should exist equally able and educated people outside the government and the state should provide the means for their education.[183]

Mill admits that determining the limits of the authority of society over individuals, while at the same time retaining as many of 'the advantages of centralized power' as it is possible 'without turning into governmental channels too great a proportion of the general activity' is 'one of the most difficult and complicated questions in the art of government'.[184]

177 Ibid., p. 110.
178 Ibid.
179 Ibid., pp. 110–111.
180 Ibid., p. 112.
181 Ibid., p. 110.
182 Ibid., p. 112.
183 Ibid., p. 113.
184 Ibid.

But he thinks that 'the practical principle' or 'standard' to be kept in mind is the following:

> [...] the greatest dissemination of power consistent with efficiency; but the greatest possible centralization of information, and diffusion of it from the centre.[185]

A remarkable phrase encapsulates Mill's argument in *On Liberty*:

> The worth of a State, in the long run, is the worth of the individuals composing it [...][186]

On Women's Emancipation

J. S. Mill's views on women were expressed in an essay entitled 'The Subjection of Women', published in 1869. This is the work where the influence of his partner, Harriet Taylor, is perhaps most apparent. There has been much controversy about the degree of this influence, whether the views Mill expressed in the essay were hers and about the extent to which her contribution was original. This is due to the discrepancy between Mill's enthusiastic comments on her 'limitless genius' and his claims that his later work owed much to her ideas, on the one hand, and the fact that she made an 'unfavorable impression' on their contemporaries, while her extant writings do not display particular originality, on the other.[187] Okin argues following H. O. Pappe that 'it is only Mill's distorted impression of her abilities that suggests that she was endowed with any qualities of genius'.[188] As Mill has said on many occasions, he was a feminist before he met Harriet Taylor. All the same, the nature of their relationship 'must

185 Ibid.
186 Ibid., p. 115.
187 S. M. Okin, *Women in Western Political Thought* (London: Virago, 1980), p. 206.
188 Ibid.

have increased the strength of his convictions'.[189] Moreover, although it is not possible to say which views were his and which hers, some light is shed on this issue by two short essays on marriage and divorce which each wrote to the other at an early stage of their relationship and by the slightly different views (if only in emphasis) expressed in the earlier essay 'The Enfranchisement of Women' and 'The Subjection of Women'. This would seem to suggest that Harriet Taylor's ideas were 'somewhat more radical than his'.[190] Perhaps Okin is right when she says:

> On most issues, however, it seems that their ideas became very much enmeshed on this subject which was so important to them both.[191]

With respect to the actual composition of the essay, Mill acknowledged the contribution of his step-daughter, Helen Taylor, as the essay was written in the winter of 1860–1861, two years after Harriet Taylor's death.[192]

I.

The essay is concerned with the legal position of women in Victorian England. This is one of subordination of women to men, a situation which, for Mill, 'is wrong in itself', as well as being an obstacle to human improvement.[193] As Mill says, this is an opinion which he had 'held from the very earliest period' when he had been able to think about social and political issues.[194] In nineteenth-century England the subjection of women was taken for granted and, as Mill acknowledges, 'the burthen is hard on those who

189 Ibid., p. 207.
190 Ibid.
191 Ibid.
192 S. Collini, 'Introduction', in J. S. Mill, *On Liberty and Other Writings* (Cambridge: Cambridge University Press, 1989), p. xviii.
193 J. S. Mill, 'The Subjection of Women', in *On Liberty and Other Writings*, ed. S. Collini (Cambridge: Cambridge University Press, 1989), p. 119.
194 Ibid.

attack an almost universal opinion'.[195] It is often believed that the adoption of a practice is owing to that practice's contribution to happiness, as the best option available at the time. But, Mill argues, this is not the case with the subjection of women to men for the following reasons: Firstly, this opinion is based on theory only, as no other arrangement has ever been tried.[196] Secondly, this state of affairs was not the result of deliberation, any social ideas 'or any notion whatever of what conduced to the benefit of humanity or the good order of society'; it is rather due to the fact that from the very beginning of human society women found themselves subordinated to men.[197] So it happens that 'Laws and systems of polity [...] convert what was a mere physical fact into a legal right'.[198] Consequently: 'Those who had already been compelled to obedience became in this manner legally bound to it.'[199] It is always like this with slavery – 'a mere affair of force' becomes 'regularised and a matter of compact'.[200] Crucially, Mill compares the condition of women with that of slaves. But, more importantly, he adds that, although gradually, as society progressed, the slavery of males was abolished, the slavery of females was merely transformed 'into a milder form of dependence'.[201] It is evident then that the inequality of rights between the sexes is based on 'the law of the strongest', which is 'a paradox', says Mill, given human improvement; for in the current stage of civilization one would have thought that 'the law of the strongest' would have been 'entirely abandoned as the regulating principle of the world's affairs'.[202]

To the argument that, no matter how an existing social institution may have arisen, 'it can only [...] have been preserved to this period of advanced civilization by a well-grounded feeling of its adaptation to human nature, and conduciveness to the general good', Mill replies that those who have

195 Ibid., p. 120.
196 Ibid., pp. 122–123.
197 Ibid., p. 123.
198 Ibid.
199 Ibid.
200 Ibid.
201 Ibid.
202 Ibid., p. 124.

power do not surrender it that easily, while it is very rare that 'those who have obtained legal power because they first had physical, have ever lost their hold of it until the physical power had passed over to the other side'. But women haven't acquired the physical power as yet.[203] The problem, so far as Mill can see, is that people do not know to what extent the 'law of force' prevailed for the greatest part of the history of humanity,[204] while they tend to forget or ignore how institutions and practices grounded on the 'law of force' continue to exist into higher stages of civilization.[205] If male domination has been more prevalent than other forms of domination, this can be explained by the fact that it is not a mere abstract doctrine but serves the interests of all men, for it comes to their home.[206] Moreover, men are safeguarded against a potential uprising, as their subjects live at home under their own eyes and with little opportunity of combining with other women against them. Pointing to the fact that women's condition is even worse than that of (male) slaves, Mill adds that, whereas in struggles for political emancipation champions are bribed or terrorized, women are 'in a chronic state of bribery and intimidation combined'.[207]

Another argument which Mill considers is the view that the power of men over women cannot be compared with other 'forms of unjust power', for these are arbitrary whereas the former natural. Mill seems to regard such an argument as a mere pretext and tells its proponents to the face: 'But was there ever any domination which did not appear natural to those who possessed it?'[208] 'unnatural generally means only uncustomary', while 'everything which is usual appears natural'.[209]

It may also be argued that the dominion of men over women differs from other forms of dominion in that women consent to it. Mill's counter-arguments to this assertion are the following: women do *not* consent to it,

203 Ibid.
204 Ibid., pp. 125–127.
205 Ibid., p. 127.
206 Ibid., p. 128.
207 Ibid., p. 129.
208 Ibid.
209 Ibid., p. 130.

in the first place;[210] second, many more women would protest, had they not been taught to repress any political aspirations 'as contrary to the proprieties of their sex';[211] third, no subjugated group asks for 'complete liberty at once'[212] – it starts to complain of the 'oppressive exercise' of power and not of 'the power itself'.[213] In fact, claims Mill, if the subjection of women differs from other forms of subjection at all, it is that 'Men do not want solely the obedience of women, they want their sentiments'.[214] As a result, women are taught to live for others.

For Mill, not only did the progression of humanity not permit the continuation of the current relation of the sexes, but required its supersession. As he emphatically puts it, 'this relic of the past is discordant with the future, and must necessarily disappear'.[215] Nothing distinguished modern from past times more than that, as opposed to the past, in modern times humans were not born to a specific place in society and there was freedom of individual choice. In the nineteenth century competition in the economic and political spheres was a well-established fact.[216] Therefore, the subjection of women, Mill argued, stood out as 'an isolated fact in modern social institutions'.[217]

According to Mill, since only the existing relation of men and women had been tried, experience could not lead anywhere; nor, for that matter, could it be possible that the true nature of men and women was known – for this is to ignore the influences that shape human character.[218] Mill must have startled his contemporaries when he argued that rarely does a man know the character of a woman, even of one of his own family.[219]

210 Ibid., p. 131.
211 Ibid.
212 Ibid.
213 Ibid., p. 132.
214 Ibid.
215 Ibid., p. 134.
216 Ibid., pp. 135–136.
217 Ibid., p. 137.
218 Ibid., pp. 138–139.
219 Ibid., p. 141.

But this was due to his belief that 'thorough knowledge of one another hardly ever exists, but between persons who, besides being intimates, are equals'.[220] Given women's subjection to men, men's knowledge of women will always be inadequate. Men can only come to know women if they allow women to tell them about themselves.[221] Therefore, women should be allowed to enter public life and the professions on equal terms as men. For Mill, competition would suffice to determine whether women were fit for a position. What women by nature could *not* do, they would not succeed in doing and it would thus be 'superfluous to forbid them from doing'. On the other hand, things that they *could* do 'but not so well as the men who are their competitors', competition alone would exclude them from doing.[222] Mill points out that the real issue is 'not lest women should be unwilling to marry', as many defenders of the existing order argued, 'but lest they should insist that marriage should be on equal conditions'.[223] This latter was surely a bold claim to make in Victorian times.

II.

Mill starts his consideration of the subject with a discussion of marriage, since this is where the relationship of man and woman is most obviously seen. He says that the marriage contract in many countries including England makes the condition of women in some cases worse even than that of slaves; women have no property rights, they have no say even in family matters, are obliged to succumb to their husbands' desires whenever the latter demand.[224] But, fortunately, he adds, the actual treatment of a wife by her husband is not as bad or cruel as the law would allow. There is, therefore, a difference between women's legal position and their treatment by their

220 Ibid., p. 142.
221 Ibid.
222 Ibid., p. 144.
223 Ibid., p. 145.
224 Ibid., pp. 146–149.

husbands.[225] In reality, many men have feelings towards their wives.[226] There are even cases when a woman influences her husband too much and often in things with which she ought not to interfere.[227] However, this does not mean that her position is made better (with regard to her *legal* position); for 'neither in the affairs of families nor in those of states is power a compensation for the loss of freedom. Her power often gives her what she has no right to, but does not enable her to assert her own rights'.[228] In fact, in the present state of affairs the wife's influence on her husband is likely to have a negative effect. Since she is meant to have no role outside the family, 'she seldom has any honest and conscientious opinion' on political matters, for instance. So her concern is unlikely to be genuine or disinterested. As Mill says: 'She neither knows nor cares which is the right side in politics, but she knows what will bring in money or invitations, give her husband a title, her son a place, or her daughter a good marriage.'[229]

It is often argued that in all voluntary association between two persons the one should by law be master. Mill shows that such an argument is unsustainable by reference to the most usual voluntary association after marriage, that of partnership in business,[230] and proceeds to argue that the 'natural arrangement' is 'a division of powers' between husband and wife, a division which should not be determined by law but by the couple themselves on the basis of the abilities of each.[231] This division of powers will in turn lead to a division of rights.[232] Anticipating any objections, Mill says that, in point of fact, the responsibilities of the wife and husband are already 'so apportioned, except in cases in which the marriage institution is a failure'.[233] As to the argument that the settlement of differences is possible

225 Ibid., p. 149.
226 Ibid., p. 154.
227 Ibid., pp. 154–155.
228 Ibid., p. 155.
229 Ibid.
230 Ibid., pp. 155–156.
231 Ibid., p. 156.
232 Ibid.
233 Ibid., p. 157.

because there is legal enforcement in the background, Mill replies that 'The despotic power which the law gives to the husband may be a reason to make the wife assent to any compromise by which power is practically shared between the two, but it cannot be the reason why the husband does.'[234]

Mill's case for the emancipation of women should be seen in connection with his principle of utility, but 'utility in the largest sense, grounded on the permanent interests of man as a progressive human being', according to the famous phrase of 'On Liberty'.[235] I think it is fair to take 'man' in the above quotation to mean 'human being', hence man *and* woman. This is where the English language can be sexist; I do not think that by 'men' Mill literally meant only men and not women. It is this 'largest sense' of utility that Mill has in mind when he says in 'The Subjection of Women' that equality of man and woman before the law is 'the only means of rendering the daily life of mankind, in any high sense, a school of moral cultivation'[236] – Mill's claim here would not make sense if 'mankind' referred to 'all men' only – and again 'the only school of genuine moral sentiment is society between equals'.[237] The human species has progressed from a 'morality of submission' at the very early stages of society to a 'morality of chivalry and generosity' at a later stage. The time is now ripe for the 'morality of justice'.[238] For Mill, justice is 'the primary virtue', founded on 'equal' and 'sympathetic association'.[239] On this basis the family would be 'the real school of the virtues of freedom'.[240] That a woman should have a right to her own property does not mean, Mill explains, that she would not be able by arrangement with her husband 'to tie up property' in order to pass it on to their offspring.[241] In fact, Mill supports a 'community of goods', provided that it does not rest on 'the doctrine, that what is mine is

234 Ibid.
235 J. S. Mill, 'On Liberty', in *On Liberty and Other Writings*, ed. S. Collini, p. 14.
236 J. S. Mill, 'The Subjection of Women', p. 159.
237 Ibid.
238 Ibid., p. 160.
239 Ibid.
240 Ibid.
241 Ibid., p. 163.

yours but what is yours is not mine',[242] as it mostly used to be the case in nineteenth-century England, placing the woman at a clear disadvantage vis-à-vis her husband.

Should she be allowed to choose for herself, Mill believes that the woman would anyway choose to get married and raise a family, not taking up any occupations which would stand in the way of her fulfilling the duties to her family.[243] That said, he adds that 'the adaptation of general rules to individual suitabilities' should be allowed.[244] It is, no doubt, in statements such as this that commentators have seen the influence of Harriet Taylor, a woman of exceptionable talent by the standards of Victorian England.

III.

Apart from the institution of marriage, Mill considers 'the other point which is involved in the just equality of women – that is, their acceptance to professions or occupations usually regarded as 'the monopoly of the stronger sex'.[245] The reason mostly given for women's exclusion from a great many occupations is not that they are mentally inferior, but that their confinement in the home is in the interest of society, which is for the most part the interest of men.[246] To make the argument for women's unsuitability plausible – not to say valid –, claims Mill, one would have to say not that 'women on the average are less gifted than men on the average' but that 'no women at all are fit' for those occupations and that 'the most eminent women are inferior in mental faculties to the most mediocre of the men on whom those functions at present devolve'.[247] Since entry to the professions is decided by competition, unfit women would not succeed anyway. However, experience shows that many women are 'capable of everything,

242 Ibid.
243 Ibid., pp. 164–165.
244 Ibid., p. 165.
245 Ibid., p. 166.
246 Ibid.
247 Ibid., p. 167.

perhaps without a single exception, which is done by men, and of doing it successfully and creditably'.[248] Mill's argument for the acceptance of women to the professions is ultimately a utilitarian one. As he rhetorically puts it:

> Is there so great a superfluity of men fit for high duties, that society can afford to reject the service of any competent person? Are we so certain of always finding a man made to our hands for any duty or function of social importance which falls vacant, that we lose nothing by putting a ban upon one-half of mankind, and refusing beforehand to make their faculties available, however distinguished they may be?[249]

In fact, not only is women's exclusion from most occupations unjust to them, it is also unjust to those who would benefit from their services.[250] To illustrate his point Mill uses the example of the suffrage, arguing that, 'If no one could vote for a member of parliament who was not fit to be a candidate, the government would be a narrow oligarchy indeed'.[251] However, this is not the case, since all men have the right to vote. Therefore, women should be given this right on exactly the same conditions.[252] What is more:

> If anything conclusive could be inferred from experience, without psychological analysis, it would be that the things which women are not allowed to do are the very ones for which they are peculiarly qualified [...][253]

Mill cites the example of able queens and empresses to this effect.[254]

One of Mill's deepest beliefs was that there is no 'human nature' *simpliciter*, but that humans are shaped by environmental and social circumstances. This belief was a properly utilitarian one. For this reason he insisted that no one can tell what women are like, since the characteristics which they now have are due to their subordination to men.[255]

248 Ibid.
249 Ibid., p. 168.
250 Ibid.
251 Ibid.
252 Ibid., p. 169.
253 Ibid., p. 170.
254 Ibid., pp. 170–172.
255 Ibid., p. 173.

In this sense, he was one of the first thinkers to pose what we nowadays call the 'nature-nurture' issue. He suggests that 'even the least contestable of the differences which now exist, are such as may well have been produced merely by circumstances, without any difference in natural capacity'.[256] But, so far as he can tell from experience, women's capacities are mostly practical;[257] they have a capacity of 'intuition',[258] quickness of apprehension or rapidity of thought,[259] a more excitable temperament[260] and mobility of mind, that is, the ability to pass from one subject to another;[261] moreover, 'a woman's mind, though it may be occupied only with small things, can hardly ever permit itself to be vacant, as a man's so often is when not engaged in what he chooses to consider the business of his life'.[262] At the same time, Mill finds arguments which account for the allegedly superior mental capacities of men on the basis of anatomical differences – such as men have larger brains, for instance – for the most part inconclusive if not absurd.[263] In any case, in his view, 'Englishmen are in peculiarly unfavourable circumstances for attempting to judge what is or is not natural, not merely to women, but to men, or to human beings altogether, at least if they have only English experience to go on'. This is because 'the English are farther from a state of nature than any other modern people. They are, more than any other people, a product of civilization and discipline [...] In England, rule has to a great degree substituted itself for nature.'[264]

As regards women's achievement in the arts, Mill concedes that women are less original than men. Yet he explains this by saying that women were not concerned with the arts in the past, while now – with so many advances

256 Ibid.
257 Ibid.
258 Ibid., pp. 174–176.
259 Ibid., p. 176.
260 Ibid., pp. 176–179.
261 Ibid., pp. 179–180.
262 Ibid., p. 180.
263 Ibid., pp. 180–182.
264 Ibid., p. 183.

already made – it is more difficult than ever for one to make an original contribution.[265] Besides, 'very few women have time for them',[266] not to mention the fact that the woman 'is expected to have her time and faculties always at the disposal of everybody'.[267] In addition, women seldom have the 'eagerness for fame', which is one of the motives for pursuing the arts.[268] This 'trait of character' is not 'inherent in women', but is 'the natural result of their circumstances'.[269] Similarly, 'The love of fame in men is encouraged by education and opinion.'[270]

Regarding moral differences between the sexes, it is said that women are better than men. But, Mill argues, if this is true at all, it only means that men admit that power is a 'corrupting influence'.[271] On the negative side, it is claimed that women are morally biased. To which Mill replies: 'Assuming it to be so, it is still to be proved that women are oftener misled by their personal feelings than men by their personal interests.'[272]

So one may well ask why women do not complain of their position. Mill's answer is that even when they do – for example, in their writings –, their complaints 'are not meant to imply blame, or to plead for any change'.[273] But this is the case with all emancipation movements in their beginnings. Each woman complains of her own husband or of those of her friends. He adds:

> Women cannot be expected to devote themselves to the emancipation of women, until men in considerable number are prepared to join with them in the undertaking.[274]

265 Ibid., pp. 184–189.
266 Ibid., p. 189.
267 Ibid., p. 191.
268 Ibid.
269 Ibid., p. 192.
270 Ibid.
271 Ibid.
272 Ibid., p. 193.
273 Ibid., p. 194.
274 Ibid.

IV.

What then are the advantages of sexual equality?

First and foremost, the most important of human relationships – 'the most universal and pervading' –, that of husband and wife, will be governed by justice instead of injustice.[275] The consequences thereof, so far as moral character is concerned, could not be overestimated, for Mill. As he notes, under the existing arrangements boys grow up to be arrogant.[276]

Second, putting forth a utilitarian argument, he says that under sexual equality the amount of human talent available will double.[277] Simultaneously, women will be allowed to expand their faculties and moral sentiments.[278] Women's influence has hitherto exerted a great influence on men and public morality in general – for example, through their opposition to war and commitment to philanthropy, 'Excellent characteristics both', but, unfortunately, 'in the particular applications' women's influence is 'at least as often mischievous as useful'.[279] Furthermore, it has often been the case that in the higher social strata the woman prevents her husband from rising above 'common public opinion'.[280] Due to women's lower cultivation, which – Mill emphasizes – is due to their current subordination, their influence on their husbands is 'deteriorating'; 'and still more so in a tolerably happy marriage than in an unhappy one.'[281] Moreover, women's influence on their husbands was greater in the nineteenth century than in previous times, as men spent more time at home.[282] It was for this reason that Mill believed that the expansion of women's faculties and sentiments following women's emancipation would lead to 'the moral regeneration' of humankind.[283]

275 Ibid., p. 196.
276 Ibid., pp. 196–199.
277 Ibid., p. 199.
278 Ibid., p. 200.
279 Ibid., pp. 203–204.
280 Ibid., p. 205; cf. ibid., p. 206.
281 Ibid., p. 210.
282 Ibid., pp. 210–211.
283 Ibid., p. 211.

Third, Mill did not fail to mention that, as well as social, there would also be individual benefits as a result of the equality of men and women, most important of which would be 'the unspeakable gain in private happiness to the liberated half of the species; the difference to them between a life of subjection to the will of others, and a life of rational freedom'.[284] What is implicit in this statement is a utilitarian argument, according to which the happiness of the liberated women – the one-half of the human species – would lead to the greatest happiness of the species as a whole. Once more, utility has to be understood in – what Mill called – 'the largest sense'.[285] And, in fact, Mill goes on to say:

> [...] the communities in which the reason has been most cultivated, and in which the idea of social duty has been most powerful, are those which have most strongly asserted the freedom of action of the individual – the liberty of each to govern his conduct by his own feelings of duty, and by such laws and social restraints as his own conscience can subscribe to.[286]

With these words Mill makes clear that the issue of sexual equality is one of liberty. The passage with which the essay on the subjection of women closes makes explicit the interrelation between Mill's principle of liberty and wider sense of utility:

> [...] every restraint on the freedom of conduct of any of their human fellow creatures [...] dries up *pro tanto* the principal fountain of human happiness, and leaves the species less rich, to an appreciable degree, in all that makes life valuable to the individual human being.[287]

Let us now look at some criticisms of Mill's views on sexual equality. According to Okin, despite his arguments in favour of equality within the family, 'it is in fact because of John Stuart Mill's assumptions and

284 Ibid., p. 212.
285 Mill, 'On Liberty', p. 14.
286 Mill, 'The Subjection of Women', p. 212.
287 Ibid., p. 217.

convictions about the family and its traditional roles that his feminism falls short of advocating true equality and freedom for married women'.[288] Specifically:

> Mill's feminist writings are, implicitly, concerned only with middle- and upper-class women, and it is the bourgeois family that is his model. Though he rejects the legalized inequalities of its patriarchal form, he regards the family itself as 'essential for humanity,' and is concerned to reassure his readers that family life has nothing to fear, but rather much to gain, from the complete political and civil equality of the sexes.[289]

Furthermore, Mill supports the traditional division of labour in marriage[290] by arguing that, although women should choose between marriage and a career, at the end of the day they would choose marriage.[291] In turn:

> Mill's acceptance of traditional sex roles within the family places serious limitations on the extent to which he can apply the principles of freedom and equality to married women.[292]

Accordingly, in the first place, 'though he argues in favor of equal property *rights* for married women, these are rights to property inherited or earned by the woman herself, not rights to equal shares in the family income'.[293] And, as another commentator notes with respect to this issue, 'the right to retain one's property ignores the fact that women earn and inherit substantially less than men'[294] – a 'situation' that 'only reinforces the wife's economic dependence on her husband', thereby making 'the legal changes which Mill advocates a merely formal improvement for the majority'.[295] In the second place, claims Okin, Mill's 'defense of traditional

288 Okin, *Women in Western Political Thought*, p. 226.
289 Ibid.
290 A criticism also made by D. H. Coole, *Women in Political Theory* (Sussex: Wheatsheaf Books & Boulder, Colorado: Lynne Rienner Publishers, 1988), p. 144.
291 Okin, *Women in Western Political Thought*, p. 226.
292 Ibid., p. 228.
293 Ibid.
294 Coole, *Women in Political Theory*, p. 144.
295 Ibid.

sex roles within the family amounts to a denial of freedom of opportunity and individual expression of talents to that majority of women whom he assumes would always choose to marry'.[296] Mill's failure to recognize that domestic responsibilities should be shared by both husband and wife and 'to question the social institutions that made such sharing practically impossible are striking', Okin argues, in view of the fact that he acknowledges that 'the principal means' by which women would gain equality was 'via success in fields formerly monopolized by men'.[297] So, Okin concludes:

> [...] although a very forward-looking feminist in many respects, he in no way perceived the injustice involved in institutions and practices which allowed a man to have a career and economic independence, *and* a home life and children, but which forced a woman to choose between the two.[298]

Coole has suggested that the inadequacy of Mill's solution to women's subjection is largely owing to his analysis of its causes. In understanding progress as 'a transition from barbarism to civilization', Mill argues that 'relations of subordination which were originally based on force' have given way to 'rational' relations based on consent. In this respect, Mill sees the relation of men and women as an exception, 'something of an anomaly' which, once exposed, will be redressed.[299] However:

> He does not appear to have recognized that there might be structural reasons for women's continued and reinforced subjugation, predicated on contemporary interests which might be perfectly rational and useful to their practitioners. He does not see that capitalism might benefit from women's domestic role nor that men may have continuing reasons for oppressing women beyond their own bad principles and barbaric legacy.[300]

296 Okin, *Women in Western Political Thought*, p. 229.
297 Ibid.
298 Ibid., p. 230.
299 Coole, *Women in Political Theory*, p. 147.
300 Ibid., p. 148.

Rather 'the subordination of women, which is embodied in the law, relies for Mill only on a tradition that has yet to be reformed according to rational principles'.[301]

Coole has also pointed out the limitations of Mill's utilitarian argument for sexual equality. In particular, Coole has noted that Mill's 'utilitarian arguments [...] dwell on the increase in the sum of happiness which will emerge from women's participation in it'.[302] As a result, Mill rarely concentrated on the advantages to women; 'the thrust of his argument is more often (as in the case of population control) designed to appeal to men's interests',[303] with the exception of a passage at the very end of the essay, where he talks about 'the unspeakable gain in private happiness to the liberated half of the species'.[304] 'This subterfuge', Coole argues, 'is made necessary by his individualistic approach to political change'.[305]

> Only when women have the jobs and votes he campaigns for, does Mill envisage them exercising power on their own behalf. It is therefore men (like himself) who must mediate women's demands, and so their support must be won.[306]

Another consequence of Mill's utilitarianism is, according to Coole, that 'it embarks upon the slippery slope of expediency', thereby inviting counter-arguments concerning the 'dysfunction' or disutility of sexual equality.[307] The danger is that the issue of women's emancipation may come 'to rely on the outcome of a cost-benefit analysis (a calculation intrinsic to utilitarianism, although one whose crudeness Mill's appeal to "man" as a "progressive being" was designed to circumvent)'.[308]

301 Ibid.
302 Ibid., p. 149.
303 Ibid.
304 Ibid., pp. 149–150; quotation from Mill, p. 150.
305 Ibid., p. 150.
306 Ibid.
307 Ibid.
308 Ibid.

On Socialism

In reading 'Chapters on Socialism' we should bear in mind that this essay is not complete. It was published in the radical journal *Fortnightly Review* six years after Mill's death (in 1879) in the form in which it was found among his papers by Helen Taylor. Given that Mill used to revise his works before sending them to the publisher and since these chapters have most probably not been revised, we should be wary about some of the statements made. It should also be noted that 'the manuscript has long since disappeared, so it is impossible to determine what the present version of the text owes to Helen Taylor's hand or even to printer's errors'.[309] All the same, many of the views expressed in the 'Chapters on Socialism' are similar to those Mill expressed in some of his other writings, especially in the *Principles of Political Economy*.

John Stuart Mill has made a reputation as a liberal thinker and politician; so one may be surprised that he should have written about socialism. Yet his socialism was not independent of his principle of utility in the wider sense of human improvement and formed part of his programme for social regeneration, not to say of his hopes for the future. His socialism envisaged a society of workers' co-operatives; his argument for such an arrangement of the economy was utilitarian; whereas under capitalism workers were not self-governing, under socialism they would actively participate in the economy.[310] Moreover, as it becomes evident from a chapter in his earlier voluminous work *Principles of Political Economy* entitled 'On the Probable Futurity of the Labouring Classes', Mill saw clear 'parallels' between 'sex and class oppression' and a 'need in both cases to abandon paternalistic protection in favour of responsible self-government'.[311]

309 S. Collini, 'Introduction', in Mill, *On Liberty and Other Writings*, p. xxii.

310 J. S. Mill, *Principles of Political Economy*, edited with an introduction by Sir William Ashley (Fairfield, N.J.: Augustus M. Kelley, 1987, Book IV, Chapter VII, esp. pp. 772–792.

311 Coole, *Women in Political Theory*, pp. 139–140.

I.

Mill begins 'Chapters on Socialism' by stressing the significance of a political fact. The 'Reform Act' of 1867 had given a considerable number of the working class the vote. Consequently, were they to exert their electoral power, workers would 'exercise, though not a complete ascendancy, a very great influence on legislation'.[312] This would have great consequences for the structure of English society, for workers did not support the institution of property, to say nothing of the 'inequalities of property'.[313] Mill seems to be willing to open the eyes of his contemporaries to recent political developments, as it were, for he goes on to say:

> [...] the greatness of this change is as yet by no means completely realised, either by those who opposed, or by those who effected our last constitutional reform. To say the truth, the perceptions of Englishmen are of late somewhat blunted as to the tendencies of political changes.[314]

However, says Mill:

> Sudden effects in history are generally superficial. Causes which go deep down into the roots of future events produce the most serious parts of their effect only slowly, and have therefore, time to become a part of the familiar order of things before general attention is called to the changes they are producing [...][315]

Owing to the political weight of the aforesaid 'Reform Act', Mill deems it essential that the political creeds of the working classes be considered and that 'every single article of them' be examined, 'so that, if possible, when the time shall be ripe, whatever is right in them may be adopted, and what is wrong rejected by general consent, and that instead of a hostile conflict, physical or only moral, between the old and the new, the best

312 J. S. Mill, 'Chapters on Socialism', in *On Liberty and Other Writings*, ed. S. Collini, p. 222.

313 Ibid.

314 Ibid.

315 Ibid., p. 223.

parts of both may be combined in a renovated social fabric'.[316] Recall Mill's position on the nature of truth:

> [...] on every subject on which difference of opinion is possible, the truth depends on a balance to be struck between two sets of conflicting reasons.[317]

Or again, the possibility – which is usual enough – that two 'conflicting doctrines, instead of being one true and the other false, share the truth between them'.[318] Therefore, like in 'On Liberty', in 'Chapters on Socialism' too the underlying rationale is a utilitarian one; one should attend to the political creeds of the workers because there may be some truth in them (albeit partial). Besides, being as always averse to violence, Mill claims that the future of humankind will be put at risk, 'if great questions are left to be fought over between ignorant change and ignorant opposition to change'.[319]

Mill saw that the 'fundamental doctrines' which were prevalent in previous times were being for the first time questioned.[320] Of these the most important was the institution of property; all political conflicts of the past had involved the propertied classes. The situation was starting to change, however, as the working classes were gaining power.[321] Although in Britain the working classes were in general opposed to *some* aspects of the proprietary system only, in European countries such as France, Germany and Switzerland, 'anti-property' doctrines had drawn a large number of workers to the socialist cause. And, as Mill makes clear, although socialism is 'a designation under which schemes of very diverse character are comprehended and confounded', it 'implies at least a remodelling generally approaching to abolition of the institution of private property'.[322] Thus, though the leaders of the English working classes call themselves socialists, they are more conscious than their continental counterparts of the

316 Ibid., p. 224.
317 Mill, 'On Liberty', p. 38.
318 Ibid., p. 47.
319 Mill, 'Chapters on Socialism', p. 224.
320 Ibid.
321 Ibid., pp. 224–225.
322 Ibid., p. 225.

fact that great changes 'in the fundamental ideas of mankind' are not to be effected 'by a *coup de main*'; thus their demands are more moderate in the first instance.[323]

In a vein similar to that of 'The Subjection of Women' Mill claims that the very fact that 'the great majority' are 'enslaved or made dependent' 'by force of poverty', though not 'by force of law' any more, 'is an evil equal to almost any of those against which mankind have hitherto struggled' and that 'the poor are not wrong in believing' this. However, he asks rhetorically: 'Is it a necessary evil?'[324] Mill firmly held the view that all arguments should be given consideration – those of the defenders of the institution of private property, those of opponents and all plans of social reformers 'for the purpose of attaining the benefits aimed at by the institution of property without its inconveniences'.[325]

II.

Mill makes clear that socialism has two aspects – 'one negative and critical' which is concerned with 'that which is to be changed', 'the other constructive' concerned with 'that which is to be changed to'.[326] As far as he can see, all strands or traditions of socialism agree on the former aspect; but, regarding the latter aspect, despite general agreement, there is 'a wide disparity' as to the particulars.[327] Turning to the critical aspect of socialism, Mill concentrates on the major 'evils' of the present order, since the socialist criticisms are too many to be exhaustively treated in the essay. First, there is 'the evil of Poverty'.[328] According to the socialist argument, even if the institution of property had at earlier stages of history enabled humans to

323 Ibid., pp. 225–226.
324 Ibid., p. 227.
325 Ibid., p. 228.
326 Ibid.
327 Ibid., pp. 228–229.
328 Ibid., p. 230.

prosper by encouraging labour and frugality, this is no longer the case.[329] Moreover, socialists argue that the prevalent view that poverty is a result of idleness or incapacity in a fair system of competition, 'even were it true, would be a very small alleviation of the evil'.[330] For:

> [...] if there be any who suffer physical privation or moral degradation [...] this, though not necessarily the crime of society, is *pro tanto* a failure of the social arrangements. And to assert as a mitigation of the evil that those who thus suffer are the weaker members of the community, morally or physically, is to add insult to misfortune.[331]

The only acceptable argument in favour of the existing order would be, so the socialist case goes, that it allows individuals to obtain 'a fair share of the fruits' of their labour. But this is not true: 'The reward, instead of being proportioned to the labour and abstinence of the individual, is almost in an inverse ratio to it'.[332] Nor is there any place for 'distributive justice' in existing society. On the contrary, an individual's fate is determined by birth, on the one hand, by accident and opportunity, on the other.[333] The second social evil, for the socialists, is 'human misconduct', which is due to 'one of three causes': the poverty of the generality of the people, the idleness of the few who are enough well-off not to need to work for a living and the bad education or the lack of it altogether of the poor and rich alike.[334] Socialists blamed the principle of individualism and competition for all the envy, hatred and mercilessness that existed in nineteenth-century capitalist society.[335] To illustrate the foregoing socialist criticisms of the existing order, Mill cites certain passages from the writings of the most prominent representatives of the socialist tradition known as 'utopian socialism' – Louis Blanc, Fourier and his followers and Owen.

329 Ibid.
330 Ibid.
331 Ibid., p. 231.
332 Ibid.
333 Ibid., pp. 231–232.
334 Ibid., p. 232.
335 Ibid., p. 233.

III.

In assessing the aforementioned socialist criticisms, Mill claims that, although many of them are indisputable, some are 'the result of errors in political economy' – that is, they arise out of 'ignorance of economic facts, and of the causes by which the economic phenomena of society as it is, are actually determined'.[336] The socialist misconceptions in respect of the nature of the capitalist system were, for Mill, the following.

First, although it is true that the wages of workers are all over Europe 'wretchedly insufficient' to supply the necessities of life, it is not correct to say, as the socialists do, that workers' wages tend to diminish. On the contrary, considered on the whole they are on the rise.[337] In addition, 'the pressure of population on subsistence, which is the principal cause of low wages, though a great, is not an increasing evil'.[338] Quite on the contrary:

> the progress of all that is called civilisation has a tendency to diminish it, partly by the more rapid increase of the means of employing and maintaining labour, partly by the increased facilities opened to labour for transporting itself to new countries and unoccupied fields of employment, and partly by a general improvement in the intelligence and prudence of the population.[339]

In any case, over-population was an issue which communism too would have to tackle.[340]

Second, socialists had 'a very imperfect and one-sided notion of the operation of competition'.[341] Specifically, they tended to forget that competition caused prizes to fall as much as to rise, that there was competition between 'the buyers of labour and of commodities' as much as between the sellers and that if competition kept the prices of labour low, yet it ensured that they did not fall still lower.[342] In point of fact, claims Mill,

336 Ibid., p. 249.
337 Ibid., p. 249; cf. p. 250.
338 Ibid., p. 250.
339 Ibid.
340 Ibid.
341 Ibid., p. 251.
342 Ibid.

> when competition is perfectly free on both sides [namely, the buyers and the sellers], its tendency is not specially either to raise or to lower the price of articles, but to equalise it; to level inequalities of remuneration, and to reduce all to a general average [...][343]

The fact that competition keeps wages down may cause the discontent of the workers, but one should bear in mind that it also keeps down the prices of commodities, which is to the advantage of wage-earners.[344] Nor is it true that the richest capitalist can get rid of all his rivals, thus coming to dominate the market. The 'commonest experience' provides evidence against the socialist fear of a 'monopoly of a few'.[345] In reality, there are only few cases in which businesses are in the hands of a small number of large producers or dealers. In any case, this concentration takes place when the possession of more capital makes possible the investment in better machinery and the production of more commodities at lower prices, which is to the benefit of the consumers and the working classes. This also leads to the diminution of 'that waste of the resources of the community so much complained by the Socialists, the unnecessary multiplication of mere distributors, and of the various other classes whom Fourier calls the parasites of industry'.[346]

Third, surely socialists have a point when they argue that competition leads to a deterioration of quality. However, Mill believes, the existing social and economic order has not employed all the means available to combat 'this evil'.[347] For him, there *are* possible remedies – the making of better laws against commercial frauds as well as the better implementation of the same laws,[348] the development of co-operative stores,[349] 'a sterner reprobation by opinion' so far as 'greater and more conspicuous economical frauds, or practices equivalent to frauds' are concerned.[350] Mill goes on to

343 Ibid. (my square brackets)
344 Ibid., pp. 251–252.
345 Ibid., p. 252.
346 Ibid.
347 Ibid., pp. 253–254.
348 Ibid., p. 254.
349 Ibid., pp. 254–255.
350 Ibid., p. 255.

say that one of the problems – a serious defect in the system – is that in cases of bankruptcy 'the primary object regarded has still been the pecuniary interest of the creditors', whereas 'criminality in the bankrupt himself, with the exception of a small number of well-marked offences gets off with impunity'.[351] And he entertained the belief that 'Until a more moral and rational mode of dealing with culpable insolvency' had been 'tried and failed', 'commercial dishonesty' could not be 'ranked among evils' which were 'inseparable from commercial competition'.[352]

Last, according to Mill, socialists misunderstood the nature of capital investment, the risks involved and the possibility of commercial crises.[353] In particular, he stresses the fact that the capitalist applies the capital to the process of production – in the form of buildings, machinery and so forth – which belongs to the workers, so that what he is left with is only the profits, which he receives 'on condition that the capital itself is employed in satisfying not his own wants, but those of the labourers'.[354] At the same time, as provider of the capital, he runs the risk of becoming bankrupt due to the change in interest rates and economic cycles.

IV.

Having considered the 'critical' aspect of socialism, Mill turns to the other, the 'constructive' aspect. Here he is careful to distinguish between two traditions: that of Owen, Fourier and other 'philosophic Socialists' (the 'utopians socialists'), who propounded a new order consisting of small co-operative communities, and 'the revolutionary Socialists' of the Continent, who proposed the overthrow of the capitalist system and the centralization of production.[355] The former programme of social reform could be

351 Ibid., p. 256.
352 Ibid.
353 Ibid., pp. 256–259.
354 Ibid., p. 257.
355 Ibid., p. 260.

established progressively,[356] whereas the latter aspired to transform the structure of society 'at a blow'.[357] Mill leaves aside the obvious differences of the aforesaid two strands of socialism in order to examine what they share in common.

First, all socialists propound the joint ownership of the instruments and means of production.[358] To which Mill provides the following counter-argument: From an economic point of view, communism would not be as efficient. Specifically, the 'strong personal motive to do their very best and utmost for the efficiency and economy of the operations, would not exist under Communism', since 'the managers would only receive out of the produce the same equal dividend as the other members of the association'.[359] Moreover, experience shows that personal interests tend to be stronger than the public interest. Mill believed that the lack of public spirit was, to a large extent, due to 'imperfect education'.[360] And improvements in education are gradual, not least 'because the future generation is educated by the present, and the imperfections of the teachers set an invincible limit to the degree in which they can train their pupils to be better than themselves'.[361] Consequently, it was to be expected that personal interest would continue to guide human behaviour for a long time to come.[362] Further, although it may be allowed that under Communism people 'directly interested in the success of the work' and with 'practical knowledge and opportunities of judgment' would appoint 'managers of greater skill than the chances of birth, which now so often determine who shall be the owner of capital', one also has to consider that in a communist society those 'most qualified for the management' would be unwilling to undertake it because of lack of incentives.[363] The only possible motive to the assumption of the manage-

356 Ibid.
357 Ibid., p. 261.
358 Ibid.
359 Ibid., p. 263.
360 Ibid.
361 Ibid., pp. 263–264.
362 Ibid., p. 264.
363 Ibid., pp. 264–265.

ment by the most competent would be to prevent it from being taken over by the incompetent. Yet 'inventors or schemers' would be accepted by the average person only with difficulty.[364] Regarding 'the ordinary workers', under Communism the workers would show more interest in their work and be more industrious, as they would work under the constant gaze of their comrades.[365] However, Mill argues,

> [...] the principal defects of the present system in respect to the efficiency of labour may be corrected, and the chief advantages of Communism in that respect may be obtained, by arrangements compatible with private property and individual competition.[366]

Mill claims that, in fact, several steps had already been taken in that direction with the introduction of piece-work and – better still – industrial partnerships, which were likely to develop into 'co-operative associations'.[367] Therefore, Mill concludes, 'as far as concerns the motives to exertion in the general body, Communism has no advantage which may not be reached under private property, while as respects the managing heads it is at a considerable disadvantage'.[368]

The second view held by all socialists is that, since different jobs are unequal in difficulty and unpleasantness, they should all be done by everyone by turns. Faithful to the teachings of classical political economy, John Stuart Mill counters this argument by saying that division of labour leads to more productivity.[369] In addition, he argues that it is 'a very imperfect standard of justice to demand the same amount of work from every one', since individuals 'have unequal capacities of work, both mental and bodily'.[370] Nor is it possible to exclude individualism altogether, *even if* it were eliminated completely from the field of 'material interests'; 'there will

364 Ibid., p. 265.
365 Ibid., p. 266.
366 Ibid., pp. 266–267.
367 Ibid., p. 267.
368 Ibid., pp. 267–268.
369 Ibid., p. 268.
370 Ibid.

still be rivalry for reputation and for personal power' – this may even be more intense and much bitter.[371] Mill also mentions that there will be many other causes of discord under communism as a result of the principle of deciding by the general voice matters that concern everyone.[372] And, obviously, as one would expect from the writer of 'On Liberty', a much greater evil would be the stifling of all individual opinions and the enforcement of unanimity.[373]

While Mill made clear that he did not wish 'to draw any inference against the possibility' of communism becoming at some point in the future 'the form of society best adapted to the wants and circumstances of mankind',[374] he was of the opinion that, to succeed, communism necessitated 'a high standard of both moral and intellectual education in all members of the community'.[375] Victorian society was not anywhere near this standard and there would be a long time before it attained it. But this does not mean that it was 'impossible for education and cultivation such as is implied in these things to be made the inheritance of every person in the nation'.[376] At least, he entertained this hope. In the meantime, he recognized that only communism could effectively prepare humankind for communism. Therefore, communism had 'to prove, by practical experiment, its power of giving this training'.[377] Practical trial was also necessary to test the possibility or practicability of 'those other forms of Socialism' which were aware of 'the difficulties of Communism' and sought 'means to surmount them', the most important of these being Fourierism.[378]

It is important to stress that, although Mill was in general sympathetic to the socialism propounded by Owen, Fourier and Saint-Simon, he rejected the demand for a radical transformation of society made by the

371 Ibid., p. 269.
372 Ibid., pp. 269–270.
373 Ibid., p. 270.
374 Ibid.
375 Ibid., p. 271.
376 Ibid.
377 Ibid.
378 Ibid.

'revolutionary socialists' of the Continent. No doubt, this was due to his opposition to social and political violence. But, apart from this, for him, the plan for the centralization of land was 'obviously chimerical'.[379] Even if the revolutionary socialists did manage to acquire all the land of the country, they would end up 'dividing it into portions, each to be made over to the administration of a small Socialist community'.[380] Mill insisted that a violent dissolution of the existing social order would lead to a Hobbesian 'state of nature'.[381] For Mill, violence would not lead anywhere. Rather he favoured a gradual transformation of social institutions.[382]

V.

Before I close, I should like to draw the reader's attention to the last five pages of 'Chapters on Socialism'. Although Mill argued that socialism was not possible in the conditions of nineteenth-century Britain and that, therefore, private property would survive for a long time, he was careful to clarify his position by emphasizing that this did not mean that the institution of private property and the laws that protected it needed to remain unmodified.[383] In these last few pages of the essay as it stands he attacks that commonest misunderstanding – that is, that private property is invariable.[384] On the contrary, he argues:

> the right of property is differently interpreted, and held to be of different extent, in different times and places [...][385]

He cites several examples to this effect. What is crucial is that 'the conception entertained of it is a varying conception, has been frequently revised,

379 Ibid., p. 273.
380 Ibid.
381 Ibid., p. 274.
382 Ibid., pp. 274–275.
383 Ibid., p. 275.
384 Ibid., p. 276.
385 Ibid., p. 278.

and may admit of still further revision.'[386] Against the 'revolutionary socialists', therefore, he wants to give the institution of private property 'a chance' to develop into a form 'more beneficial to that large portion of society' which at the time of writing benefited least.[387]

386 Ibid., pp. 278–279.
387 Ibid., p. 279.

CHAPTER 5

Jean-Jacques Rousseau

Rousseau was writing in the middle of the eighteenth century. At the time France was a semi-feudal economy and was governed by an absolute monarchy. Like many French intellectuals of his day, he was critical of the Ancien Régime. But, although he came to be associated with the 'Philosophes' in the literary *salons* of Paris, he later distanced himself from them. The latter believed that reason could lead to human progress and their views were expressed in the bulky volumes of this momentous work of the Enlightenment, the *Encyclopaedia*. By contrast, Rousseau wished to emphasize the importance of feelings and emotions and argued that political communities could not be based only on reason; a people had to be bound by sentimental ties too.

The *Discourse on Inequality*

Rousseau dedicated his *Discourse on the Origins and the Foundations of Inequality Among Men* to the citizens of Geneva, a republic which he regarded as a model. In the eighteenth century Geneva was a city-state, a single political entity with a population slightly exceeding 25,000.[1] The *Discourse on Inequality* is an essay written in response to the question proposed by the Dijon Academy in a competition 'What is the origin of the

1 M. Cranston, 'Introduction', in his translation of J.-J. Rousseau's *A Discourse on Inequality* (Harmondsworth: Penguin, 1984), p. 9.

inequality among men, and is it authorized by natural law?'[2] The *Discourse* is a polemic, its purpose being to demonstrate how civilization corrupts the natural goodness, happiness and freedom of humans. As Rousseau writes at the very beginning of the second *Discourse*, there are two kinds of inequality among humans:

> [...] the first [...] natural or physical because it is established by nature, and consists of differences in age, health, strength of the body and qualities of the mind and soul; the second [...] moral or political inequality because it derives from a sort of convention, and is established, or at least authorized, by the consent of men.[3]

It is to 'moral or political' inequality, consisting of social privileges, that Rousseau objects. Like Hobbes and Locke before him, Rousseau makes use of the category of the 'state of nature'. However, it is important to bear in mind that Rousseau uses the 'state of nature' in a different way. For him, it refers to the original condition of humans; this does not mean that the 'state of nature' is an historical fact; it is rather hypothetical, intended to explain how inequality arose among human beings.[4] Rousseau describes humans in the 'state of nature' as savages living among other animals in the wild.[5] The 'state of nature' is not *im*moral but *a*moral; that is to say, there is no morality in the 'state of nature'.[6] However, as Rousseau says:

> [...] let us not conclude with Hobbes that man is naturally evil just because he has no idea of goodness, that he is vicious for want of any knowledge of virtue, that he

2 Jean-Jacques Rousseau, *A Discourse on Inequality*, translated with an introduction and notes by M. Cranston (Harmondsworth: Penguin, 1984), p. 73.

3 Ibid., p. 77.

4 Ibid., p. 78; cf. 'If I have dwelled so long on the hypothesis of this primitive condition, it is because, having ancient errors and inveterate prejudices to eliminate, I thought I ought to dig down to the roots, and provide a picture of the true state of nature, to show to what extent inequality, even in its natural form, is far from having in that state as much reality and influence as our writers claim.' Ibid., p. 105.

5 Ibid., pp. 81ff.

6 'It would seem at first glance that men in the state of nature, having no kind of moral relationships between them, or any known duties, could be neither good nor evil, and that they could have neither vices nor virtues'. Ibid., p. 98.

> always refuses to do his fellow-men services which he does not believe he owes them, or that on the strength of the right he reasonably claims to things he needs, he foolishly imagines himself to be the sole proprietor of the whole universe [...] that writer ought to have said that the state of nature, being the state where man's care for his own preservation is least prejudicial to that of others, is the one most conducive to peace and the most suited to mankind. Hobbes said precisely the opposite as a result of introducing, illogically, into the savage man's care for his own preservation the need to satisfy a multitude of passions which are the product of society and which have made laws necessary.[7]

Unlike Hobbes, Rousseau believed that 'savages are not wicked precisely because they do not know what it is to be good; for it is neither the development of intelligence nor the restraint of the laws, but the calm of the passions and the ignorance of vice which prevents them from doing evil'.[8] Rousseau's opposition to liberalism as well as to the Enlightenment is evident in his emphasis on the passions. As he puts it:

> Whatever our moralists say, human understanding owes much to the passions, which, by common consent, also owe much to it. It is by the activity of the passions that our reason improves itself; we seek to know only because we desire to enjoy [...] The passions, in turn, owe their origin to our needs and their development to our knowledge, for one can desire or fear a thing only if one has an idea of it in the mind – unless one is responding to a simple impulsion of nature.[9]

Hobbes and Locke had argued that human beings in the 'state of nature' possessed reason. By contrast, Rousseau argues as follows:

> The savage man, deprived of any sort of enlightenment, experiences passions only [...] his desires do not go beyond his physical needs.[10]

Consequently, as a commentator has observed, 'Natural Law, understood as rational, universal moral principles, is simply inapplicable in

7 Ibid.
8 Ibid., p. 99.
9 Ibid., p. 89.
10 Ibid.

Rousseau's primitive state of nature'.[11] This is because humans in their original condition 'would lack the reasoning ability to apprehend such rational principles'.[12]

In Rousseau's 'state of nature' human beings have 'self-love' (*amour de soi*) – which is not a selfish sentiment, but a concern for oneself (self-preservation) – and 'pity' (*pitié*), empathy or compassion for others of their kind.[13] According to Rousseau, Hobbes ignored that *pitié* gives human beings 'an innate repugnance against seeing a fellow creature suffer'.[14] Further, 'it is pity which in the state of nature takes the place of laws, morals and virtues, with the added advantage that no one there is tempted to disobey its gentle voice'.[15] For this reason it has been noted that 'self-love' and 'pity' perform in Rousseau's depiction of the natural condition of humankind 'something of the same role which other philosophers attribute to Natural Law'.[16]

Nor is Rousseau's 'state of nature' characterized by a 'war of all against all', as it is in Hobbes. For these 'proto-humans' were 'wild rather than wicked, and more intent on protecting themselves from the harm that might be done to them than tempted to do harm to others'. Therefore, 'they were not prone to especially dangerous quarrels'.[17] Moreover, since they had 'no experience of vanity, consideration, esteem or contempt; [...] not the least idea of *meum* and *tuum*, or any authentic idea of justice'; since they considered violence 'an injury easily healed rather than an insult to be punished; and since they did not even dream of vengeance, except perhaps mechanically and on the spot', their 'disputes would seldom have had bloody consequences, provided there was no more sensitive subject than food'.[18]

11 J. I. MacAdam, 'The Discourse on Inequality and the Social Contract', *Philosophy*, Vol. 47 (1972), p. 311.
12 Ibid.
13 Rousseau, *A Discourse on Inequality*, p. 101.
14 Ibid., p. 99.
15 Ibid., p. 101.
16 MacAdam, 'The Discourse on Inequality and the Social Contract', p. 311.
17 Rousseau, *A Discourse on Inequality*, p. 102.
18 Ibid.

For Rousseau too, as for Hobbes and Locke, the 'state of nature' is *a*social; each cares for oneself. However, what this means for him is that in the 'state of nature' human beings are free and independent. Crucially:

> [...] since the bonds of servitude are formed only through the mutual dependence of men and the reciprocal needs that unite them, it is impossible to enslave a man without first putting him in a situation where he cannot do without another man, and since such a situation does not exist in the state of nature, each man there is free of the yoke, and the law of the strongest is rendered vain.[19]

Unlike Hobbes, Rousseau argued that human beings develop over time; human nature is not static but changeable. In fact, what distinguishes human beings from beasts is '*the faculty of self-improvement*'.[20] Thus humans come to develop out of the 'state of nature'. What brings them into civil society is property.[21] At any rate, by that time human beings had reached a stage of their development beyond which they could not go on to live in the same way; 'for the idea of property, depending on many prior ideas which could only have arisen in successive stages, was not formed all at once in the human mind.'[22] With the growth of population, the difficulties (i.e. scarcity) with which humans were confronted also multiplied.[23] These factors combined made human beings sociable.[24] At this early stage of social life language was very basic; different and more sophisticated languages evolved through the ages.[25] And with the passage of time 'The more the mind became enlightened, the more industry improved.'[26] According to Rousseau, the formation of families marked the 'first revolution', while within the family a division of labour between the sexes occurred.[27] Natural

19 Ibid., p. 106.
20 Ibid., p. 88.
21 Ibid., p. 109.
22 Ibid.
23 Ibid., p. 110.
24 Ibid., pp. 110–111.
25 Ibid., pp. 111–112.
26 Ibid., p. 112.
27 Ibid.

phenomena such as floods and earthquakes separated groups of humans from each other, each group subsequently developing their own language.[28] So, as MacAdam has put it, 'man progressed from a state of primitive savagery but only by responding to his physical and social environment rather than, through reason, attempting to take control of it'.[29] According to Rousseau, what is more important is that in civil society humans cease to be independent of each other; they become dependent on others, specifically on other people's opinion of themselves. In his words:

> Each began to look at the others and to want to be looked at himself; and public esteem came to be prized […] this was the first step towards inequality and at the same time towards vice. From those first preferences there arose, on the one side, vanity and scorn, on the other, shame and envy, and the fermentation produced by these new leavens finally produced compounds fatal to happiness and innocence.[30]

This is the point at which morality emerged and 'although men had come to have less fortitude, and their natural pity had suffered some dilution', still Rousseau characterized this epoch as 'the golden mean between the indolence of the primitive state and the petulant activity of our own pride […] the happiest epoch and the most lasting'.[31]

The development of metallurgy and agriculture was the second revolution.[32] The cultivation of the land was followed by its division, whence arose property; 'and from property once recognized arose the first rules of justice.'[33] Like Locke, Rousseau argued that labour legitimized property.[34] However, Rousseau did not view the introduction of property so favourably as Locke; for talents are not equal; nor is it possible, for that matter, for the use of iron and the consumptions of foodstuffs to balance each other:

28 Ibid., p. 113.
29 MacAdam, 'The Discourse on Inequality and the Social Contract', p. 312.
30 Ibid., p. 114.
31 Ibid., p. 115.
32 Ibid., p. 116.
33 Ibid., p. 117.
34 Ibid., p. 118.

> [...] the stronger did more productive work, the more adroit did better work, the more ingenious devised ways of abridging his labour: the farmer had greater need of iron or the smith greater need of wheat, and with both working equally, the one earned plenty while the other had hardly enough to live on. It is thus that natural inequality merges imperceptibly with inequality of ranks [...][35]

In other words, 'natural or physical' inequality becomes 'moral or political inequality'. Avarice and the desire to accumulate all the more property led to a Hobbesian 'war of all against all';[36] as Rousseau puts it:

> There arose between the right of the stronger and the right of the first occupant a perpetual conflict which ended only in fights and murders. Nascent society gave place to the most horrible state of war [...][37]

Thus Rousseau appears as a 'critic of civil society'.[38]

The personal or moral dependence of humans soon becomes a political dependence too, as the rich conspire against the poor, making them the 'defenders' of their property.[39] According to Rousseau:

> Such was, or must have been, the origin of society and of laws, which put new fetters on the weak and gave new powers to the rich, which irretrievably destroyed natural liberty, established for all time the law of property and inequality, transformed adroit usurpation into irrevocable right, and for the benefit of a few ambitious men subjected the human race thenceforth to labour, servitude and misery.[40]

The constitutions set up to remedy these inequalities actually contribute to their perpetuation.[41] This 'fraudulent' social contract should be distinguished from the 'genuine' social contract advocated in the work entitled *The Social Contract*. For Rousseau, 'the establishment of law and the right

35 Ibid.
36 Ibid., pp. 119–120. Rousseau himself does not use this expression.
37 Ibid., p. 120.
38 See L. Colletti, 'Rousseau as Critic of Civil Society', in his *From Rousseau to Lenin: Studies in Ideology and Society* (New York: Monthly Review Press, 1972).
39 Rousseau, *A Discourse on Inequality*, p. 121.
40 Ibid., p. 122.
41 Ibid., p. 124; cf. ibid., pp. 130–131.

of property was the first stage' of inequality, 'the institution of magistrates the second, and the transformation of legitimate into arbitrary power the third and last stage'. Accordingly,

> the status of rich and poor was authorized by the first epoch, that of strong and weak by the second, and by the third that of master and slave, which is the last stage of inequality [...][42]

Rousseau believed that 'political distinctions' led to 'civil distinctions', so that 'The growing inequality between the people and its chiefs' was paralleled by inequality between individuals, where it took different forms 'according to passions, talents and circumstances'.[43] After all,

> citizens allow themselves to be oppressed only so far as they are impelled by a blind ambition; and fixing their eyes below rather than above themselves, come to love domination more than independence, and agree to wear chains for the sake of imposing chains on others in turn.[44]

Put differently, citizens accept to be ruled on condition that they in turn rule or command others. Everyone comes to be dependent on the others to such an extent that 'dependence may even be mistaken for independence'.[45] According to Rousseau, in 'the last stage of inequality',

> [...] all individuals become equal again because they are nothing [...] subjects have no longer any law but the will of the master, nor the master any other rule but that of his passions [...] notions of the good and principles of justice vanish once more. Here everything is restored to the law of the strongest, and consequently to a new state of nature different from the one with which we began only that that one was the state of nature in its pure form and this one is the fruit of an excess of corruption.[46]

42 Ibid., p. 131.
43 Ibid.
44 Ibid., p. 132.
45 MacAdam, 'The Discourse on Inequality and the Social Contract', p. 316.
46 Rousseau, *A Discourse on Inequality*, pp. 134–135.

MacAdam notes that for Rousseau humans are dependent in the following senses. 'Each man is dependent upon every other in the sense that his existence as a self, as a person is so dependent.'[47] This is what Rousseau means when he says that, as opposed to 'the savage' who 'lives within himself', 'social man lives always outside himself; he knows how to live only in the opinion of others, it is, so to speak, from their judgement alone that he derives the sense of his own existence'.[48] Furthermore, says MacAdam, for Rousseau 'in the course of seeking a self, each becomes subject to passions, unruly and unreasonable passions of greed, vanity and ambition. Finally, independence, in the sense of not being subject to one's will, is mistaken for domination, which means the control of one person over another'.[49]

If modern society corrupts human beings, what alternative social organization could there be? Rousseau's answer is given in *The Social Contract*.

The Social Contract

The Social Contract was published in 1762. In France it was banned at once, while in Geneva it was condemned as seditious and burnt. As Rousseau says in the Foreword, *The Social Contract* – subtitled *or Principles of Political Right* – is part of a longer work, *Political Institutions* (*Institutions Politiques*), which he never completed. He sets forth the aim of the treatise as follows:

> My purpose is to consider if, in political society, there can be any legitimate and sure principle of government, taking men as they are and laws as they might be.[50]

47 MacAdam, 'The Discourse on Inequality and the Social Contract', p. 316.

48 Rousseau, *A Discourse on Inequality*, p. 136.

49 MacAdam, 'The Discourse on Inequality and the Social Contract', pp. 316–317.

50 Jean-Jacques Rousseau, *The Social Contract*, translated and introduced by M. Cranston (Harmondsworth: Penguin, 1968), p. 49.

The phrase 'taking men as they are' is at least ambiguous: does Rousseau mean as they are in their original condition or as they now are in society, what he terms the 'new state of nature'?[51] It has been noted that, considering what he says in the *Discourse on Inequality*, Rousseau cannot mean that the views expressed in *The Social Contract* will leave human beings as they are. This is made clear in Book II, Chapter 7,[52] which deals with the 'lawgiver'. The famous phrase 'Man was born free, and he is everywhere in chains'[53] can be read in light of the *Discourse on the Origins of Inequality*. But, as Maurice Keens-Soper has observed, although Rousseau had given 'a speculative account' of the progress from freedom to slavery in the *Discourse on Inequality*, here he denies all knowledge of how this historical transformation has taken place.[54] Rousseau says:

> How did this transformation come about? I do not know.[55]

'He presents this transformation as a movement of depravation.'[56] Like Hobbes and Locke, Rousseau employs the categories of 'state of nature', 'social contract' and 'civil society'; humans develop out of the 'state of nature' and through the 'social contract' enter 'civil society'. However, Rousseau makes use of these categories differently; the 'state of nature' and the 'social contract' in particular have a different function in Rousseau's political theory.

According to Rousseau, human beings are by nature independent and self-sufficient: 'Man's first law is to watch over his own preservation; his first care he owes to himself'.[57] Therefore, all humans are born free and no

51 Rousseau, *A Discourse on Inequality*, p. 134.

52 MacAdam, 'The Discourse on Inequality and the Social Contract', p. 317.

53 Rousseau, *The Social Contract*, p. 49.

54 M. Keens-Soper, 'Jean-Jacques Rousseau: *The Social Contract*', in M. Forsyth and M. Keens-Soper (eds), *The Political Classics: A Guide to the Essential Texts from Plato to Rousseau* (Oxford & New York: Oxford University Press, 1992), p. 174.

55 Rousseau, *The Social Contract*, p. 49.

56 Keens-Soper, 'Jean-Jacques Rousseau: *The Social Contract*', p. 174.

57 Rousseau, *The Social Contract*, p. 50.

one has 'any natural authority over his fellows';[58] nor is political society 'a natural right', for that matter.[59] The 'only natural' as well as the 'oldest of all societies' is the family. But, again, 'children remain tied to their father by nature only so long as they need him for their preservation. As soon as this need ends, the natural bond is dissolved' and 'both parties equally regain their independence'.[60] Freedom being the natural condition of humankind, 'To renounce freedom is to renounce one's humanity, one's rights as a man and equally one's duties.'[61] It may be that humans have been subjected to political rule by those who were stronger and able to exact obedience by force. However, Rousseau writes:

> So long as a people is constrained to obey, and obeys it does well; but as soon as it can shake off the yoke, and shakes it off, it does better; for since it regains its freedom by the same right as that which removed it, a people is either justified in taking back its freedom, or there is no justifying those who took it away.[62]

In no case does 'might' make 'right' and 'the duty of obedience is owed only to legitimate powers'.[63] For this reason conquest cannot found legitimate rule; for 'The right of conquest has no other foundation than the law of the strongest.'[64] Rousseau insists that morality cannot be based on mere force, which is 'a physical power'.[65] Similarly, for Rousseau, there can be no justification of slavery whatsoever.[66] The issue is: how can political right be made legitimate? He believes he can answer this question.[67] And he is eager to show that:

58 Ibid., p. 53.
59 Ibid., p. 50.
60 Ibid.
61 Ibid., p. 55.
62 Ibid., p. 50.
63 Ibid., p. 53.
64 Ibid., p. 57.
65 Ibid., p. 52.
66 Ibid., pp. 53–58.
67 Ibid., p. 49.

> [...] the social order is a sacred right which serves as a basis for all other rights. And as it is not a natural right, it must be one founded on covenants. The problem is to determine what those covenants are.[68]

It is important that one distinguishes 'between subduing a multitude and ruling a society', Rousseau says.[69] This distinction rests on the difference between a mere 'aggregation' and an 'association'.[70] In the former case, there is no common concern between rulers and ruled; the interest of the ruler always remains 'a personal interest'.[71] A 'body politic' is an 'association', in which rulers and ruled recognize 'a common good'.[72] Grotius[73] is attacked for supposing that a people may willingly submit to a king. Rousseau notes that a people must first be *a* people in order to be able to give itself to a ruling authority. For how could otherwise the decision of the majority be binding to the minority? An 'earlier agreement' is necessary. What is crucial, therefore, is that we examine the act whereby a people comes to being, as it is this act which is the basis of political society.[74]

Rousseau argues that human beings reach a stage in their development 'where the obstacles to their preservation in a state of nature prove greater than the strength that each man has to preserve himself in that state'.[75] As a matter of fact, 'Beyond that point, the primitive condition cannot endure, for then the human race will perish if it does not change its mode of existence.'[76] In order to overcome the new difficulties they encounter, humans combine their individual powers so that these 'are directed by a single motive and act in concert'.[77] The social contract is meant to give a solution to the following problem:

68 Ibid., p. 50.
69 Ibid., p. 58.
70 Ibid.
71 Ibid., pp. 58–59.
72 Ibid., p. 58.
73 Grotius is also attacked for his views on slavery at ibid., p. 54.
74 Ibid., p. 59.
75 Ibid.; cf. Rousseau, *A Discourse on Inequality*, pp. 109–110.
76 Rousseau, *The Social Contract*, p. 59.
77 Ibid., pp. 59–60.

> How to find a form of association which will defend the person and goods of each member with the collective force of all, and under which each individual, while uniting himself with the others, obeys no one but himself, and remains as free as before.[78]

One cannot fail to notice the demanding requirements of this venture: the individual and the collectivity as well as freedom and obedience to law should be combined. Certainly, the complexity of the above requirements means that a slight amendment can invalidate the social contract concerned. The articles of the social contract are such that are valid everywhere the same, tacitly accepted and recognized; while, should the social pact ever be broken, human beings regain their 'original rights' and 'natural freedom', which they had exchanged for 'civil freedom'.[79] Important here is the distinction Rousseau draws between 'natural' and 'civil' freedom. As Rousseau makes clear:

> These articles of association, rightly understood, are reduced to a single one, namely the total alienation by each associate of himself and all his rights to the whole community.[80]

Specifically: Firstly, as every individual gives himself completely, the same conditions apply to all and, therefore, no one has an interest in making these conditions more demanding to others; secondly, given that the 'alienation' is absolute, the union is as complete as it can be and no member of the association has any individual rights any longer; thirdly, since everyone give themselves to all, they give themselves to no one, thereby everyone receiving the equivalent of what they lose.[81] Rousseau writes:

> The public person thus formed by the union of all other persons was once called the *city*, and is now known as the *republic* or the *body politic*.[82]

78 Ibid., p. 60.
79 Ibid.
80 Ibid.
81 Ibid., pp. 60–61.
82 Ibid., p. 61.

For Rousseau, ideal republics were the historical cities of Rome and Sparta. In the modern world his birthplace, Geneva, approximated the ideal. Considered in its 'passive role' the republic 'is called the *state*', while when considered in its 'active role' 'it is the *sovereign*'.[83] It is 'a *power*' among other republics and internally an association of '*a people*' – the latter calling themselves '*citizens*' in the sense that they are the sovereign and '*subjects*' in the sense that they obey the laws of the state.[84]

The 'act of association' is 'a reciprocal commitment' between each individual and political society, so that each, in making a contract with oneself, becomes 'doubly committed': 'first, as a member of the sovereign body in relation to individuals, and secondly as a member of the state in relation to the sovereign.'[85] Obviously, although, given the foregoing, a 'public decision' is binding on the subjects, there is no decision binding on the sovereign as a body; for the sovereign is in a similar 'position of a private person making a contract with himself'.[86] Rousseau calls the sovereign a 'body politic' and this is more than a metaphor; for it consists of individuals united in 'a single body' in such a way that an injury of one of them implies an injury of the whole.[87] This is an organic conception of the state. The sovereign cannot act against the wishes of its members taken as a collectivity; thus guarantees are not necessary. However, it is possible for an individual to have 'a private will' contrary to the 'general will'.[88] In this case, there is a split between the individual in his public and private roles; should he 'seek to enjoy the rights of a citizen without doing the duties of a subject', injustice would creep in and the body politic would be led to its destruction.[89] It is for this reason that Rousseau insists that 'whoever refuses to obey the general will shall be constrained to do so by the whole body', or, in one of the most celebrated phrases of *The Social*

83 Ibid., pp. 61–62.
84 Ibid., p. 62.
85 Ibid.
86 Ibid.
87 Ibid., p. 63.
88 Ibid.
89 Ibid., p. 64.

Contract, 'he shall be forced to be free'.[90] No doubt, Rousseau has 'civil freedom', as opposed to 'natural freedom', in mind here. Yet the idea that one should be forced to be free has led many scholars to accuse Rousseau of totalitarianism. The relationship between the 'individual' and 'general' will does remain problematic in Rousseau's political philosophy.

As already mentioned, the social contract just described should not be confused with the 'fraudulent' social contract laid out in the *Discourse on Inequality*.[91] The 'true' social contract enables human beings to pass from the 'state of nature' to 'civil society', a progress which transforms them; justice comes to replace instinct as a motive for action, while human actions assume a 'moral quality' which they did not have before.[92] Rousseau wishes to show that '*civil* liberty, which is limited by the general will' is superior to '*natural* liberty, which has no limit than the power of the individual concerned', and that freedom implies justice and obedience to 'a law one prescribes to oneself'.[93] For Rousseau, civil society also legitimizes '*property*', based on 'a legal title', as opposed to '*possession*' which is founded on force alone.[94] At the moment civil society is established by the social contract each individual gives not only himself to it but 'his resources, including all his goods' as well.[95] Undoubtedly, individuals become more dependent on the state this way. But this does not mean to say that they lose their possessions; on the contrary, the latter become 'lawful'.[96] Furthermore:

> Since every owner is regarded as a trustee of the public property, his rights are respected by every other member of the state, and protected with its collective force against foreigners [...][97]

90 Ibid.
91 Rousseau, *A Discourse on Inequality*, pp. 121ff.
92 Rousseau, *The Social Contract*, p. 64.
93 Ibid., p. 65.
94 Ibid.
95 Ibid.
96 Ibid., p. 67.
97 Ibid., p. 68.

According to Rousseau, sovereignty can neither be alienated[98] nor divided.[99] It cannot be alienated because sovereignty is 'the exercise of the general will', 'a collective being' which 'cannot be represented by anyone but itself'; therefore, although 'power may be delegated', the 'general will' cannot.[100] For the same reason sovereignty is 'indivisible'; 'for either the will is general or it is not.'[101] Thus for Rousseau political theorists are wrong when they divide sovereignty into the legislative and executive powers.[102] This mistake is due to a misunderstanding as to the nature of 'sovereign authority', a failure to distinguish between the law itself and its application.[103] Rousseau's elaboration will come shortly. For the moment, it is important to bear in mind another significant distinction which Rousseau draws – that between 'the will of all' and 'the general will'. The difference lies therein: whereas the 'general will' refers to the 'common interest', the 'will of all' is merely 'the sum of individual desires'.[104] Now, if one subtracts 'the pluses and minuses' which annul themselves from the sum of the individual wills, 'the balance which remains is the general will'.[105] Should there be factions in political society, the will of each is 'general in relation to its own members and private in relation to the state'.[106] It follows that in that case the 'general will' is derived from the will of these different groups and, inevitably, is bound to be less general than when it is the result from individual votes. Clearly, when one faction becomes so large and powerful that it can prevail over all others, there will no longer be a 'general will' and 'a private opinion' will be dominant instead.[107] It is for this reason that Rousseau urges that:

98 Ibid., pp. 69–70.
99 Ibid., pp. 70–72.
100 Ibid., p. 69.
101 Ibid., p. 70.
102 Ibid.
103 Ibid., p. 71.
104 Ibid., p. 72.
105 Ibid., pp. 72–73.
106 Ibid., p. 73.
107 Ibid.

> [...] if the general will is to be clearly expressed, it is imperative that there should be no sectional associations in the state, and that every citizen should make up his own mind for himself [...][108]

This is what Lycurgus, the lawgiver of Sparta, had achieved.[109] Should there be sections in political society, Rousseau advised that their number be increased and inequality among them checked. This is what the famous Athenian statesman, Solon, among others, had done.[110] Should these safety measures against the predominance of particular interests be implemented, Rousseau was convinced that the 'general will' could never be wrong;[111] 'the general will is always rightful and always tends to the public good'.[112] In other words, the 'general will' cannot be contrary to the interests of individual citizens. Yet Rousseau admitted that, although humans will what is beneficial to them, they do not always discern it: 'The people is never corrupted, but it is often misled; and only then does it seem to will what is bad'.[113]

Rousseau's concept of the 'general will' implies that there is a complete identification of the citizens with the state. At the same time, the 'general will' cannot relate to particular individuals or groups.[114] Rousseau stresses that the 'general will' is such not because of 'the number of voices' but because of 'the common interest which unites them':

> for the general will is an institution in which each necessarily submits himself to the same conditions which he imposes on others; this admirable harmony of interest and justice gives to social deliberations a quality of equity [...][115]

108 Ibid.
109 Ibid.
110 Ibid., pp. 73–74.
111 Ibid., p. 74.
112 Ibid., p. 72.
113 Ibid.
114 Ibid., p. 75.
115 Ibid., p. 76.

However, Rousseau also recognized that there are limits to sovereign power; in particular, the sovereign should not demand of subjects anything that is not necessary to political society.[116] But, of course, it falls on the sovereign to decide what is of communal concern.[117]

The social contract having established civil society is not enough to preserve it; this purpose is fulfilled by the law.[118] 'Positive' laws are necessary because humans are not aware of divine, universal, justice.[119] Once again, Rousseau emphasizes that 'the province of the law is always general';[120] the law does not legislate with any individual citizen or action in view.[121] Consequently, 'laws are acts of the general will'.[122] This being so, Rousseau calls a 'republic' any state which is governed by law, whatever the form of government;

> for then, and then alone, does the public interest govern and then alone is the 'public thing' – the *res publica* – a reality.[123]

What is surprising is Rousseau's sudden distrust of humans to formulate their own laws. As he says:

> Individuals see the good and reject it; the public desires the good but does not see it. Both equally need guidance. Individuals must be obliged to subordinate their will to their reason; the public must be taught to recognize what it desires. [...] Hence the necessity of a lawgiver.[124]

The lawgiver is 'a superior intelligence' and his nature resembles that of the Gods.[125] His task is tremendous, since he is called 'to change human

116 Ibid., p. 75.
117 Ibid., p. 74.
118 Ibid., p. 80.
119 Ibid., pp. 80–81.
120 Ibid., p. 81.
121 Ibid., p. 82.
122 Ibid.
123 Ibid., p. 82.
124 Ibid., p. 83.
125 Ibid., p. 84.

nature, to transform each individual, who by himself is entirely complete and solitary, into a part of a much greater whole'.[126] The office of the lawgiver is special, because does not form part of either the sovereign or the government; nor is it part of the constitution.[127] It is above all these and superior to them. Thus the task of the lawgiver is beset by a contradiction; it is 'beyond human powers and a non-existent authority for its execution'.[128] Another significant difficulty is that 'a newly formed people' is not able to understand 'wise principles of politics and to follow the basic rules of statecraft', as they lack 'the social spirit' which is necessary to this purpose.[129] Consequently, the lawgiver 'must have recourse to an authority of another order, one which can compel without violence and persuade without convincing'.[130]

In this context, it has been noted that

> Rousseau is, however, doing something more than highlighting an intellectual defect even though it remains unclear how far he realized the full purport of his argument. The figure of the Lawgiver comes as such an intrusion and its implications for the idea of a social contract are so disastrous, that one is led to question whether the true significance of the Lawgiver is perhaps that it signals Rousseau's release from a way of thinking quite at odds with the spirit of his convictions. While remaining attached to the idiom of the social contract, the content of Rousseau's reasoning is surely incompatible with it.[131]

Many commentators have put forth a similar argument. The same author has also observed that 'Although at the beginning of the book Rousseau says that he would treat "men as they are and laws as they might be", the task of creating a body politic is now described as demanding a change of human nature'.[132] Besides, 'It is not always clear whether Rousseau believes 'a people'

126 Ibid.
127 Ibid., p. 85.
128 Ibid., p. 86.
129 Ibid., pp. 86–87.
130 Ibid., p. 87.
131 Keens-Soper, 'Jean-Jacques Rousseau: *The Social Contract*', pp. 185–186.
132 Ibid., p. 186.

has to be 'created' out of hitherto unrelated individuals, or 'recreated' out of men deformed by the servitudes of dependence.'[133] These are some problems that the introduction of the lawgiver poses. At any rate, the lawgiver should legislate bearing the temperament of the people for whom he legislates in mind.[134] Vaughan has pointed out that, whereas in the earlier parts of *The Social Contract* Rousseau is rather Platonic (particularly, in his conception of the 'general will'), from this point onwards he is influenced by Montesquieu.[135] In his celebrated *The Spirit of the Laws* (published in 1748) Montesquieu argued that the identity of political communities is related to their institutions, which are to a large extent influenced by natural and historical factors. Rousseau makes a similar argument in Chapters 8 to 10 of Book II. He maintains that a state should be 'neither too large to be well-governed nor too small to maintain itself';[136] there should be a balance between the size of the land and the number of inhabitants, which should be determined on the basis of geographical and climatic differences;[137] the people for whom the laws are made should already have a common identity, but its customs and beliefs should not be so deep-rooted that they cannot be changed.[138] Rousseau believed that only one European country was 'fit to receive laws', the island of Corsica.[139]

Rousseau classified laws into 'political' (what we would call 'constitutional'), 'civil' and 'criminal' laws.[140] What is more important, however, is the fourth category of laws, which is engraved in 'the hearts of the citizens' – this is 'morals, customs and, above all, belief', a category most political theorists ignore; this sustains all the other laws. For this reason this is the

133 Ibid.

134 Rousseau, *The Social Contract*, pp. 88–90.

135 C. E. Vaughan (ed.), *The Political Writings of Jean-Jacques Rousseau* (Cambridge: Cambridge University Press, 1915; reprinted Oxford: Basil Blackwell, 1962); cited in Keens-Soper, 'Jean-Jacques Rousseau: *The Social Contract*', p. 187.

136 Rousseau, *The Social Contract*, p. 90.

137 Ibid., p. 93.

138 Ibid., p. 95.

139 Ibid., p. 96.

140 Ibid., pp. 98–99.

category 'on which the great lawgiver bestows his secret care'.[141] Therefore, for Rousseau the laws are articles of *civic virtue*.

We have seen that for Rousseau sovereignty cannot be alienated; nor can the 'general will' be delegated; 'the legislative power belongs, and can only belong, to the people'.[142] But 'executive power' cannot belong to the people, for it 'is exercised only in particular acts which are outside the province of law and therefore outside the province of the sovereign which can act only to make laws'.[143] Put differently, 'executive power' is concerned with the implementation of the laws and is delegated. Thus a government is set up, which is defined by Rousseau as follows:

> An intermediary body established between the subjects and the sovereign for their mutual communication, a body charged with the execution of the laws and the maintenance of freedom, both civil and political.[144]

Rousseau calls the members of the government 'magistrates', '*kings*' or '*governors*' and 'the whole body' '*prince*'. So, crucially, in Rousseau 'prince' refers to the government and not necessarily to a single person – it depends on the type of régime. Specifically, '"government" or "supreme administration"' is 'the legitimate exercise of the executive power', while '"prince" or "magistrate" the man or the body charged with that administration'.[145] The influence of Montesquieu is evident when Rousseau says:

> [...] there is only one good government possible for any state; but as a thousand events may change the relations within a nation, different governments may not only be good for different peoples, but good for the same people at different times.[146]

What is important is that in Rousseau's political philosophy the government is 'a new body within the state', but, whereas 'the state exists in itself', 'the

141 Ibid., p. 99.
142 Ibid., p. 101.
143 Ibid.
144 Ibid., p. 102.
145 Ibid.
146 Ibid., p. 103; see also Book III, Chapter 8: 'That All Forms of Government Do Not Suit All Countries', ibid. pp. 124–129.

government exists only through the sovereign';[147] therefore, the government 'has only a kind of borrowed and subordinate life'.[148] Rousseau is eager to distinguish between the 'sovereign' and the 'government'.

Regarding the different forms of government, Rousseau accepts the traditional classification into democracy – when the government is placed 'in the hands of the whole people, or of the greater part of the people' –, aristocracy – when the government is put in 'the hands of a few' – and monarchy – when it is placed 'in the hands of one single magistrate'.[149] That said, all forms of government – especially, democracy and aristocracy – have a certain 'elasticity', in that they 'can be had in greater or lesser degrees'.[150] In addition, all forms can be combined to produce many different 'mixed forms'.[151] Rousseau holds the view that 'the number of supreme magistrates should be in inverse ratio to the number of citizens', from which it follows that, generally, democracy is suitable to small states, aristocracy to states of medium size and monarchy to large states.[152]

Rousseau is rather suspicious of democracy because, above all, it collapses the distinction between the legislative and executive powers.[153] Moreover, democracy presupposes too much – a very small state, very simple manners and morals, social and economic equality, and as little luxury as possible.[154] Further, it is the form of government most susceptible to civil war.[155] In general, 'A government so perfect is not suited to men.'[156] Rousseau favours an elective aristocracy.[157] As he puts it: 'it is the best and most natural arrangement for the wisest to govern the multitude, if we are

147 Ibid., p. 105.
148 Ibid., p. 106.
149 Ibid., p. 110.
150 Ibid., p. 111.
151 Ibid.
152 Ibid.
153 Ibid., p. 112.
154 Ibid., p. 113.
155 Ibid.
156 Ibid., p. 114.
157 Ibid., pp. 114–116.

sure that they will govern it for its advantage and not for their own.'[158] But elections ensure that 'honesty', 'sagacity' and 'experience' prevail.[159] As for monarchy, its merits lie in the fact that 'all the levers of the machine are in the same hands', which guarantees a strong government, but an inherent danger is that 'Kings want to be absolute', thus posing a great threat to the 'general will'.[160]

Rousseau strikes a blow to liberalism by insisting that there cannot be representatives of the people. Rousseau writes:

> Sovereignty cannot be represented, for the same reason that it cannot be alienated; its essence is the general will, and will cannot be represented [...] Thus the people's deputies are not, and could not be, its representatives; they are merely its agents [...][161]

Therefore, the English people is wrong to consider itself to be free; 'it is free only during the election of Members of Parliament', and 'as soon as the Members are elected, the people is enslaved'. What is worse, 'In the brief moments of its freedom, the English people makes such a use of that freedom that it deserves to lose it.'[162]

Rousseau was convinced that the 'general will' is 'indestructible';[163]

> Upright and simple men are difficult to deceive precisely because of their simplicity; stratagems and clever arguments do not prevail upon them; they are not indeed subtle enough to be dupes.[164]

When sectional interests gain the upper hand, 'the common interest' may become 'corrupted', but not the 'general will', which 'is always unchanging, incorruptible and pure'. What happens is that 'it is subordinated to other wills which prevail over it'.[165] According to Rousseau:

158 Ibid., p. 115.
159 Ibid.
160 Ibid., p. 117.
161 Ibid., p. 141.
162 Ibid.
163 Ibid., pp. 149ff.
164 Ibid., p. 149.
165 Ibid., p. 150.

> The greater harmony that reigns in public assemblies, the more [...] that public opinion approaches unanimity, the more the general will is dominant; whereas long debates, dissensions and disturbances bespeak the ascendance of particular interests and the decline of the state.[166]

Ancient republicanism was his ideal. For Rousseau, only the 'social pact' requires 'unanimous consent'.[167] All other laws become binding once they have been voted by the majority. This means that 'The citizen consents to all the laws, even to those that are passed against his will, and even to those which punish him when he dares to break any of them'.[168] This is because when a law is proposed in the assembly, citizens are not called to approve or disapprove of the proposition but to determine 'whether it is in conformity with the general will which is theirs'.[169] Commentators have not failed to notice the totalitarian implications of this and Rousseau has been criticized for holding totalitarian views on many occasions.[170] Liberals have noted that the theory of the 'general will' lives no room for individual rights.

Rousseau was aware of the fact that what held a body politic together was beliefs and attitudes. For this reason he argued that a 'censorial tribunal' was necessary to maintain public morality 'by preventing opinions from being corrupted, by preserving their integrity [...] and sometimes even by settling points on which opinion is uncertain'.[171] However, the task of the censorial office was to preserve morals, not to restore them.[172] For this reason it must be set up 'while the laws are still vigorous; for as soon as the vigour is lost, everything is hopeless'.[173] More importantly, common beliefs and values are inculcated in citizens' minds by what he calls 'civil religion'.[174]

166 Ibid., p. 151.
167 Ibid., p. 152.
168 Ibid., p. 153.
169 Ibid.
170 See e.g. J. L. Talmon, *The Rise of Totalitarian Democracy* (Boston: Beacon Press, 1952).
171 Ibid., p. 175.
172 Ibid., pp. 174–175.
173 Ibid., p. 175.
174 Ibid., pp. 176ff.

He is careful to differentiate this from the 'religion of the man' and the 'religion of the priest'. The 'religion of the man' is the 'inward devotion to the supreme God and the eternal obligations of morality', the religion of the Gospel, associated with 'divine natural law'. By contrast, the 'religion of the citizen' is the religion of a single country, its Gods and 'tutelary deities', and has its own dogmas, rituals and ways of external worship; this is 'civil or positive divine law'. Lastly, the 'religion of the priest', which includes Catholic Christianity among others, preaches 'two legislative orders, two rulers, two homelands', the kingdom of the earth and the kingdom of god.[175] Hobbes had been right in so far as he had recognized that the reunification of the state and religion was necessary for the restoration of political unity. Yet he was wrong in thinking that Christianity was the religion concerned.[176] For Rousseau, what was needed was the 'religion of the citizen' or 'civil religion', which was appropriate to republicanism; such was also the religion of the Romans. The 'civil religion' is 'a profession of faith' and its dogmas are not religious but 'expressions of social conscience, without which it is impossible to be either a good citizen or a loyal subject'.[177] In other words, it is a secular or humanist religion, whose purpose is political socialization – that is, the identification of the citizens with the laws and institutions of the body politic. Although no one can be forced to believe in the articles of faith of the 'civil religion', Rousseau argued that the sovereign could send into exile those who did not believe them – not for being impious but for being 'antisocial'. And he who does not observe the dogmas of the 'civil religion', after having publicly acknowledged them, should be condemned to death; for he has lied before the law, 'the greatest crime' of all.[178] It is of the utmost importance that the dogmas of the 'civil religion' should be 'simple and few in number', expressed in exact terms, without clarifications and comments. Negative dogmas should be restricted to one, 'no intolerance', by which is meant both 'civil' and 'theological' intolerance,

175 Ibid., p. 181.
176 Ibid., p. 180.
177 Ibid., p. 186.
178 Ibid.

as the two are connected.[179] Rousseau held that, since in modern times there was not, nor could there be, a national religion, all religions should be tolerated, provided they themselves tolerated others and their dogmas did not run counter to one's civil duties.[180]

It is generally believed that Rousseau's ideas in *The Social Contract* inspired the French Revolution. What is more, in the period November 1793 to July 1794 the Jacobins attempted to organize government on the basis of principles drawn from Rousseau's *The Social Contract*. I shall now turn to look at Hegel's discussion of Rousseau's notion of the 'general will' and the French Revolution in the *Phenomenology of Spirit*. Hegel was a student at the time of the French Revolution and, together with many other students, he was enthusiastic about the events taking place in France. These young people shared the feelings of many intellectuals in Germany, for whom the French Revolution marked the beginning of a new age. By the time he came to write the *Phenomenology of Spirit* in 1806, however, Hegel was more skeptical about the success of the French Revolution; in particular, he had become very critical of the Robespierrists and their policies during the radical phase of the Revolution.

Hegel on Rousseau and the French Revolution

The 'general will' is a lived experience, 'a real general will, the will of all *individuals* as such'. As such, the 'general will' does not accept 'a representative'. Therefore, it is as an 'undivided Substance' that the 'general will' 'ascends the throne of the world without any power being able to resist it'.[181] Upon seizing power, the Republicans abolished all social distinctions

179 Ibid.
180 Ibid., p. 187.
181 G. W. F. Hegel, *Phenomenology of Spirit*, trans. A. V. Miller (Oxford: Oxford University Press, 1977), p. 357.

– the Nobility, the Third Estate and the Clergy – and the 'general will' as 'negativity' came to penetrate French society.[182] There is now no distinction between the 'individual' and 'universal', as there is a perfect identification of the individual with political society. As Hegel puts it:

> [...] this *individual* consciousness is no less directly conscious of itself as universal will; it is aware that its object is a law given by that will and a work accomplished by it; therefore, in passing over into action and in creating objectivity, it is doing nothing individual, but carrying out the laws and functions of the state.[183]

Power is concentrated and no room is left for a separation of the legislative, executive and judiciary branches of government.[184]

However, says Hegel, the 'general will' 'cannot achieve anything positive'. Its absolute freedom is self-contradictory; in not allowing anything to exist independently of itself, no 'universal works of language or reality' can be created nor 'laws and general institutions of *conscious* freedom' can be established.[185] In other words, the 'general will' is empty, an abstraction. Hegel criticizes the radical phase of the French Revolution (1792–1794) when the Jacobins attempted to implement Rousseau's principles. Absolute freedom, for Hegel, is abstract and for this reason destructive; to be able to transform the world, it should be able to embody itself in social and political institutions. This would imply the separation of state functions (into a legislature, executive and judiciary) and the division of society into different strata. But the French Revolutionary Government, in espousing absolute freedom, would not allow this and freedom remained a mere 'negativity', a destructive power.[186]

For Hegel, not only is 'absolute freedom' as implied in the notion of the 'general will' unable to form the basis of a new social order, but even worse it is not able to accomplish anything. This is because the very idea of a 'general will' entails that 'Before the universal can perform a deed it

182 Ibid.

183 Ibid., p. 358.

184 Ibid.

185 Ibid.

186 Ibid., pp. 358–359.

must concentrate itself into the One of individuality'.[187] This can only lead to political inaction or to the adoption of a measure which is not approved by all the citizens, since this could happen only if there were unanimity. Inevitably 'absolute freedom' – as mere universal, abstract freedom – is reduced to a '*fury* of destruction'.[188] According to Hegel, this is the contradiction implicit in Rousseau's conception of the 'general will' and in the view that 'The citizen consents to all the laws, even to those that are passed against his will', for a citizen's failure to vote a law enacted by the majority suggests that he has misunderstood the 'general will'.[189]

Another contradiction implicit in the notion of 'absolute freedom', says Hegel, is that sooner or later divisions or splinter groups will arise in the state. What is more, having 'completed the destruction of the actual organization of the world', 'absolute freedom' exists for its sake and hence proceeds to an annihilation of its individual expressions.[190] Eventually, it turns into terror. In Hegel's words:

> The sole work and deed of universal freedom is therefore *death*, a death too which has [...] no more significance than cutting off a head of cabbage or swallowing a mouthful of water.[191]

Rousseau himself had recognized that executive power cannot belong to the people taken as a totality, for executive power carries out *particular* measures which, being particular, do not fall into the jurisdiction of the law nor of the sovereign, for that matter.[192] He had, therefore, argued that the 'general will' ought to set up a government, an intermediate body between the subjects and the sovereign, whose task would be to implement the laws and maintain freedom.[193] But, as Hegel says, in practice:

187 Ibid., p. 359.
188 Ibid.
189 Rousseau, *The Social Contract*, p. 153.
190 Hegel, *Phenomenology of Spirit*, pp. 359–360.
191 Ibid., p. 360.
192 Rousseau, *The Social Contract*, p. 101.
193 Ibid., p. 102.

> What is called a government is merely the *victorious* faction, and in the very fact of its being a faction lies the direct necessity of its overthrow.[194]

Consequently, for the Jacobins the defeat of the French Army in Holland and the treason of its commander was a pretext for throwing out the Girondins, who were soon tried and executed. For the 'general will', the revolutionary government established by the Jacobins under the leadership of Robespierre was 'a crime committed against it'.[195] Unable to prove the guilt of its opponents, this government could merely suspect 'traitors' whom it led to the guillotine. Only in this way could the Jacobins secure an objective existence for themselves. Surely, 'absolute freedom' finds the régime of terror to be 'quite different from what its own Notion of itself was, viz. that the universal will is merely the *positive* essence of personality'.[196] As 'pure insight', it cannot but oscillate between two equally abstract ideals, namely, 'the predicateless Absolute as pure *Thought* and as pure *Matter*',[197] exemplified in the Jacobins' institutionalization of a 'Cult of the Supreme Being' – this being their interpretation of the 'civil religion' propounded by Rousseau in *The Social Contract* – and their enactment of laws which decreed a radical redistribution of confiscated property, respectively.

However, as Hegel proceeds to say, Robespierre's group being only a faction among others could not remain in power for long; for it represented a private interest as distinct from the 'general will'. It was therefore a matter of time before the Robespierrists were overthrown in turn by the remaining members of the 'Revolutionary Convention'. The experience of Terror makes individuals ready to submit to a power that can put an end to it. It was for Napoleon Bonaparte, following the *coup d' état* of Brumaire (1799), to bring an end to anarchy by consolidating social institutions.[198]

194 Hegel, *Phenomenology of Spirit*, p. 360.
195 Ibid.
196 Ibid., p. 361.
197 Ibid.
198 Ibid.

CHAPTER 6

Edmund Burke

Edmund Burke was born in Dublin in 1729 and lived until 1797. His father was a Protestant attorney, while his mother was Catholic. In the eighteenth century Ireland was beset by religious conflict and during Burke's lifetime Catholicism was repressed.

Burke was not a philosopher. He was a practising Whig politician and worked for the Marquis of Rockingham and with Charles James Fox. He made a reputation as a commentator on current political affairs. His writings are, therefore, those of a politician with extensive experience of political reality. For this reason they are characterized by pragmatism rather than by theoretical rigorousness. He supported the American Revolution, as well as the rebellions of the Corsicans, Poles and Indians, because these were attempts to reaffirm the political identity of a given people. On the other hand, he came to condemn the French Revolution, as it was disruptive of the history and ties of the French people.

Burke's most famous work is *Reflections on the Revolution in France*, published in 1790 and immediately becoming a best-seller. Eleven editions of it were published within ten months.[1] It is on this work, therefore, that this chapter shall concentrate.

1 L. G. Mitchell, 'Introduction' in E. Burke's *Reflections on the Revolution in France* (Oxford & New York: Oxford University Press, 1993), p. vii.

The Nature and Sources of the *Reflections*

As Mitchell has said:

> That Burke should write about a French theme at all was remarkable. Unlike most members of the Whig party, Burke had shown very little interest in France or its politics. He may have crossed the Channel in 1757. He certainly spent two months there in 1773, but this was a poor record compared to that of the Whig grandees who were his patrons in politics. Even when he ventured into France, Burke unfashionably avoided Paris, preferring to spend his time among the provincial clergy and gentry of Auxerre. These people became his principal informants on French affairs. While Fox, Rockingham, and Grey spoke to Mirabeau, Talleyrand, and Lafayette, Burke listened to the views of men and women whose names are barely known to history.[2]

Given his sources, Burke has been criticized for being biased and of limited intelligence,[3] but I think that this may well be one of the strengths of his work; that is, he was able to take into account the opinions of the man-in-the-street.

The *Reflections* is based on a letter Burke had written in reply to a young man at Paris, Charles-Jean-Francois Depont. Depont had met Burke in England in 1785 and in 1789 wrote to him asking him for his opinions on the events taking place in France. Burke wrote an answer in October 1789, but he did not send it right away, as he did not deem it safe to do so. Later Burke set out to elaborate on this topic with the purpose to publish it and decided not to change the form of address, as this would also possibly mean a change in style.[4]

Of course, its style makes the book difficult to analyze. The book does not have a coherent structure and Burke's views on politics are not presented in an organized manner; one has to extricate them from the prose. Despite its lack of a formal structure, however, the work can be divided in the following parts for analytical purposes: a prologue, a first part which

2 Ibid.
3 Ibid.
4 Ibid., p. 3.

focuses on Price's sermon; a second part which deals with religion and the relationship of Church and State in England and France; a third part which concentrates on the Jacobin state; and an epilogue.[5] That said, Burke does introduce a lot of themes whenever he feels like introducing them and on many occasions he leaves a topic in order to come back to it at some later point.

In the first part Burke subjects the Reverend Richard Price's sermon 'On the Love of Our Country' to criticism. This was preached before a dinner of the Revolution Society, a group of radical clerics who applauded the Glorious Revolution of 1688. Burke recognized that the position of these radical clerics was similar to that of their counterparts in France. In France religious nonconformists did not have any civil rights and were outsiders to the French Establishment. These were mainly Protestants and Jews who, precisely because they were on the fringes of French society, supported the ideals of the French Revolution. So, as it has been noted, 'When Burke uses quotations from Rabaut de St. Etienne, he was aware that he was using the words of a Protestant pastor'.[6] Similarly, in England dissenting priests had joined the reform movements of the 1780s. And:

> Either as nonconformist divines protesting against exclusion, or as renegade clergy within the established Church seeking to benefit from a redistribution of episcopal and monastic wealth, they were all prepared to peddle nonsense ideas about the rights of man.[7]

What Burke found fundamentally wrong was Dr. Price's attempt to draw an analogy between the Glorious Revolution of 1688 and the French Revolution. According to Burke, far from changing English social and political institutions, the English Revolution 'was made to preserve our *antient* indisputable laws and liberties, and that *antient* constitution of

5 I. Hampsher-Monk, *A History of Modern Political Thought: Major Political Thinkers from Hobbes to Marx* (Oxford & Cambridge, Massachusetts: Blackwell, 1992), p. 264.

6 L. G. Mitchell, 'Introduction' in E. Burke's *Reflections on the Revolution in France*, p. xi.

7 Ibid., pp. xi–xii.

government which is our only security for law and liberty'.[8] Regarding the succession of William and Mary, Burke argued that undoubtedly, it was 'a small and a temporary deviation from the strict order of a regular hereditary succession, but it is against all genuine principles of jurisprudence to draw a principle from a law made in a special case'.[9] For Burke, 'If the *principles* of the Revolution of 1688 are any where to be found, it is in the statute called the *Declaration of Right*'. This was a 'most wise, sober, and considerate declaration, drawn up by great lawyers and great statesmen, and not by warm and inexperienced enthusiasts', in which 'not one word is said, nor one suggestion made, of a general right "to choose our own *governors*; to cashier them for misconduct; and to *form* a government for *ourselves*"'.[10] On the contrary, it has always been 'the uniform policy' of the English Constitution 'to claim and assert our liberties, as an *entailed inheritance* derived to us from our forefathers, and to be transmitted to our posterity [...] We have an inheritable crown; an inheritable peerage; and an house of commons and a people inheriting privileges, franchises, and liberties, from a long line of ancestors'.[11]

His Criticism of Natural Rights

Burke was critical of the French 'Declaration of the Rights of Man and Citizen'. His criticism was based on the conviction that all talk of 'natural rights' is empty; 'natural rights' in themselves are mere abstractions. He insisted that 'Government is not made in virtue of natural rights', which

8 E. Burke, *Reflections on the Revolution in France*, edited with an introduction by L. G. Mitchell (Oxford & New York: Oxford University Press, 1993), p. 31.

9 Ibid., p. 17.

10 Ibid., p. 16.

11 Ibid., p. 33.

allegedly exist independently of it.[12] Rather 'rights', for Burke, can be understood only within the context of a political society; as he says:

> Government is a contrivance of human wisdom to provide for human *wants*. Men have a right that these wants should be provided for by this wisdom.[13]

Burke would agree with Hobbes that the 'natural right' of human beings is to judge for themselves. But in passing to political society, each person gives up 'the first fundamental right of uncovenanted man, that is, to judge for himself, and to assert his own cause'.[14] He also surrenders 'the right of self-defence, the first law of nature'; this he does in return for justice and liberty.[15] Thus political society is established – a power out of humans in order to restrain their passions and secure their liberties, which in this sense are their rights. However, Burke points out, the restrictions on human passions and liberties are not the same at all times and circumstances, which makes all talk of abstract natural rights meaningless.[16] Crucially then, for Burke, 'natural rights' are not compatible with political society. He held the view that each political society is a specific historical community based on convention, from which derived its law and institutions.[17] He objected to the French idea of 'the rights of men', because this was no longer a standard by which to judge the abuse of government, but had gradually come to be used against all forms of government. As he says:

> The objections of these speculatists [...] are as valid against such an old and beneficent government as against the most violent tyranny, or the greenest usurpation. They are always at issue with governments, not on a question of abuse, but a question of competency, and a question of title.[18]

12 Ibid., p. 60.
13 Ibid.
14 Ibid., p. 59.
15 Ibid., p. 60.
16 Ibid.
17 Ibid., p. 59.
18 Ibid., p. 58.

The French revolutionaries and their English supporters tended to link 'natural' with 'civil' rights in such a way that political society became impossible; specifically, they translated the 'natural right' to judge for oneself into the 'civil' right to decide on political matters in political society – in effect, to participate in government.[19] But Burke denies that 'the share of power, authority, and direction which each individual ought to have in the management of the state' is 'amongst the direct original rights of man in civil society'. This is something to be determined by convention.[20] Besides, 'Men cannot enjoy the rights of an uncivil and of a civil state together.'[21] What underlies Burke's criticism of the radical conception of natural rights is the idea that human beings are social beings and, as such, cannot exist without political society. Echoing Aristotle's famous phrase 'the human being is by nature a political animal [that is, destined to live in the *polis*],'[22] Burke says that outside 'civil society man could not by any possibility arrive at the perfection of which his nature is capable'.[23] But 'natural rights', if they existed independently of political society, presuppose the separation of human beings from each other. To the abstract 'rights of man' Burke opposes his own conception of natural rights; these are what he terms 'the *real* rights of men'[24] – that is, *concrete*, as opposed to *abstract*, rights which consist in the 'advantages' humans enjoy within political society. Accordingly, in political society humans have 'a right' to live by a rule; 'they have a right to justice' vis-à-vis their fellows; 'They have a right to the fruits of their industry [...] They have a right to the acquisitions of their parents; to the nourishment and improvement of their offspring; to instruction in life, and to consolation in death.'[25] Burke rejects the idea of 'natural rights' as

19 Cf. C. Parkin, *The Moral Basis of Burke's Political Thought: An Essay* (Cambridge: Cambridge University Press, 1956), p. 12.

20 Burke, *Reflections on the Revolution in France*, p. 59.

21 Ibid., p. 60.

22 Aristotle, *Politica*, reviewed briefly and with critical notes by W. D. Ross (Oxford, 1957), 1253a.

23 Burke, *Reflections on the Revolution in France*, p. 98.

24 Ibid., p. 58.

25 Ibid., p. 59.

propounded by the French revolutionaries for yet another reason. Radical 'natural rights' allow licence; as he says: 'By having a right to every thing they [humans] want every thing.'[26] For Burke, this is the reason why the French revolutionaries were led to the excesses which characterized the period of Terror. The role of political society is to restrain human passions. Yet in revolutionary France passion reigned supreme and untrammelled freedom had become a mere negative, destructive force.[27] This criticism is similar to Hegel's.

Let us now look at Burke's conception of the state.

His Version of Contract Theory

According to Vaughan, Burke rejects social contract theory completely. This is because, Vaughan argues, Burke does not accept the idea of 'natural rights', which seems to be a necessary assumption of contractarian thought. Rather Burke's thought rests on a doctrine of 'expediency'.[28] However, others have – rightly – contested this view.[29] In Burke the social contract has a more extended meaning, with religious and cosmological implications. As he says: 'Society is indeed a contract.' But, as opposed to liberal thinkers, Burke insists that the state is not merely 'a partnership agreement in a trade of pepper and coffee, callico or tobacco, or some other such low concern, to be taken up for a little temporary interest, and to be dissolved

26 Ibid., p. 60 (my square brackets).

27 '[T]he "all-atoning name" of liberty [...] But what is liberty without wisdom, and without virtue? It is the greatest of all possible evils; for it is folly, vice and madness, without tuition and restraint.' Ibid., p. 246.

28 C. E. Vaughan, *Studies in the History of Political Philosophy Before and After Rousseau* (Manchester: Manchester University Press, 1925), Vol. II, Chapter I, p. 59. Cited in Parkin, *The Moral Basis of Burke's Political Thought*, p. 10.

29 E.g. Parkin, *The Moral Basis of Burke's Political Thought*; Parkin vs. Vaughan, p. 10.

by the fancy of the parties'.[30] Leaving the rhetoric aside, what Burke means is that the state is not the minimal one propounded by the liberals, its task being to provide the rules of the game, as it were, and to arbitrate between competing individual interests. For Burke, the state should be revered,[31] for its existence is owing to God's will.[32] Human beings may well enter into secondary contractual relationships in order to satisfy their economic needs, but the state is superior to all these. As Burke says:

> It is a partnership in all science; a partnership in all art; a partnership in every virtue, and in all perfection.[33]

More importantly:

> As the ends of such a partnership cannot be obtained in many generations, it becomes a partnership not only between those who are living, but between those who are living, those who are dead, and those who are to be born. Each contract of each particular state is but a clause in the great primaeval contract of eternal society, linking the lower with the higher natures, connecting the visible and invisible world, according to a fixed compact sanctioned by the inviolable oath which holds all physical and all moral natures, each in their appointed place.[34]

So Burke's social contract transcends time and place; it becomes a contract of humanity – past, present and future. In effect, this 'great primaeval contract of eternal society', as Burke calls it, is 'the order of the universe' and resembles Plato's, but also Aristotle's, cosmological scheme. A first principle, namely, God, is the source of the cosmic edifice, where each being occupies his, her (or, for that matter, its) specific, pre-ordained place. This superior law cannot be changed by human will, nor should it, Burke thought, for this would lead to chaos. Only a 'supreme necessity', beyond the control of

30 Burke, *Reflections on the Revolution in France*, p. 96.
31 Ibid.
32 'He who gave our nature to be perfected by our virtue, willed also the necessary means of its perfection – He willed therefore the state'. Ibid., p. 98.
33 Ibid., p. 96.
34 Ibid., pp. 96–97.

human beings, can change the structure of this cosmic order;[35] this necessity is to be understood as God's will. However, as a commentator has said, Burke retains 'the element of individual consent even in this ultimate contract. The order of things within which human life is held is not imposed on us, or alien to our nature; it is made to us, and we are made to it'.[36]

According to Burke, this cosmic order is also a moral order. The rights and duties of each human being are defined by his status in it. Within this great order the most basic community is that of the family, to which humans are bound by sentimental ties. Next comes civil society, to which humans have moral obligations. But family and society are interdependent, as family ties form the basis of civil society, in the sense that humans get to know the feelings which sustain a political community within the family.[37] For Burke, the 'natural aristocracy' has an important function to perform in the hierarchical society. Being wiser and wealthier than the other social strata, its task is to lead or direct society. Burke identified the aristocratic order with the landowners and he believed that they were best suited to discern the good of the political community because their possession of land meant that they had a long-term interest in stability.[38] But, as Parkin emphasizes, Burke defends a 'natural aristocracy' for its place and role in securing the unity of a hierarchical society and 'not for its own sake'.[39]

For Burke, chivalry, illusions and prejudice are what hold a political society together. He deplores the fact that 'the age of chivalry is gone' and 'That of sophisters, oeconomists, and calculators, has succeeded'.[40] The feudal moral code, which comprised such values as chivalry, was important, for Burke, because it formed the ethical basis of political society; it gave meaning to moral relationships – everyone knew the rights and duties appropriate to their station; for this reason it contributed to the stability of the social order. This social equilibrium is contrasted with the anarchy

35 Ibid., p. 97.
36 Parkin, *The Moral Basis of Burke's Political Thought*, p. 26.
37 Ibid., pp. 31–32.
38 Ibid., pp. 33–35.
39 Ibid., p. 35.
40 Burke, *Reflections on the Revolution in France*, p. 76.

which results from the individualism of modern market relationships. Moreover, Burke believed that 'illusions' sustained the social structure by making 'power gentle, and obedience liberal'.[41] But reason has led to the collapse of all social distinctions, to the effect that 'a king is but a man; a queen is but a woman; a woman is but an animal; and an animal not of the highest order'.[42] The supremacy of reason leaves no solid foundation of moral standards and laws, which (laws) can from now on be enforced only by terror or observed whenever they accord with individuals' private interests.[43] Burke goes on:

> On the principles of this mechanic philosophy, our institutions can never be embodied [...] in persons; so as to create in us love, veneration, admiration, or attachment.[44]

More importantly,

> [...] that sort of reason which banishes the affections is incapable of feeling their place. These public affections, combined with manners, are required sometimes as supplements, sometimes as correctives, always as aids to law.[45]

In effect, in the absence of feudal values humans 'have no compass to govern' their affairs.[46] What is worse:

> When the old feudal and chivalrous spirit of *fealty*, which, by freeing kings from fear, freed both kings and subjects from the precautions of tyranny, shall be extinct in the minds of men, plots and assassinations will be anticipated by preventive murder and preventive confiscation. [...] Kings will be tyrants from policy when subjects are rebels from principle.[47]

With these words Burke anticipates the dissolution of political society.

41 Ibid., p. 77.
42 Ibid.
43 Ibid.
44 Ibid.
45 Ibid., pp. 77–78.
46 Ibid., p. 78.
47 Ibid.

But, not only does Burke contrast the feudal moral code with the individualism of the emergent commercial economy, what is more important he stresses the fact that feudal values contributed to the development of the modern economy. Therefore, he argues, should these values be lost, human beings will return to barbarism.[48] Two values in particular have characterized European civilization over the centuries, namely, 'the spirit of a gentleman, and the spirit of religion'.[49] I shall discuss Burke's views on the role of religion shortly. But first let us look at what Burke has to say about prejudice. Together with chivalry and illusions, prejudice fulfils a significant role in society; specifically, it is a motive of moral behaviour. Despite the connotations that the term 'prejudice' has for us today, for Burke 'prejudice' was not an irrational belief. On the contrary, 'prejudice' was collective wisdom, accumulated through the ages. For him, 'prejudice' had two advantages over pure reason: Firstly, the very fact that a prejudice has survived attests to its usefulness in political society; thus the longer a prejudice has survived, the more beneficial it has been to a people. Secondly, prejudice is a rule of thumb, as it were, readily available in an emergency and as such 'does not leave the man hesitating in the moment of decision, sceptical, puzzled, and unresolved'.[50] In addition, prejudice makes virtue a matter of habit, so that, thanks to prejudice, one comes to conceive of one's duty as part of one's nature.[51]

In a few words then, chivalry, illusions and prejudice are, for Burke, the moral pillars of the social order, making political society possible. By contrast, reason destroys the fabric of political society. His conception of political society is a traditional, hierarchical one and for this reason he has been called the 'Father of modern Conservatism'.

48 Ibid., p. 79.
49 Ibid., pp. 78–79.
50 Ibid., p. 87.
51 Ibid.

On Religion

In the second part of the *Reflections* Burke discusses the role of religion in political society. As he says: 'religion is the basis of civil society, and the source of all good and of all comfort.'[52] So Burke is a conservative in yet another respect – in the significance he attaches to religion and the place of an Established Church in the state. Not only should there be an interdependence between Church and State; crucially, Burke believed that the Established Church consecrates the state. For him, this 'consecration of the state, by a state religious establishment, is necessary [...] to operate with an wholesome awe upon free citizens'.[53] Therefore, religion has an important civic role – to instill awe as well as some sense of duty and responsibility to statesmen and other public figures, so that they acknowledge 'that they act in trust; and that they are to account for their conduct in that trust to the one great master; author and founder of society', namely God.[54] For Burke, it was even more important that this sense of duty and responsibility be impressed on the minds of statesmen in democratic states, for in a democracy it was much easier for a politician to get away with irresponsibility by making other members of the government responsible.[55] Besides, religion renders the people 'conscious that they exercise [...] the power', according 'to that eternal immutable law, in which will and reason are the same', so that 'they will be more careful how they place power in base and incapable hands'.[56] Accordingly:

> In their nomination to office, they will not appoint to the exercise of authority, as to a pitiful job, but as to an holy function; not according to their sordid selfish interest, nor to their wanton caprice, nor to their arbitrary will; but they will confer that

52 Ibid., p. 90.
53 Ibid., p. 92.
54 Ibid., p. 93.
55 Ibid.
56 Ibid., p. 94.

> power (which any man may well tremble to give or to receive) on those only, in whom they may discern that predominant proportion of active virtue and wisdom [...][57]

Burke believed that the merit of the English Constitution was precisely that it recognized an Established Church in the state and criticized the French revolutionaries for religious fanaticism and sacrilege. As he says:

> If our religious tenets should ever want a further elucidation, we shall not call on atheism to explain them. We shall not light up our temple from that unhallowed fire. It will be illuminated with other lights. It will be perfumed with other incense, than the infectious stuff which is imported by the smugglers of adulterated metaphysics.[58]

In England, Burke goes on: 'We are protestants, not from indifference but from zeal.'[59] Burke believed that, just as humans are social beings,[60] they are 'religious' animals too;[61] for this reason the English recognized that atheism is contrary not only to their reason but also to their instincts.[62] And

> [...] instead of quarrelling with establishments, as some do, who have made a philosophy and a religion of their hostility to such institutions, we cleave closely to them. We are resolved to keep an established church, an established monarchy, an established aristocracy, and an established democracy, each in the degree it exists, and in no greater.[63]

For the English, the Church Establishment was their major prejudice, but, as Burke is careful to make clear, 'not a prejudice destitute of reason, but involving in it profound and extensive wisdom'.[64]

Obviously, there is a personal reason why Burke should feel so strongly about religion and its role in political society. He was Irish and had first-hand

57 Ibid.
58 Ibid., p. 90.
59 Ibid.
60 Ibid., p. 98.
61 Ibid., pp. 90–91.
62 Ibid., p. 91.
63 Ibid.
64 Ibid.

experience of the consequences of religious dogmatism, fanaticism and dissention. It is important to note that, for him, religion was both a matter of faith and social utility.[65]

Pragmatism vs. Metaphysics

Before I turn to Burke's discussion of the institutions of the Jacobin state, I should like to say a few things about Burke's approach to politics. Some points with regard to this issue appear early on in the *Reflections*, in Burke's reply to the Reverend Dr. Price's sermon. But scattered comments are found throughout the book.

In his criticism of the notion of abstract 'natural rights' Burke makes two remarks regarding the nature of politics. Firstly:

> The science of constructing a commonwealth, or renovating it, or reforming it, is, like every other experimental science, not to be taught *à priori*. Nor is it a short experience that can instruct us in that practical science; because the real effects of moral causes are not always immediate [...][66]

This is a criticism of abstract theorizing about politics. In Burke's view, one cannot establish social and political institutions on the basis of *a priori* principles – that is, assumptions or statements taken to be true. The idea of 'natural rights' was just such an assumption. An *a priori* science of politics is not possible; it is not possible because the consequences of political action often come to the surface much later. In such a practical science as politics experience is, therefore, necessary. Secondly:

> The science of government being therefore so practical in itself, and intended for such practical purposes, a matter which requires experience, and even more experience than any person can gain in his whole life, however sagacious and observing

65 Cf. Hampsher-Monk, *A History of Modern Political Thought*, p. 278.

66 Burke, *Reflections on the Revolution in France*, p. 61.

> he may be, it is with infinite caution that any man ought to venture upon pulling down an edifice which has answered in any tolerable degree for ages the common purposes of society, or of building it up again, without having models and patterns of approved utility before his eyes.[67]

So the very continuity of a political practice implies its utility – it has served, and continues to serve, a purpose. Tradition is to be valued precisely because it has proven to be beneficial to political society. It is, therefore, wrong to destroy a social and political structure which has passed the test of time, as it were, and has contributed to human well-being. Besides, Burke argues, politics deals with 'human passions and concerns', and these are complex. Abstract political theorizing starts by postulating certain 'metaphysic rights', which are unchangeable and universal. Yet, given the complexity of human passions and interests, 'the primitive rights of men' undergo so much change 'that it becomes absurd to talk of them as if they continued in the simplicity of their original direction.'[68] Due to the intricacy of human nature, political issues are also complex; it follows that 'no simple disposition or direction of power can be suitable either to man's nature, or to the quality of his affairs.'[69] In point of fact, Burke argues, 'The simple governments are fundamentally defective, to say no worse of them.'[70] As we have already seen, for Burke, 'The rights of men in governments are their advantages'; these rights 'are in a sort of *middle*', that is, 'often in balances between differences of good; in compromises sometimes between good and evil, and sometimes, between evil and evil.'[71] Because of this, claims Burke, far from being abstract,

> Political reason is a computing principle; adding, subtracting, multiplying, and dividing, morally and not metaphysically or mathematically, true moral denominations.[72]

67 Ibid.
68 Ibid.
69 Ibid., pp. 61–62.
70 Ibid., p. 62.
71 Ibid.
72 Ibid.

What underlies all the above statements is Burke's conviction that politics is intimately connected with morality; or, as he once said, 'the principles of true politics are those of morality enlarged'.[73]

Burke adopted a pragmatic approach to politics and valued tradition because he believed that only in this way could progress be made and the continuity of social and political life be maintained. For, if a state were to be changed 'as often, and as much, and in as many ways as there are floating fancies or fashions, the whole chain and continuity of the commonwealth would be broken. No one generation could link with the other'; and 'Men would become little better than the flies of a summer'.[74] In fact, for Burke, this continuity and historical precedent was so valuable that he argued that, even in cases where English lawyers had proven to be wrong in supposing that English constitutional law had existed since time immemorial, this was only proof of 'the powerful prepossession towards antiquity [...] and the stationary policy of this kingdom in considering their most sacred rights and franchises as an *inheritance*'.[75] According to Burke, 'the science of jurisprudence' was 'the pride of the human intellect'; despite 'all its defects, redundancies, and errors', it was 'the collected reason of ages'.[76]

Burke's pragmatism also made him an advocate of cautious and gradual change;

> By a slow but well-sustained progress, the effect of each step is watched; the good or ill success of the first, gives light to us in the second; and so, from light to light, we are conducted with safety through the whole series.[77]

Actually, he argued, once humans have got used to a certain way of life and come to respect the laws of their country, 'it is unjust in legislature,

73 E. Burke, *Correspondence*, edited by C. William, Earl Fitzwilliam and Sir R. Bourke (London: Francis & John Rivington, 1844), Vol. I, p. 332. Quoted in Parkin, *The Moral Basis of Burke's Political Thought*, p. 1.

74 Burke, *Reflections on the Revolution in France*, p. 95.

75 Ibid., p. 32.

76 Ibid., p. 95.

77 'It is one of the excellencies of a method in which time is amongst the assistants, that its operation is slow, and in some cases almost imperceptible.' Ibid., p. 169.

by an arbitrary act, to offer a sudden violence to their minds and their feelings'.[78] Rather

> [...] a good patriot and a true politician, always considers how he shall make the most of the existing materials of his country.[79]

By 'the existing materials' Burke means current custom, social and political institutions, as well as a people's moral sentiments. And, as he puts it:

> If circumspection and caution are a part of wisdom, when we work only upon inanimate matter, surely they become a part of duty too, when the subject of our demolition and construction is not brick and timber, but sentient beings, by the sudden alteration of whose state, condition, and habits, multitudes may be rendered miserable.[80]

This is a criticism of the destruction caused by the French revolutionaries. For Burke, the 'standard of a statesman' is a 'disposition to preserve, and an ability to improve, taken together'.[81] This combination of preservation and improvement exemplifies Burke's pragmatic approach to politics.[82] As Burke says with reference to the British Constitution:

> I would not exclude alteration [...] but even when I changed, it should be to preserve. I should be led to my remedy by a great grievance. In what I did, I should follow the example of our ancestors. I would make the reparation as nearly as possible in the style of the building.[83]

This contrasts sharply with the attitude of the members of the Revolution Society in England, who like 'this continual talk of resistance and revolution, or the practice of making the extreme medicine of the constitution its daily bread. It renders the habit of society dangerously valetudinary:

78 Ibid., pp. 156–157.
79 Ibid., p. 157.
80 Ibid., p. 169.
81 Ibid., pp. 157–158.
82 Cf. ibid., p. 169.
83 Ibid., p. 248.

it is taking periodical doses of mercury sublimate, and swallowing down repeated provocatives of cantharides to our love of liberty.'[84]

His Criticism of the French Revolutionary Government

In the third and last part of the *Reflections* Burke examines in great detail and criticizes the institutions of the Jacobin state. This part is interesting from an historical rather than a theoretical point of view. However, a few points are worth our attention.

To begin with, Burke accuses the members of the French Assembly of incompetence. Their only concern is to remain in power;[85] moreover, they attempt to apply in practice their abstract theories, which, being abstract, are inapplicable to the sphere of human affairs:

> [...] in all the regulations relative to the public good [...] they commit the whole to the mercy of untried speculations; they abandon the dearest interests of the public to those loose theories, to which none of them would chuse to trust the slightest of his private concerns.[86]

The system of government they have established is not the result of a coherent plan, but of chance. What is more, 'Their purpose every where seems to have been to evade and slip aside from *difficulty*'.[87] Yet, difficulty, for Burke, 'is a severe instructor', as it is through trying to cope with difficulty that humans sharpen their understanding and skills, and get to know their subject-matter better.[88] This inability to tackle difficulty is to blame for the

84 Ibid., p. 63.
85 Ibid., p. 166.
86 Ibid.
87 Ibid., p. 167.
88 Ibid.

Assembly's resort to 'abolition and total destruction'.[89] 'But is it in destroying and pulling down that skill is displayed?',[90] Burke asks rhetorically.

Regarding the legislature in the French revolutionary state, Burke believed that it defeated the notion of universal human rights, which the revolutionaries proclaimed. The legislature was to be based on 'the *basis of territory*', 'the *basis of population*' and 'the *basis of contribution*'.[91] Accordingly, the French divided the country into '*Departments*', subdivided into '*Communes*' and these into '*Cantons*'.[92] If they were to adhere to their own principles, the French should have proceeded from the idea that 'Men [...] are strictly equal, and are entitled to equal rights in their own government'. Everyone would then have a vote 'and every man would vote directly for the person who was to represent him in the legislature'.[93] However, as Burke notes, the French were not prepared to go all the way with their principles. 'But soft – by regular degrees, not yet'. This metaphysic principle, to which law, custom, usage, policy, reason, were to yield,' had first 'to yield itself to their pleasure.' There had to be 'many degrees, and some stages, before the representative can come in contact with his constituent'. And, in fact, this contact would never happen.[94] For, starting from the smallest division, the '*Canton*', the voters who would compose the '*primary assemblies*' were to have a '*qualification*'; this, in effect, would reduce the electorate and undermine the idea of 'rights of men'.[95] The primary assemblies of the '*Canton*' would then elect deputies to the '*Communes*'; here another qualification would be introduced.[96] The '*Communes*' would then elect deputies to the '*Department*' and the deputies of the '*Department*' would subsequently elect deputies to the '*National Assembly*'. A third qualification would be introduced for every deputy elected to the National Assembly.

89 Ibid., p. 168.
90 Ibid.
91 Ibid., p. 173.
92 Ibid., pp. 173–174.
93 Ibid., p. 175.
94 Ibid.
95 Ibid.
96 Ibid., pp. 175–176.

Clearly, the property qualification undermined the alleged equality of humans, as proclaimed by the French revolutionaries.[97] In this connection, it should be mentioned that some commentators have observed that Burke's description of the electoral process is wrong, as he appears to have mixed up the electoral system with that of local government.[98] That said, according to Burke, the principle of contribution was unjust to the wealthy too, because, by giving more electoral weight to the district which contributed more to the national revenue *as a whole*, the rich *individually* were not given more representation.[99]

Concerning the executive branch of government of the French revolutionary state, Burke regarded the constitutional king as 'a degraded king',[100] 'a machine, without any sort of deliberative discretion in any one act of his function'.[101] In effect, his powers were so diminished that he had no authority any longer. He cannot exercise any power over the judiciary; at the same time, 'Every thing in justice that is vile and odious is thrown upon him.'[102] He does not have the power to award any titles or distinctions; but coercion and repression are tasks left to him. Thus:

> If relief is to be given to any municipality, the assembly gives it. If troops are to be sent to reduce them to obedience to the assembly, the king is to execute the order; and upon every occasion he is to be spattered over with the blood of his people.[103]

In other words, the King has come to be associated with cruelty and oppression, thereby losing the aura of glory which should be attached to the highest officer in the state. Nor does the King choose his own ministers. These are chosen by the National Assembly and made to work for him.[104]

97 Ibid., p. 176.
98 L. G. Mitchell, 'Explanatory Notes', in E. Burke's *Reflections of the Revolution in France*, p. 311.
99 Burke, *Reflections on the Revolution in France*, pp. 177–179.
100 Ibid., p. 199.
101 Ibid., p. 200.
102 Ibid.
103 Ibid., p. 201.
104 Ibid., p. 203.

As for the ministers, they are accountable to the National Assembly, yet they are not allowed to sit in it.[105]

So far as the judiciary is concerned, Burke's criticism is that it is not independent;[106] the National Assembly appoints the judges and subjects them to its rules.[107] Lastly, 'the administrative bodies are carefully exempted from the jurisdiction of' the tribunals; which means, Burke says, that 'those persons are exempted from the power of the laws, who ought to be the most entirely submitted to them'.[108]

Finally, Burke considers the military of the Jacobin state. Having 'destroyed all the opinions, and prejudices, and [...] all the instincts which support government', the French revolutionary government has no other solution but to resort to force to maintain social and political stability.[109] The French 'must rule by an army';[110] however, at the same time, they have instilled in the military principles which make them unable to use it for the purposes they want.[111] For 'They have destroyed the principle of obedience in the great essential link between the officer and the soldier'.[112] All this metaphysical talk of 'the rights of man and citizen' has taught the soldier that 'he is a citizen, and has the rights of man and citizen'; that these rights mean that he should 'be his own governor' and agree 'to be ruled only by those to whom he delegates that self-government'. Therefore, the soldier will come to think 'that he ought most of all to have his choice where he is to yield the greatest degree of obedience'.[113]

In the epilogue Burke concedes that 'among an infinite number of acts of violence and folly, some good may have been done'. For '[t]hey who destroy every thing certainly will remove some grievance. They who

105 Ibid.
106 Ibid., p. 207.
107 Ibid., p. 209.
108 Ibid., p. 210.
109 Ibid., p. 222.
110 Ibid.
111 Ibid., pp. 222–223.
112 Ibid., p. 221.
113 Ibid.

make every thing new, have a chance that they may establish something beneficial.'[114] Thus:

> Some usages have been abolished on just grounds; but they were such that if they had stood as they were to all eternity, they would little detract from the happiness and prosperity of any state. The improvements of the national assembly are superficial, their errors fundamental.[115]

By contrast, the British Constitution, Burke says, is 'an invaluable treasure'. For this reason:

> I think our happy situation owing to our constitution; but owing to the whole of it, and not to any part singly; owing in a great measure to what we have left standing in our several reviews and reformations, as well as to what we have altered or superadded.[116]

So the merit of the British Constitution, for Burke, is that it combines tradition with cautious reform and renovation, as well as balancing monarchical, aristocratic and democratic elements, unifying them into a whole.[117]

114 Ibid., p. 248.
115 Ibid.
116 Ibid.
117 See: 'We are resolved to keep an established church, an established monarchy, an established aristocracy, and an established democracy, each in the degree it exists, and in no greater.' Ibid., p. 91. Also: 'We see, that the parts of the system do not clash [...] We compensate, we reconcile, we balance. We are enabled to unite into a consistent whole the various anomalies and contending principles that are found in the minds and affairs of men. From hence arises, not an excellence in simplicity, but one far superior, an excellence in composition.' Ibid., p. 170.

CHAPTER 7

G. W. F. Hegel

Georg Wilhelm Friedrich Hegel was born in Stuttgart in 1770. He studied theology at the University of Tübingen. After his studies he worked as a private tutor to a well-off family in Berne and later on as a university tutor in Frankfurt. From 1801–1807 Hegel was a lecturer at the University of Jena and it was during this period that he wrote his first philosophical works, the most significant of which is the *Phenomenology of Spirit*, written during 1806 and published in 1807. Hegel had to leave Jena due to war – the troops of Napoleon Bonaparte had started occupying the city; in fact, there is a saying that Hegel was writing the last pages of the *Phenomenology of Spirit* as Napoleon's troops were entering Jena and he then had to send the last sections of the work which made his reputation to the publisher by a carriage which passed through the battlefield. For a year (1807–1808) he edited a pro-French newspaper in Bamberg and then became headmaster of a *Gymnasium* in Nuremberg. He held this position for eight years (1808–1816) until he was appointed to a professorship of philosophy at the University of Heidelberg (1816). In 1818 he became a professor of philosophy at the University of Berlin; he was appointed to the chair that had been occupied by Johann Gottlieb Fichte. It was during this period that Hegel wrote the *Philosophy of Right*, his work on political philosophy.

The Structure of the *Philosophy of Right*

The *Philosophy of Right* consists of three parts, which should be understood as 'moments' or aspects of the whole – namely, 'Abstract Right', 'Morality' and 'Ethical Life'. Essentially, what we have is – in Hegelian terminology – a development from immediacy or abstract universality through particularization and difference to a differentiated unity. In fact, 'ethical life', more precisely, its highest 'moment', the state, is the beginning, in the sense that it is the whole within which the earlier parts of the *Philosophy of Right* should be understood. The development from 'Abstract Right' through 'Morality' to 'Ethical Life' is a logical one. Hegel's purpose is to show that 'Ethical Life' is *presupposed* by 'Abstract Right' and 'Morality'; that is, 'Abstract Right' and 'Morality' do not make sense outside the context of 'Ethical Life', this being their determining ground. But the reason why Hegel begins from 'Abstract Right' rather than 'Ethical Life' is because he wishes to philosophize without foundations. In other words, rather than positing 'Ethical Life' in an *a priori* manner, he presents 'Ethical Life' as arising out of the contradictions implicit in 'Abstract Right' and 'Morality'; so what we have is a development of a simple conception of right ('Abstract Right') through a more comprehensive understanding of human relations ('Morality') to a yet more comprehensive understanding of these relationships ('Ethical Life'). The point Hegel wishes to make is that the state, as the highest 'moment' of 'Ethical Life', determines what is right and wrong as well as morality. Moreover, in real life the individual can live only with other individuals within a political community. Human beings are from birth *already* situated *within* a given political community and can lead their lives only within it; they are embedded in specific social practices and depend on the institutional framework of the particular historical community in which they find themselves and which 'cultivates' or 'educates' them (the Hegelian word is *bilden*), as well as shaping their identity and lives. What is distinctive in Hegel is that only through relating oneself to another can a human being be constituted as a self; thus one's identity is one's relation to another. This is what Hegel means by 'recognition' or self-recognition in another.

Here I shall discuss the sections on 'Abstract Right' and 'Morality' only briefly. I shall then examine in more detail the section on 'Ethical Life'.

Abstract Right

At the beginning of the section on 'Abstract Right' Hegel articulates the implications of the notion of the 'absolutely free will'.[1] This free will is in its immediacy – it simply exists; it is *un*determined and for this reason abstract. It is 'personality' conceived in abstraction – that is, as simple 'self-relation'.[2] In order to determine itself, the will must give itself a content and thus become particularized. Human will actualizes itself in property, because in property ('a thing') it becomes something concrete and particular.[3] This is why, according to Hegel's account, property is so important; for it allows the will to determine itself, thereby actualizing itself. By 'right' is meant the possibility of the will's determination in an object; as Hegel puts it:

> An existent of any sort embodying the free will, this is what right is. Right is therefore by definition freedom as Idea.[4]

Now in the contract the will of a person is recognized by another. Therein lies the significance of the contract; it expresses the mutual recognition of the contracting parties as property owners.[5] However, the contract is an agreement of two abstract wills and there is no authority or third party to mediate between them. This is why the 'moment' of 'Abstract Right' is inadequate. There not being a mediating party it is likely that the claims of right of the contracting parties will clash and negate each other. This clash of right claims is not necessarily malicious; it may well be innocent. The inadequacy of the sphere of right, Hegel says, lies in the lack of a framework

1 G. W. F. Hegel, *Philosophy of Right*, translated with notes by T. M. Knox (Oxford: Oxford University Press, 1967), § 34, p. 37.

2 Ibid., § 35, p. 37.

3 Ibid., §§ 41–42, p. 40.

4 Ibid., § 29, p. 33.

5 Ibid., § 71, p. 57.

which defines what right is (gives it a meaning) and provides the rules of the game. In the absence of social and political institutions, the notion of right turns out to be contradictory. This comes to the fore in Hegel's discussion of 'wrong'. 'Wrong' is the negation of right.[6] It can take the form of an innocent clash of wills, of fraud and of coercion.[7] Punishment becomes necessary in order to safeguard 'will', 'right', 'property' and 'contract'. The importance of punishment lies, not simply in the negation of a given right, but in its defence – assertion – of the very principle of right.[8] Hegel says with regard to punishment:

> The injury [the penalty] which falls on the criminal is not merely *implicitly* just – as just, it is *eo ipso* his implicit will, an embodiment of his freedom, his right; on the contrary, it is also a right *established* within the criminal himself, i.e. in his objectively embodied will, in his action.[9]

This may strike the reader as odd. How can the criminal have willed his punishment? And what does it mean that it is 'a right *established* within the criminal himself [...] in his action'? What Hegel means is that, in the absence of a social and political context and of institutions giving meaning to 'right', 'property', 'contract' and 'crime', 'crime' turns out to be implicit in a person's assertion of right – that is to say, it is a possibility. For this reason 'Abstract Right' is an inadequate understanding of human relations and it passes over to the sphere of 'Morality'.[10] The 'moment' of 'Abstract Right' is superseded, in the double Hegelian sense of overcome and yet preserved.

6 Ibid., § 82, p. 64.
7 Ibid., §§ 84–86, 87–89 and 90 ff, respectively.
8 Ibid., §§ 97 & 99.
9 Ibid., § 100, p. 70.
10 Ibid., § 104, pp. 73–74.

Morality

'Morality' consists in an attempt to overcome the difficulties involved in 'Abstract Right'. It conceives of the same concepts and relationships in a more comprehensive manner. From the moral point of view, the will does not pertain to a personal or private right only; it is self-reflective, the will of a subject.[11] A subject has self-consciousness, whereas the person at the level of 'Abstract Right' is merely an abstraction. The moral will, as opposed to the abstract will, has the very principle of right in view, not merely the notion of right, which is abstract. It is, therefore, an advance over 'Abstract Right', a more comprehensive and adequate conception of the will. As such, the 'right of the moral will' has three 'aspects', namely, purpose, intention and good.[12] Hegel uses these categories in the usual sense, purpose being a willingness to bring about a state of affairs, while intention being what underlies the purpose (the motive); as for the 'good', it is 'the unity of the concept of the will with the particular will'.[13] Implicit in the notion of the 'good' is both right and the welfare of others:

> Welfare without right is not a good. Similarly, right without welfare is not the good [...][14]

Yet, without a social and political context to define the good, the only criterion of goodness is the subject; moral standards are subjective. 'Conscience' is one's inner conviction that what one does is good; it is the 'subjective self-consciousness' that knows 'in itself and from within itself what is right and obligatory',[15] or for that matter what is wrong. There is no doubt that

11 Ibid., § 105, p. 75.
12 Ibid., § 114, p. 79.
13 Ibid., § 129, p. 86.
14 Ibid., § 130, p. 87.
15 Ibid., § 137 [A], p. 91.

in this section Hegel renders explicit the implications of Kantian morality.[16] So, in unmasking the contradictions implicit in the standpoint of 'Morality', Hegel is in effect criticizing Kant. The inadequacy of Kantian morality is that it claimed to derive objective, universal standards of morality from the subjective will. But there is nothing to determine between different sets of rules. Therefore, morality remains abstract, devoid of any specific content whatsoever. Ultimately, what gives morality a content is 'Ethical Life' – that is to say, a social and political culture and institutions. So 'Morality' too is superseded in the double Hegelian sense of overcome and preserved. In this way the transition from 'Morality' to 'Ethical Life' is effected.[17]

Ethical Life

'Ethical life' has three 'moments', namely, the family (an immediate, unreflective unity), civil society (a formal unity, mediated by particularity) and the state (a reflective unity in difference).

The Family

The family is an immediate, unreflective unity, because its members are bound together by sentimental ties. What characterizes family relationships is love.[18] Hegel articulates the development of the family in three phases: marriage, family property and capital, the education of children

16 See I. Kant, *Foundations of the Metaphysics of Morals*, 2nd revised edition, translated with an introduction by L. W. Beck, Library of Liberal Arts (New York: Macmillan, 1990).

17 Hegel, *Philosophy of Right*, para. 141, pp. 103–104.

18 Ibid., § 158, p. 110.

and the dissolution of the family.[19] From the standpoint of nature, marriage expresses the necessity of human reproduction but what makes it an *ethical* institution is its translation of a natural impulse into a spiritual (*geistig*) relationship, 'a union on the level of mind, into self-conscious love'.[20] There are different roles for men and women; man's consciousness is more suitable to 'conceptual thought and the volition of the objective final end', while woman's consciousness is more emotional and family centred.[21] The essence of marriage is monogamy.[22] To actualize itself, the family, just as the 'abstract will', must possess property. Therein lies the significance of family capital.[23] The unity of marriage is implicit – it is 'only a unity of inwardness and disposition'; outwardly, this unity is split into two partners, a man and a woman. For this reason marriage attains an explicit, perfect, unity in a third party who arises out of the union of the other two, namely, the child. Thus the child or children are 'the embodiment' of the parents' 'substance'.[24] As soon as the child or children become of age, the family dissolves. The children become legal persons in civil society and found families of their own.[25] In many cases, their parents separate through divorce.[26] The family dissolves in yet another, more extended, sense: historically, the family in the wider sense of the tribe either disintegrates or expands to such an extent that it no longer is a family but becomes a 'people' or 'nation'.[27] In all of the above senses, following the dissolution of the family the transition to civil society is effected.

19 Ibid., § 160, p. 111.
20 Ibid., § 161, p. 111.
21 Ibid., § 166, p. 114.
22 Ibid., § 167, p. 115.
23 Ibid., § 169, p. 116.
24 Ibid., § 173, p. 117.
25 Ibid., § 177, p. 118.
26 Ibid., § 176, p. 118.
27 Ibid., § 181, p. 122.

Civil Society

Civil society (*bürgerliche Gesellschaft*) contains 'difference' or 'particularity'; at the same time, it brings this particularity to a formal or external universality. It is the economic sphere, where every person pursues his own interests and aims; but, since in pursuing his own goals the individual enters into relationships with other individuals, he comes to be related to them. It is in this sense that a formal universality is attained.[28] Specifically, Hegel says:

> In the course of the actual attainment of selfish ends [...] there is formed a system of complete interdependence, wherein the livelihood, and legal status of one man is interwoven with the livelihood, happiness, and rights of all. [...] This system may be prima facie regarded as the external state, the state based on need, the state as the Understanding envisages.[29]

According to Hegel, the 'Understanding' considers things separately, bringing them in a unity, which however is external. It is external because the 'understanding' emphasizes distinction; it is not able to discern the *necessary* relations between things. For this reason in civil society 'the Idea is present only as a relative totality'.[30] Although entering into relations with others – in the form of economic transactions, for example –, individuals retain their independence. Therefore, civil society is a unity of externally related atoms. 'Civil society contains three moments': the system of needs, the administration of justice and the public authority (or 'police') as well as corporations.[31]

The 'system of needs' is economic relations. Hegel points out that, unlike animals, human beings multiply their needs and means of satisfying them, as well as dividing a concrete need into different parts.[32] Due to their multiplication and sophistication, as well as to the different ways of

28 Ibid., § 182, pp. 122–123.
29 Ibid., §183, p. 123.
30 Ibid., § 184, p. 123.
31 Ibid., § 188, p. 126.
32 Ibid., § 190, p. 127.

satisfying them, needs gradually become 'abstract'.[33] Here Hegel seems to have in mind the way(s) in which one's needs come to depend on those of others or even the way(s) in which others come to impose a need on an individual. But, as soon as needs and their satisfaction become abstract, interpersonal relations too become abstract.[34] Needs can be satisfied through material things. And to acquire these, one has to work. Work transforms 'the raw material directly supplied by nature', adapting it to human ends.[35] Work is *social* when there is no direct link between one's need and its satisfaction. According to Hegel's account, in modern society there is a division of labour, whereby each works toward the satisfaction of one's own as well as others' needs; this is the 'universal and objective element in work'.[36] In this way humans come to be interrelated and mutually dependent. By doing one's own specific job, each individual produces commodities or goods which satisfy others' needs. Hegel is, of course, aware of the consequences of this specialization: 'the abstraction of one man's production from another's makes work more and more mechanical, until man is able to step aside and install machines in his place'.[37] The complexity of the relations of production and exchange becomes 'crystallized' into different social groups or 'class-divisions'.[38] Accordingly, there are three classes in civil society: the '*substantial* or immediate' agricultural class, the 'reflecting or *formal*' business class and the '*universal* class' of civil servants.[39] The three classes, as different aspects of civil society, are characterized by immediate unreflective unity, formal unity mediated by particularity and reflective unity, respectively. Surely, Hegel says, to which class one belongs is to a certain extent determined by birth, natural factors such as ability and other circumstances. However, what distinguishes modernity from previous historical periods is the opportunity it affords individuals to choose a

33 Ibid., § 191, p. 127.

34 Ibid., § 192, p. 127.

35 Ibid., § 196, pp. 128–129 (quote p. 129).

36 Ibid., § 198, p. 129.

37 Ibid.

38 Ibid., § 201, pp. 130–131.

39 Ibid., § 202, p. 131.

job and thereby their social position.[40] Membership of a class is essential, for an individual 'actualizes himself only in becoming something definite, i.e. something specifically particularized; this means restricting himself exclusively to one of the particular spheres of need'.[41] In other words, one obtains a social identity, comes to be recognized by others, as a member of a class. Crucially, as a member of a class, the individual is raised above his private interests (particularity) to a consideration of the interests of others (that is, other members of the class) and thus to universality.

In civil society 'the right of property', presented as 'Abstract Right' at the beginning of the book, 'is no longer merely implicit but has attained its recognized actuality as the protection of property through the administration of justice'.[42] Within the context of civil society this right, firstly, is known by all individuals and, secondly, is recognized by all as valid – so it is 'universally valid'.[43] In civil society there is a legal system which formulates the laws. 'Right' is no longer an 'abstract right' but takes the form of 'law' and here Hegel plays with the etymology of the German word for 'law' (*Gesetz*): *Gesetz* is something which has been posited, *gesetzt*;[44] 'the right becomes positive law in general'.[45] The implication here is that in civil society 'wrongdoing [...] becomes an infringement, not merely of what is subjectively infinite' – namely, an abstract free will – 'but of the universal thing which is existent with inherent stability and strength' – that is, the social whole. On the one hand, 'the magnitude of the wrongdoing' is greater, since the wrongdoing now affects society as a whole; on the other, however, the significance of the wrongdoing is less, given the strength of the social structure and social institutions.[46] Moreover, punishment is now administered by the system of justice and ceases to have the character of mere revenge.[47]

40 Ibid., § 206, p. 132.
41 Ibid., § 207, p. 133.
42 Ibid., § 208, p. 134; cf. § 209, p. 134.
43 Ibid., § 210, p. 134.
44 Ibid., § 211, p. 134.
45 Ibid., § 211, p. 135; cf. §§ 212–214 & 217, pp. 136–138 & 139, respectively.
46 Ibid., § 218, p. 140.
47 Ibid., § 220, p. 141.

The task of the 'court of justice' is the application of the law to 'a particular case'.[48] This is necessary because a law is by definition universal, a general rule, while each particular case is different. Thus the law needs to be adapted to the specific circumstances of the case. To this purpose, the nature of the case, its uniqueness, must first be determined, and subsequently the case must be subsumed under the general law.[49] So the administration of justice combines or synthesizes the particular with the universal. This is recognized by the citizens. Moreover, therein lies the significance of public proceedings and the jury.[50]

To sum up, the system of justice brings particularity and universality into unity; it is thus an attempt to overcome the particularity and individualism of civil society. Yet, Hegel says, this is not enough, because at best particularity is overcome and universality achieved only in those cases which are dealt with by the courts. This unity is brought forward more effectively by the 'public authority' or 'police' and the corporations.[51]

Hegel is aware of the fact that in the economic sphere success is due both to one's capacity or talent and to other factors beyond one's control. So he sees a public authority intervening in order to correct the deficiencies of the 'system of needs'. This intervention takes the form, first, of a removal of accidental obstacles to personal goals and, second, of the securing of every person's welfare by considering it a right.[52] It should be made clear that by 'police' Hegel does not mean what we would normally understand by the term. Hegel also refers to a 'public' or 'universal' authority and this is what we should take 'police' to mean. In so far as civil society is characterized by particularity, the 'public authority' is 'restricted to the sphere of contingencies' and remains 'an external organization'.[53] Civil society is a realm of contingencies because the lawful actions of an individual agent may harm others for reasons beyond that actor's control.[54] Hegel is thinking how one

48 Ibid., § 219.
49 Ibid., § 225, pp. 142–143.
50 Ibid., §§ 227–228, pp. 143–145.
51 Ibid., § 229, p. 145.
52 Ibid., § 230, p. 146.
53 Ibid., § 231, p. 146.
54 Ibid., § 232, p. 146.

person's success in business may lead to another's bankruptcy, for instance. So there is a need for public control of trade and commerce.[55] The family is a 'substantive whole' which caters for its members. However, 'civil society tears the individual from his family ties', as in the economic arena individuals are recognized as 'self-subsistent persons'. Therefore, '[...] the individual becomes a son of civil society which has as many claims upon him as he has rights against it'.[56] Accordingly, the role of the 'public authority' or 'police' is to be responsible for the individual's education;[57] to prevent the individual from leading a licentious life;[58] and to look after the poor; in the latter case, the public authority does not merely provide the necessaries of life to the poor, but also seeks to transform their moral disposition which may well have been a contributing factor to their poverty.[59] Hegel recognized the structural nature of poverty, for poverty afflicted not only the unemployed but also the unskilled workers; it was a consequence of 'the subdivision and restriction of particular jobs'[60] and tended to lead to the emergence of what he called 'a rabble of paupers', the destitute who lived on the margins of civil society and so did not share in its benefits or advantages.[61] Hegel's insight so far as the nature of poverty is concerned is remarkable. He saw how a commercial society leads to a 'concentration of disproportionate wealth in a few hands'.[62] He also saw that the extreme polarization of civil society – between rich and poor – could not be solved internally;[63] it therefore drove civil society 'to push beyond its own limits and seek markets'.[64] Colonization becomes necessary as a means of exporting surplus goods and surplus population.[65]

55 Ibid., § 236, pp. 147–148.
56 Ibid., § 238, p. 148.
57 Ibid., § 239, p. 148.
58 Ibid., § 240, p. 148.
59 Ibid., § 241, pp. 148–149.
60 Ibid., § 243, p. 149.
61 Ibid., § 244, p. 150.
62 Ibid.
63 Ibid., § 245, p. 150.
64 Ibid., § 247, p. 151.
65 Ibid., §§ 247–248, pp. 151–152.

The life of the agricultural class, the traditional class of landowners, is based on nature – due to its possession of land – and centred around the family. For this reason, says Hegel, the agricultural class expresses 'the concrete universal' within civil society – that is to say, their way of life is characterized by an immediate, unreflective unity, since it is rooted in custom and tradition. The class of civil servants, by contrast, expresses 'the universal explicitly', that is, a reflective unity. As for the business class, situated between the agricultural class and the class of civil servants, it expresses 'the particular', since each of its members pursues their own interests. It is in this class that the corporations have a role to fulfil.[66] One should bear in mind that it is not only entrepreneurs that belong to the business class but also skilled workers. This is important in order to understand what a corporation is. A corporation is an association of producers and skilled workers who work in a specific branch of industry. As a result, they broadly lead the same way of life and have some common concerns. The role of the corporation is significant, for it raises each individual from particularity to universality. Surely, corporations are set up on the basis of selfish interests, but, as individuals engaged in the same kind of activity come together in an association, they are transformed. They now have a universal purpose in view, although admittedly this is still restricted in scope.[67] Corporations operate 'under the surveillance of the public authority' and, Hegel says, have four rights: to provide for the interests of the industrial sector concerned; to choose new members on the basis of their skills and moral disposition, as well as according to the needs of the economy and society at large – thus a corporation has the right to restrict the number of new entrants to a specific industrial sector to prevent a surplus of labour; to protect the members of the sector from the fluctuations of the economy; and to offer the training which is necessary for others to be able to acquire the requisite skills and join the sector.[68] According to Hegel's account, what is important is that in the corporation the individual comes to identify with a whole, so 'he

66 Ibid., § 250, p. 152.
67 Ibid., § 251, p. 152.
68 Ibid., § 252, pp. 152–153.

commands the respect due to one in his social position.'[69] In other words, the individual acquires a social identity, a social status. Further, within the corporation the right of exercising one's skill ceases to be 'natural' and becomes 'rational'[70] – it is therefore lifted from 'immediacy' and becomes reflective, conscious. Crucially, the corporation is the second ethical basis of the state, the family being the first.[71]

However, 'The end of the Corporation is restricted and finite' and the 'public authority' is 'an external organization' and as such 'a merely relative identity' of the individual with the social whole.[72] Liberal political thought from Hobbes and Locke onwards has regarded the state as an arbitrator between individual interests. In this sense the liberal conception of the state corresponds to what Hegel sees as civil society; this way of viewing the state is proper to the 'understanding', which attempts to unite what it considers to be separate elements. However, this is *not* the essence of the state, Hegel says. Rather the state is a 'substantial unity',[73] the ground of human existence. 'Hence the sphere of civil society passes over into the state.'[74]

The State

In Hegel's words, 'The state is the actuality of the ethical Idea.'[75] What Hegel means by this is that the state is the Idea fully developed; it is the objectification of human reason and will in political institutions, this objectification being at the same time reflective in the sense that it is conscious. Put differently, individuals are conscious of the fact that it is *they* who create social and political institutions, and that these very institutions express their

69 Ibid., § 253, p. 153.
70 Ibid., § 254, p. 154.
71 Ibid., § 255, p. 154.
72 Ibid., § 256, p. 154.
73 Ibid., § 258, p. 156.
74 Ibid., § 256, p. 154.
75 Ibid., § 257, p. 155.

will. In a very important paragraph (para. 258) Hegel says that the state, as a 'substantial unity', is 'absolute unmoved end in itself';[76] it is 'absolute' because it does not depend on anything else and it is 'unmoved' for the same reason – it is not moved by anything without itself, but is a self-moving totality, an 'end in itself'. It is within this organic whole that 'freedom comes into its supreme right'.[77] Hegel has in mind freedom as self-determination; political institutions are the product of the conscious human will and as such an expression of human freedom; simultaneously, in being aware that political institutions are the product of their will, humans recognize that these very institutions are the embodiment of their freedom. This is what Hegel means when he says 'The state is the actuality of concrete freedom'.[78] In this sense in social and political institutions individuals recognize themselves.[79] So one's identity is a relation of oneself to another or recognition in another. This recognition becomes concretized in the institutions of the state and for this reason individuals are identified with this larger whole. Like Aristotle, Hegel emphasizes that the state 'is the end immanent within' humans,[80] so that human beings cannot exist independently of the state. Humans are rational beings and human consciousness has by nature two aspects: on the one hand, each human being conceives himself as an individuality; on the other, each human being conceives himself as universality, as part of a whole.[81] However, this identity of the individual with the state is not immediate – that is, unreflective – as, indeed, it was in the ancient Greek *polis* or as it is in the family; it is not therefore an undifferentiated identity but an identity which includes difference. This is because within the state the principle of individuality is allowed. The sphere of civil society is superseded by the state, yet what this supersession implies is both an overcoming and preservation. In civil society individuality has its place; at the same time, civil society is subsumed within a larger,

76 Ibid., § 258, p. 156.
77 Ibid.
78 Ibid., § 260, p. 160.
79 Ibid.
80 Ibid., § 261, p. 161.
81 Ibid., § 264, p. 163.

more comprehensive and substantial whole, the state. And the state, as the embodiment of 'reason' is a unity in difference.[82] This is the fundamental Hegelian insight. The achievement of the modern state, for Hegel, is precisely that it is able to comprehend the distinctively modern principle of individual subjectivity, yet at the same time raising this to a universality. For this reason it expresses what was best in antiquity and what is best in modernity.

Hegel does not put forth a *theory* of the state; he does not prescribe what the state should be like, nor does he construct a political edifice on the basis of some assumption or assumptions. As mentioned above, his is a philosophy without foundations and the structure of the *Philosophy of Right* attests to this; what we have is an attempt to show how less adequate conceptions of interpersonal relationships can have a meaning only in more comprehensive contexts. The state is a presupposition of 'Abstract Right' and 'Morality', in the sense that it is their ultimate, determining ground – that is to say, what gives them meaning. In this sense the book could have been structured the other way round. The reason why it is structured this way is to make plain to the reader that it is impossible to understand human relations fully outside the context of the state; an attempt to do so can only lead to contradictions. So, rather than constructing a theory, Hegel renders *explicit* what is *implied* in the notion of the state. What is meant by the modern state? This is what he is trying to articulate. Accordingly, questions such as how all states or a particular state and its institutions originate historically, whether the state has emerged out of patriarchalism, whether it is based on divine right, contract or custom are irrelevant for Hegel's purposes. Hegel is not concerned with the state's foundations; 'all these questions are no concern to the Idea of the state'.[83] Rather:

82 The Hegelian distinction between 'reason' and 'understanding' is crucial. 'Reason' (*Vernunft*) is the synthesizing faculty which perceives the interconnections between different aspects of reality. 'Understanding' (*Verstand*) is the analytical thinking which breaks reality down into isolated elements, while failing to bring these elements together in an harmonious manner (i.e. in unity). 'Reason' characterizes the state, whereas 'understanding' characterizes civil society.

83 Hegel, *Philosophy of Right*, § 258, p. 156 [A].

> We are dealing here exclusively with the philosophic science of the state, and from that point of view all these things are mere appearance and therefore matters for history. So far as the authority of any existing state has anything to do with reasons, these reasons are culled from the forms of the laws authoritative within it.[84]

And 'The philosophical treatment of these topics is concerned only with their inward side, with the thought of their concept'.[85]

The 'Idea of the state' has three 'moments': the constitution or constitutional law, its relation to other states (international law) and its actualization or realization in world history.[86]

Regarding the first 'moment', the constitution, this should be understood as the structure of the state – a structure which does not consist of the state in the strict sense of the word only, but includes civil society, the family, morality and all legal rules.[87] So the categories discussed abstractly in the section on 'Abstract Right' are rooted in a specific political context. Hegel praised Montesquieu for acknowledging that laws are dependent on the nature of each specific state and for examining the part in its relation to the whole.[88] And when Hegel says that the state is the 'spirit' of a nation ('the mind of a nation'), first, as the law governing human relations within the state and, second, as the manners and consciousness of the citizens,[89] he means 'spirit' in the sense of Montesquieu's *L'Esprit des Lois*. The constitution is rational (*vernünftig*) in so far as each of its parts is interrelated with the others into a coherent whole (unity in difference or differentiated unity).[90] So theories of a separation of powers *mis*understand the nature of the constitution, in assuming that each power – the legislative, executive

84 Ibid.
85 Ibid.
86 Ibid., § 259, p. 160.
87 See 'The constitution of the state is, in the first place, the organization of the state and the self-related process of its organic life, a process whereby it differentiates its moments within itself and develops them to self-subsistence.' Ibid., § 271, p. 174.
88 Ibid., § 261, p. 161 [A].
89 Ibid., § 274, pp. 178–179.
90 Ibid., § 272, p. 174.

and judiciary – is independent of the others and acts as a check to them.[91] Internally the state has three 'moments': the legislature (the universal element), the executive (which subsumes particularity under the universal) and the crown (the element of subjectivity).[92]

In respect of the latter, Hegel says:

> The power of the crown contains in itself the three moments of the whole [...] viz. (α) the *universality* of the constitution and the laws; (β) counsel, which refers the *particular* to the universal; and (γ) the moment of ultimate decision, as the *self-determination* to which everything else reverts and from which everything else derives the beginning of its actuality.[93]

The significance of the crown lies in its symbolism; he symbolizes the 'substantial unity'[94] of the state in an individual will,[95] as the monarch ratifies the decisions of the assembly and the civil servants. Hegel is rationalizing the Prussian monarchy in the *Philosophy of Right*, a monarchy which, he believed, exemplified modern monarchy generally. Modern monarchy is hereditary,[96] yet at the same time constitutional, not arbitrary. And it is a rational institution, in so far as it comprises all the elements found in the state (subjectivity, particularity and universality).[97] Thus:

> [...] sovereignty depends on the fact that the particular functions and powers of the state are not self-subsistent or firmly grounded either on their own account or in the particular will of the individual functionaries, but have their roots ultimately in the unity of the state as their single self.[98]

Regarding the executive, its task is to subsume the particular under the universal. This task is also performed by the judiciary and the 'police' or

91 Ibid., § 272, p. 175 [A].
92 Ibid., § 273, p. 176.
93 Ibid., § 275, p. 179.
94 Ibid., § 276, p. 179.
95 Ibid., § 279, p. 181.
96 Ibid., § 280, p. 184.
97 Ibid., §§ 275–277, p. 179.
98 Ibid., § 278, pp. 179–180.

'public authority'.[99] Therefore, there are two aspects in the judiciary and the public authority – one pertaining to civil society, the sphere of individual interests, and another which relates to the universal, namely, the state.[100] Executive power consists of the civil servants and higher advisory officials.[101] The organization of the officials is the following: first, some of them – the officials lower down the hierarchy such as corporation officers, for example – are popularly elected; second, there are administrative officials in different departments; third, departments are supervised by a supreme official.[102] Civil servants are appointed on the basis of merit;[103] they are nominated by the monarch,[104] while their tenure is conditional on their fulfilment of the duties it involves.[105] Civil servants and the members of the executive form 'the greater part of the middle class'.[106] Obviously, there is a tendency among civil servants to develop a distinctive culture and to consider themselves as a caste within the state,[107] but Hegel sees this tendency checked by the sovereign from above and the corporations from below.[108]

As for the legislature, firstly, it formulates or amends the laws as and when appropriate; secondly, it concerns itself with the internal affairs of the state.[109] In relation to individuals, its tasks are, first, to formulate laws providing for private rights, the rights of communities, corporations and organizations; second, to exact services from them in the form of taxation.[110] What is important is the legislature's composition; the monarch, the executive and the Estates sit in it.[111] What is meant by 'Estates' is the

99 Ibid., § 287, pp. 188–189.
100 Ibid., § 288, p. 189.
101 Ibid., § 289, p. 189.
102 Ibid., § 290, p. 190.
103 Ibid., § 291, p. 190.
104 Ibid., § 292, pp. 190–191.
105 Ibid., § 294, pp. 191–192.
106 Ibid., § 297, p. 193.
107 Ibid., § 295, pp. 192–193.
108 Ibid., § 297, p. 193.
109 Ibid., § 298, p. 193.
110 Ibid., § 299, p. 194.
111 Ibid., § 300, p. 195.

political representation of the classes of civil society, while their significance lies in that they bring before the state the subjective consciousness of individuals, as well as allowing these to participate in public affairs.[112] Therefore, 'the Estates stand between the government in general on the one hand and the nation broken up into particulars (people and associations) on the other'. Simultaneously, in giving political representation to the citizens, the Estates 'prevent individuals from having the appearance of a mass or an aggregate and so from acquiring an unorganized opinion' contrary to the universal interest of the state.[113] So far as the landed gentry is concerned, Hegel sees this as the 'moment' of mediation between the crown and civil society. This is because, like the monarchy, their status too is hereditary and also the exercise of their private will (that is, their private interests) does not affect the rest of civil society.[114] As for the business class, it elects its own deputies to the legislature.[115] Thus there are two houses in the assembly of the estates – the agricultural class being members of an upper house, while the commercial or business class being represented in a lower house.[116]

Let us now look at the state in its external aspects. Hegel has been criticized for being in favour of war but, I think, this is a misunderstanding. Hegel does *not* prescribe a foreign policy. What he *does* is articulate the implications of the modern state in the international arena. The nature of the modern state, as this has unfolded in the previous pages of the *Philosophy of Right*, is that '[…] the state has individuality, and individuality is in essence an individual, and in the sovereign an actual, immediate individual'.[117] Like a human individual, the state as individual, can attain its identity only through relation to another. As Hegel puts it:

112 Ibid., § 301, p. 195; cf. Addition 179, p. 292.
113 Ibid., § 301, p. 197.
114 Ibid., §§ 305–307, pp. 199–200.
115 Ibid., §§ 308–311, pp. 200–203.
116 Ibid., § 312, p. 203.
117 Ibid., § 321, p. 208.

> Individuality is awareness of one's existence as a unit in sharp distinction from others. It manifests itself here in the state as a relation to other states, each of which is autonomous *vis-à-vis* the others. This autonomy embodies mind's actual awareness of itself as a unit and hence it is the most fundamental freedom which a people possesses as well as its highest dignity.[118]

Given the state's nature, war is inevitable, Hegel says. It is a necessity because the state has to actualize itself. As the interests of different states are different, this leads to conflict. Moreover, in time of war the citizens become aware of the contingency of their position; they realize that their 'rights and interests' are 'a passing phase'. They come to appreciate the fact that they owe their very existence to the state[119] and are prepared to defend it at the risk of their lives.[120] If we bear in mind what international relations were like in the nineteenth and the beginning of the twentieth centuries (until the First World War), Hegel proved to be right. The nation-states as they emerged in the course of the seventeenth, eighteenth and nineteenth centuries pursued aggressive foreign policies. What is interesting is that Hegel did not think that the modern state as it had developed at the time he was writing could, or would, ever be able to supersede this stage in a league of nations, for example. Articulating what was implied in the modern notion of the state, Hegel says that states cannot become interdependent in the same way as individuals; to satisfy their needs, individuals enter into economic relationships within the sphere of civil society; by contrast 'autonomous states are principally wholes whose needs are met within their own borders'.[121] In other words, states are self-sufficient unities and for this reason they do not develop ties of interdependence. All they need is recognition, that is, that they exist as absolute authorities and for this reason they occasionally engage in war. At the time Hegel was writing the economic system was very different from ours; there was not an international economy. Nowadays, of course, it has become increasingly difficult for a

118 Ibid., § 322, p. 208.
119 Ibid., § 324, p. 209.
120 Ibid., § 325, p. 210.
121 Ibid., § 332, p. 213.

state to survive in isolation from other states, precisely because states are no longer self-sufficient, due to the existence of an international economy.

Finally, the state has an historical dimension. World history is not a series of accidental events; rather it has a rational purpose, in so far as it is made by rational human beings. Human reason becomes concretized in historical developments.[122] The notion of freedom as self-determination becomes clearer now. *Geist* (spirit) – sometimes misleadingly translated as 'mind' – is human consciousness as concretized in culture and social-cum-political institutions at different times in history *as well as* the way(s) humans come to understand these and to reflect on them. Each historical stage is a 'necessary moment' in the development of the world spirit.[123] To begin with, in the Oriental world human civilization was centred around the freedom of one individual, the despot, who ruled arbitrarily.[124] The next significant stage in the development of human civilization was the Greek world; this was a civilization based on the freedom of the few, the citizens (democracies of ancient Greek city-states).[125] Human civilization developed in Rome (a republic and then an empire), where interpersonal relationships were formal and legal categories abstract and fixed.[126] At the time Hegel was writing human civilization had developed in the modern Germanic state, where freedom is enjoyed by all.[127] Although Hegel refers to the modern state as 'Germanic', what he really means is northern-European.

122 Ibid., §§ 341–343, pp. 216–217.
123 Ibid., §§ 345–346, p. 217.
124 Ibid., § 355, pp. 220–221.
125 Ibid., § 356, p. 221.
126 Ibid., § 357, pp. 221–222.
127 Ibid., §§ 358–360, pp. 222–223.

CHAPTER 8

Karl Marx

Karl Marx was born into a middle-class family in Trier, a very old city, in 1818. At the beginning of the nineteenth century Trier was the commercial centre of the Moselle district, a district known for its production of wine. His father was a lawyer and exemplified the 'typical rationalist of the Enlightenment'.[1] It has been suggested that there are two reasons why Marx came to adopt a critical attitude towards the society in which he was born and brought up. Firstly, he was of Jewish origin; his father had been baptized into Protestantism for fear of losing his job, while his mother was very pious. Secondly, the Rhineland, being the most advanced German region industrially and economically was opposed to the predominance of semi-feudal Prussia; simultaneously, it was strongly influenced by the ideals of the French Revolution, as it had been annexed by Napoleon. So the Rhineland was the most progressive German region both in terms of economic organization and ideas.[2]

At the age of seventeen Marx left home in order to study law at the University of Bonn. However, when his father realized that Karl was not taking his studies seriously, he sent him to the more prestigious and rigorous in its academic standards University of Berlin a year later. In Bonn the young Marx had become acquainted with romanticism; but his interest in romantic literature had been aroused earlier by the Baron von Westphalen, the father of his fiancée. The Baron had also introduced Marx to French utopian socialism, especially Saint-Simonian politics.[3] Thus when he arrived in Berlin in 1936 in order to study at the University there, Marx

1 D. McLellan, *Marx* (London: Fontana, 1975), p. 10.

2 Ibid.

3 Ibid., pp. 10–11.

had moved away from the Enlightenment rationalism of his father towards romanticism; over the past year or so he had spent a lot of time writing poems which he dedicated to Jenny von Westphalen. However, in Berlin he came under another influence, Hegelianism. The late Hegel had been professor of philosophy in Berlin since 1818 – which is, incidentally, the year Marx was born – and had died only five years before Marx arrived there. So Hegel's philosophy was still dominant; in fact, it had become a sort of an orthodoxy, Hegelian ideas having been espoused not only by philosophers but by academic lawyers, historians and theologians as well. The Hegelian influence spread well beyond the university walls, as Hegelianism had permeated the German intellectual circles. Of course, this influence was much more strongly felt in Berlin.

At the beginning the young Marx was frustrated by Hegelianism, 'the grotesque craggy melody of which', as he wrote to his father, did not appeal to him.[4] Actually, Marx eventually got sick partly, as he wrote, 'as the result of nagging annoyance at having had to make an idol of a view that I hated'.[5] However, while ill, he 'got to know Hegel from beginning to end, together with most of his disciples'.[6] Marx describes his conversion to Hegelianism as follows:

> From the idealism which, by the way, I had compared and nourished with the idealism of Kant and Fichte, I arrived at the point of seeking the idea in reality itself. If previously the gods had dwelt above the earth, now they became its centre.[7]

Soon he joined the 'Doctors' Club', which consisted mainly of university lecturers who interpreted Hegel in a radical way and who discussed Hegel's philosophy at their meetings in a small café. Out of this Club emerged the 'Young Hegelians'.[8]

4 *The Marx-Engels Reader*, ed. R. C. Tucker, 2nd edition (New York & London: W. W. Norton & Co., 1978), p. 7.
5 Ibid., p. 8.
6 Ibid.
7 Ibid., p. 7.
8 Ibid., p. 8 (and footnote 2).

In 1841 Marx submitted his doctoral thesis, entitled 'The Difference Between the Democritean and Epicurean Philosophies of Nature'.[9] Marx was perhaps interested in the philosophies of Democritus and Epicurus for the following reason: they were both materialist philosophies and allowed him to move from the idealism of Hegel towards a materialistic conception of the world. Like other 'Young Hegelians' Marx drew an analogy between Aristotelian philosophy in antiquity and Hegelian philosophy in modernity; as Aristotelianism was succeeded by materialist philosophy, so after Hegelianism philosophy would be materialistic. In other words, there was to be a similarity (analogy) between post-Aristotelian and post-Hegelian philosophy.[10] What is important for our understanding of Marx's intellectual development is that his doctoral thesis hints at the way in which Marx was to make Hegel's *thought practical* – his concern with applying Hegel's *thought* to *practice*. Marx wrote the thesis intending to pursue an academic career. However, his views were too radical for the conservative/reactionary Prussian government, so the doors of academia were closed to him, as it were. Bruno Bauer, a leading figure of the 'Young Hegelian' movement and member of the 'Doctors' Club', who had been a lecturer in theology at the University of Berlin, and with whom Marx had come to associate – in fact, Marx had hoped that Bauer would help him secure an academic position – was dismissed for unorthodoxy in 1842.[11] As his hopes to obtain a university teaching post were dashed, Marx turned to journalism instead. He started contributing articles to the *Rheinische Zeitung*, a leading opposition daily newspaper backed by liberal Rheinish industrialists, and in a few months he became editor.[12] Journalism offered the young Marx the opportunity to grapple with contemporary economic issues. Soon the newspaper was suppressed and this was the time Marx turned to a re-assessment of Hegel's political philosophy (summer of 1843).

9 Ibid., pp. 9–11.

10 Cf. McLellan, *Marx*, p. 11.

11 Ibid.

12 Ibid., p. 12.

His Critique of Hegel's Political Philosophy

According to Hegel's account in the *Philosophy of Right*, the state is the determining ground of civil society and the institution of the family; it is the comprehensive whole which supersedes them in the double sense of overcoming and preserving them. This means, Marx says, that, as Hegel sees matters, 'The family and civil society are parts of the state'.[13] Articulating what was implied in the modern notion or concept of the state, Hegel said that it was the state that determined what was right and wrong as well as morality. The state as the fully developed 'idea' – that is, as the concretization of human reason and simultaneously human reflection on social and political institutions – includes civil society, the family, morality and all legal rules. The state, as the fully developed ethical idea, is a differentiated unity or unity in difference because it contains the 'moment' of particularity which manifests itself in the sphere of civil society. However, claims Marx, 'Family and civil society constitute *themselves* as the state. They are the driving force.' In fact, 'there can be no political state without the natural basis of the family and the artificial basis of civil society; they are for it a *condition sine qua non*'.[14] Therefore, for Marx, the state is dependent on civil society. At this early stage Marx did not spell out wherein lies the state's dependence on civil society. His criticism of Hegel's philosophical articulation of the notion of the modern state is reduced to the following: Hegel mystifies the state – the state becomes a 'mystical substance'.[15] But, claims Marx, 'The state is an abstraction. The people alone is what is concrete.'[16] As he says, whereas in monarchy the people 'is subsumed under one of its particular modes of being, the political constitution', 'In democracy the *constitution itself* appears only as *one* determination, that

13 K. Marx, 'Contribution to the Critique of Hegel's *Philosophy of Right*', in *The Marx-Engels Reader*, p. 16.
14 Ibid., p. 17.
15 Ibid., p. 18.
16 Ibid.

is, the self-determination of the people'; while in monarchy there is 'the people of the constitution', in democracy there is 'the constitution of the people'.[17] In other words, democracy inverts the relationship between humans and the state, as it is presented in Hegel's political philosophy. As Marx puts it, 'Hegel starts from the state and makes man the subjectified state' – by which is meant that he starts from the idea of the state and makes man a result of this idea –, whereas 'democracy starts from man and makes the state objectified man' – by which is meant that the state is the product of man.[18] In fact, Marx's reading of Hegel's *Philosophy of Right* is not altogether correct; Hegel intended the relationship between humans and the state as a two-way process; after all, it is humans who make social and political institutions and, simultaneously, reflect on them; political institutions are the product of the conscious human will and as such an expression of human freedom; at the same time, in being aware that political institutions are the product of their will, humans recognize that these very institutions are the embodiment of their freedom (freedom as self-determination). This is what Hegel means when he says 'The state is the actuality of concrete freedom'.[19] In this sense in social and political institutions individuals recognize themselves.[20] Anyway, according to Marx, '[…] it is not the constitution which creates the people but the people which creates the constitution'.[21] As opposed to Hegel, Marx argues that only democracy 'is the true unity of the general and the particular', as in monarchy 'political man has his particular mode of being alongside unpolitical man, man as a private individual'. In monarchy

> Property, contract, marriage, civil society, all appear […] as *particular* modes of existence alongside the *political* state, as the *content* to which the *political state* is related as *organising form* […][22]

17 Ibid., p. 20.
18 Ibid.
19 G. W. F. Hegel, *Philosophy of Right*, translated with notes by T. M. Knox (Oxford: Oxford University Press, 1967), § 260, p. 160.
20 Ibid.
21 Marx, 'Contribution to the Critique of Hegel's *Philosophy of Right*', p. 20.
22 Ibid., p. 21.

By contrast, 'In democracy the *formal* principle is at the same time the *material* principle'.[23] For this reason 'democracy is the *essence of all state constitutions* – socialized man as a *particular* state constitution'.[24] Marx also challenged Hegel's description of the bureaucracy as a 'universal class', that is to say, a class which mediated between the different classes of civil society. For him, the bureaucracy developed its own interests against those of the political community at large.[25] Specifically:

> In the bureaucracy the identity of state interest and particular private aim is established in such a way that the *state interest* becomes a *particular* private aim over against other private aims.[26]

The Critique of Liberalism

After he had written the 'Contribution to the Critique of Hegel's *Philosophy of Right*' (which remained unpublished), the young Marx moved to Paris (in the autumn of 1843). Obviously, Marx was led to this decision by political considerations; Paris was the centre of radical, socialist politics and ideas. In Paris he published a Franco-German journal together with another 'Young Hegelian', Arnold Ruge. In this journal, entitled *Deutsch-Französiche Jahrbücher*, he published two essays, 'On the Jewish Question' and an introduction to the 'Contribution to the Critique of Hegel's *Philosophy of Right*', which he intended to publish at a later time.

Regarding the former essay,[27] despite its title, it is actually a critique of liberalism. This criticism is developed in the form of a critical analysis of Bauer's views on Jewish emancipation. According to Bruno Bauer, 'The

23 Ibid., pp. 20–21.
24 Ibid., p. 20.
25 Ibid., pp. 23–25.
26 Ibid., p. 25.
27 K. Marx, 'On the Jewish Question', in *The Marx-Engels Reader*, pp. 26–52.

Christian state, *by its very nature*, is incapable of emancipating the Jew'. Equally, 'the Jew, by his very nature, cannot be emancipated', because he cuts himself off 'from the rest of humanity'.[28] In other words:

> As long as the state remains Christian, and as long as the Jew remains a Jew, they are equally incapable, the one of conferring emancipation, the other of receiving it.[29]

The main barrier to the solution of the Jewish question, for Bauer, was religion; in particular, the major issue was the relation between religion and the state.[30] Therefore, Bauer suggested, on the one hand, that the Jew give up his religion, and, on the other hand, that the state cease to be Christian.[31] However, for Marx, this solution was not enough; it overlooked the real matter, which was *human* emancipation.[32]

> To be *politically* emancipated from religion is not to be finally and completely emancipated from religion, because political emancipation is not the final and absolute form of *human* emancipation.[33]

Even if state religion is abolished, religion continues to exist in the private lives of human beings – and Marx cites the example of the United States.[34] What underlies Marx's critical attitude to religion is his belief that religion is a projection of material conditions. He says:

> [...] since the existence of religion is the existence of a defect, the source of this defect must be sought in the *nature* of the state itself. Religion no longer appears as the basis, but as the *manifestation* of secular narrowness.[35]

28 Ibid., p. 27.
29 Ibid.
30 Ibid., p. 28.
31 Ibid., p. 29.
32 Ibid., p. 31.
33 Ibid., p. 32.
34 Ibid., p. 31.
35 Ibid., p. 31.

And this is as far as he goes. At this stage Marx does not elaborate this. The real problem, for Marx, lies in the fact that in modern times human beings lead a *social* life in the '*political community*' and a *private* life in '*civil society*'.[36] This, in effect, amounts to a criticism of the liberal distinction between state and civil society – that is to say, politics and the economy –, the public and private spheres. It follows that in the liberal state one can be a citizen and participate in political affairs, while, at the same time, continuing to profess one's religion as a private individual in civil society. A truly human emancipation would end all these liberal divisions.[37]

In a similar vein, Marx criticized the liberal conception of the 'rights of man'. For Bauer, the Jews would be emancipated if the state adopted the 'rights of man'. But against the liberal belief in the *universality* of the rights of man Marx insists that

> The idea of the rights of man was only discovered in the Christian world, in the last century. It is not an innate idea; on the contrary, it is acquired in a struggle against the historical traditions in which man has been educated up to the present time. The rights of man are not, therefore, a gift of nature, nor a legacy from past history, but the reward of a struggle against the accident of birth and against the privileges which history has hitherto transmitted from generation to generation.[38]

Moreover, the 'rights of man' as proclaimed by the American and French revolutionaries consist partly in '*political rights*' and as such do not dispense with religion, which they confine to the private sphere. What is more, the French 'Declaration of the Rights of Man and of the Citizen' (1791) presupposes the distinction between the 'citizen' and 'man', that is to say, the human being in his public and private existence.[39] Accordingly:

> [...] the so-called *rights of man*, as distinct from the *rights of the citizen*, are simply the rights of a *member of civil society*, that is, of egoistic man, of man separated from other men and from the community.[40]

36 Ibid., p. 34.
37 Ibid., pp. 34–40.
38 Ibid., p. 40.
39 Ibid., p. 41.
40 Ibid., p. 42.

As regards the liberal conception of liberty, it is claimed to be 'the power which man has to do anything which does not harm the rights of others', which, for Marx, meant that man was 'regarded as an isolated monad, withdrawn into himself'.[41] Thus 'Man is far from being considered, in the rights of man, as a species-being'[42] – Marx borrowed the term 'species-being' from Feuerbach, 'species-being' meaning a communal or social being. According to Marx, 'The *political revolution* dissolves civil society into its elements without *revolutionizing* these elements themselves or subjecting them to criticism'.[43] However, 'human emancipation' required the abolition of the divide between the state and civil society, public man or citizen and private individual – a divide still maintained by 'political emancipation'. As he puts it:

> Human emancipation will only be complete when the real, individual man has absorbed into himself the abstract citizen; when as an individual man, in his everyday life, in his work, and in his relationships, he has become a *species being*; and when he has recognized and organized his own powers [...] as *social* powers so that he no longer separates this social power from himself as *political* power.[44]

In the second part of the essay 'On the Jewish Question' Marx criticizes contemporary economics (capitalism), with which he associates the Jews.[45] (As is well-known, the Jews were very successful businessmen; it is for this reason that Marx directs his attack against Judaism.) He concludes this section by saying that:

> The *social* emancipation of the Jew is the *emancipation of society from Judaism*.[46]

Put differently, social emancipation consists in the emancipation from capitalism.

41 Ibid.
42 Ibid., p. 43.
43 Ibid., p. 46.
44 Ibid.
45 Ibid., pp. 47–52.
46 Ibid., p. 52.

His Revolutionary Strategy

The second essay Marx published in the *Deutsch-Französische Jahrbücher* was entitled 'Contribution to the Critique of Hegel's *Philosophy of Right*: Introduction';[47] Marx intended to publish the critique of Hegel's political philosophy later. The essay is important for two reasons. For one thing, in it Marx sets forth his views on religion. As he says:

> [...] *man makes religion*; religion does not make man. Religion is indeed man's self-consciousness and self-awareness so long as he has not found himself or has lost himself again.[48]

The influence of Hegel is evident here. For Hegel, religion was a less adequate (form of) understanding of the world than philosophy. When human beings have a religious conception of the world, in their reflection of their collective identity they do not recognize themselves in their practices and institutions (the practices and institutions *they* have produced). This is because in religion humans represent their community (collective identity) to themselves by means of pictures. This does not allow humans to reflect on the reflection of their relationships and institutions. However, in religion is *implicit* the content of philosophy. Human beings become able to reflect on their reflection of themselves (social relationships), once they come to realize that it is they themselves who have created the object of their worship (namely, God) as well as their collective identity, which has become concretized in social institutions and practices. Only then are humans able to understand that, in worshipping God, they are actually reflecting on their identity (i.e. social identity, self-recognition in another) and the social and political institutions they have created. The human community that has reached the standpoint of philosophy 'is in communion

47 K. Marx, 'Contribution to the Critique of Hegel's *Philosophy of Right*: Introduction', in *The Marx-Engels Reader*, pp. 53–65.

48 Ibid., p. 53.

with itself in *its* otherness as such'.[49] So religion is a 'representation' of the truth of philosophy; religion grasps by means of symbols what philosophy grasps conceptually. As a more comprehensive understanding of reality, philosophy comes to supersede religion in the double sense of overcoming and preserving it.[50] Marx uses Hegel's interpretation of religion in a more radical way. So when he says in the above quotation 'Religion is indeed man's self-consciousness and self-awareness so long as he has not found himself or has lost himself again' he means, in Hegelian terms, that religion is human self-consciousness so long as it does not recognize itself in social and political institutions (institutions which *it* has created) – or spirit which is not adequate to its essence. However, Marx goes on,

> [...] *man* is not an abstract being, squatting outside the world. Man is *the human world*, the state, society. This state, this society, produce religion which is an *inverted world consciousness*, because they are an *inverted world*.[51]

It follows that 'The struggle against religion is [...] indirectly a struggle against *that world* whose spiritual *aroma* is religion'.[52] In a famous, oft-quoted passage Marx says:

> Religion is the sigh of the oppressed creature, the sentiment of a heartless world, and the soul of soulless conditions. It is the *opium* of the people.[53]

In laying out his views on religion, Marx draws on another Hegelian term, 'alienation' ('*Entfremdung*'). Hegel had used this term in the *Phenomenology of Spirit* to refer to the state of those forms of human self-consciousness which were not able to recognize themselves in their creations (whether

49 G. W. F. Hegel, *Phenomenology of Spirit*, trans. A. V. Miller (Oxford: Oxford University Press, 1977), p. 479.

50 See transition from section C. ('The revealed religion') of Chapter VII (CC.) to Chapter VIII (DD.) ('Absolute Knowing') in Hegel's *Phenomenology of Spirit*.

51 K. Marx, 'Contribution to the Critique of Hegel's *Philosophy of Right*: Introduction', p. 53.

52 Ibid., p. 54.

53 Ibid.

these be custom, culture, social and political institutions, or nature as transformed by humans); therefore, human self-consciousness was alienated in so far as it regarded the objective world as independent of – even opposed to – itself. For Marx, religion is alienation because it masks the imperfections of this world by turning humans' attention to a beyond which promises an '*illusory* happiness'; and, although this beyond is a human construct (i.e. religion is made by humans), humans are not conscious of this. For this reason, Marx argued:

> The immediate *task of philosophy*, which is in the service of history, is to unmask human self-alienation in its *secular form* now that it has been unmasked in its *sacred form*.[54]

The unmasking of 'human self-alienation [...] in its *sacred form*' is a reference to Feuerbach's criticism of religion. And Marx continues:

> Thus the criticism of heaven is transformed into the criticism of earth, the *criticism of religion* into the *criticism of law*, and the *criticism of theology* into the *criticism of politics*.[55]

There is a second reason why Marx's introduction to the critique of Hegel's political philosophy is important: Marx expounds his revolutionary politics. Marx was aware of the fact that Germany was politically backward. But, like Hegel, he believed that the Germans had achieved in *thought* what other nations – particularly the French – had achieved in *practice*. Consequently, a criticism of German philosophy would point to the future of human society.[56] To be sure, he says:

> Material force can only be overthrown by material force; but theory itself becomes a material force when it has seized the masses. Theory is capable of seizing the masses [...] as soon as it becomes radical. To be radical is to grasp things by the root. But for man the root is man himself. What proves beyond doubt the radicalism of German theory, and thus its practical energy, is that it begins from the resolute *positive* abolition of religion. The criticism of religion ends with the doctrine that *man is the*

54 Ibid.
55 Ibid.
56 Ibid., pp. 54–60.

> *supreme being for man*. It ends, therefore, with the *categorical imperative to overthrow all those conditions* in which man is an abased, enslaved, abandoned, contemptible being [...][57]

Now 'Revolutions need a *passive* element, a *material* basis'.[58] For Marx, this was the 'proletariat', a class 'which has *radical chains*, a class in civil society which is not a class of civil society' but 'the dissolution of all classes'. The proletariat has 'a universal character because its sufferings are universal' and 'does not claim a *particular redress* because the wrong which is done to it is not a *particular wrong* but *wrong in general*'.[59] At the time Marx was writing the proletariat did not yet exist as a class in Germany; so Marx called for its formation. As a famous Marxist scholar has said, 'the proletariat was destined to assume the universal role that Hegel had misleadingly assigned to the bureaucracy'.[60] And, in fact, Marx anticipated that the proletariat would form an alliance with German philosophy, to the effect that 'Just as philosophy finds its *material* weapons in the proletariat, so the proletariat finds its *intellectual* weapons in philosophy'.[61] One only had to wait for 'the inner conditions' to 'ripen' and '*the day of German resurrection* will be proclaimed by *the crowing of the Gallic cock*'.[62]

The Theory of Alienation

Until the beginning of 1844 Marx had been concerned solely with politics. However, an essay by Engels, which was published together with Marx's two essays in the *Deutsch-Französische Jahrbücher*, made Marx turn his

57 Ibid., p. 60.
58 Ibid., p. 61.
59 Ibid., p. 64.
60 McLellan, *Marx*, p. 32.
61 Marx, 'Contribution to the Critique of Hegel's *Philosophy of Right*: Introduction', p. 65.
62 Ibid.

attention to economic issues. Engels's essay was entitled 'Outlines of a Critique of Political Economy'. Marx's early ideas on the capitalist economy are laid out in his notebooks, written in the spring/summer of 1844, unpublished during his lifetime and entitled by their first editors 'Economic and Philosophic Manuscripts of 1844'. One can discern the influence of Engels, German romantics such as Schiller and Feuerbach in them.[63] The 'Economic and Philosophic Manuscripts'[64] consist of three sections: a critique of classical political economy, a section on communism and a critique of Hegelian philosophy. More important for an understanding of Marx's social and political thought is the first section, in particular the part on alienated or 'estranged labour'.[65] According to Marx, in capitalist society 'the distinction between capitalist and land-rentier, like that between the tiller of the soil and the factory-worker, disappears' and society comes to be divided into two classes, 'the property-*owners* and the propertyless *workers*'.[66] Marx took classical political economy to task for failing to explain the origin of capitalism, 'the source of the division between labour and capital, and between capital and land';[67] the relation 'between exchange and competition, value and the devaluation of men, monopoly and competition' – phenomena which liberal economics simply took for granted, considered to be immutable or unchangeable; liberal economists did not consider 'the connection between this whole estrangement and the *money*-system'.[68] So how is the worker dehumanized in capitalist society? Marx's theory of 'estranged' or 'alienated' labour is the following. The worker's alienation has four aspects. Firtsly, the worker is alienated or estranged from the products of his labour, because his products come to acquire an existence independent of the worker who created them and to confront the worker as alien (that is, strange) objects. The material which the worker uses

63 D. McLellan, *Marx*, pp. 32–33.
64 K. Marx, 'Economic and Philosophic Manuscripts of 1844', in *The Marx-Engels Reader*, pp. 66–125.
65 Ibid., pp. 70–81.
66 Ibid., p. 70.
67 Ibid.
68 Ibid., p. 71.

to create a product is nature. Thus the worker mixes his creative energy with 'the *sensuous external world*'.[69] But, having created the product, he loses it, for he does not appropriate it; rather the product comes to stand opposed to the worker, as it were, as capital. Put simply, the products created by the worker do not remain his own, as they are taken away from him and sold in the market as commodities.[70] Secondly, the worker is alienated 'in the *act of production* – within the *producing activity* itself',[71] for he does not obtain satisfaction in his work;

> The worker therefore only feels himself outside his work, and in his work feels outside himself. He is at home when he is not working, and when he is working he is not at home. His labour is therefore not voluntary, but coerced; it is *forced labour*. It is therefore not the satisfaction of a need; it is merely a *means* to satisfy needs external to it.[72]

In writing this, Marx has the nature of work in nineteenth-century factories in mind. The work of an individual worker consisted of a specified, repetitive task, which could be done almost mechanically and which the worker would do for hours on end. As he later put it in the *Communist Manifesto*:

> Owing to the extensive use of machinery and to division of labour, the work of the proletarians has lost all individual character, and consequently, all charm for the workman. He becomes an appendage of the machine [...][73]

Thirdly, in his work the worker is alienated from nature as well as other humans – that is, from his '*species life*'[74] (a Feuerbachian term). The human being is a '*species*', that is, *social* or *communal* being and as such can only live together with other members of its kind. Moreover, the human being is destined to live in a harmonious relationship with nature; for nature is 'his *inorganic* body – both inasmuch as nature is (1) his direct means of life, and

69 Ibid., p. 72.
70 Ibid., pp. 71–73.
71 Ibid., p. 73.
72 Ibid., p. 74.
73 K. Marx, 'Manifesto of the Communist Party', in *The Marx-Engel Reader*, p. 479.
74 Marx, 'Economic and Philosophic Manuscripts of 1844', p. 76.

(2) the material, the object, and the instrument of his life-activity'.[75] But in his work the worker becomes estranged or alienated from both his social essence and nature; from his social essence because his work is not social – in the factory the worker leads an '*individual existence*',[76] the social aspect of his self (his social consciousness) is suppressed; from nature because – as already said – the objects, in which his power is mixed with the material of nature, are taken away from him. Fourthly, the worker is alienated from other human beings,[77] because in his work he is confined to a single task, which he performs alone, without entering into relationships with others. This being Marx's analysis of 'alienated labour', what is the alternative? This is put forth in a passage which follows a note on James Mill, not included in most editions of the 'Economic and Philosophic Manuscripts'. The alternative is exactly the opposite of each of the four foregoing aspects of 'estranged labour' and reads as follows:

> Supposing that we had produced in a human manner; each of us would in his production have doubly affirmed himself and his fellow men. I would have: (1) objectified in my production my individuality and its peculiarity and thus both in my activity enjoyed an individual expression of my life and also in looking at the object have had the individual pleasure of realizing that my personality was objective, visible to the senses and thus a power raised beyond all doubt. (2) In your enjoyment or use of my product I would have had the direct enjoyment of realizing that I had both satisfied a human need by my work and also objectified the human essence and therefore fashioned for another human being the object that met his need. (3) I would have been for you the mediator between you and the species and thus been acknowledged and felt by you as a completion of your own essence and a necessary part of yourself and have thus realized that I am confirmed both in your thought and in your love. (4) In my expression of my life I would have fashioned your expression of your life, and thus in my own activity have realized my own essence, my human, my communal essence.[78]

75 Ibid., p. 75.
76 Ibid., p. 77.
77 Ibid.
78 Quoted in McLellan, *Marx*, pp. 34–35.

His Theory of History

Marx put forth his 'materialist conception of history' in *The German Ideology*,[79] in which he distinguished his views from those of Feuerbach. According to Marx, the starting-point of history is humans' interaction with nature. As he says:

> The premises from which we begin [...] are the real individuals, their activity and the material conditions under which they live, both those which they find already existing and those produced by their activity.[80]

In other words, there is a dialectical relation between human nature as determined by the conditions of life and the transformation of those conditions by humans through their labour. Human beings 'themselves begin to distinguish themselves from animals as soon as they begin to *produce* their means of subsistence'.[81] There is no fixed human 'essence'; rather humans create themselves through their productive activity. The first premise of all history is that humans must live to be able to make history; that is, they must provide themselves with the necessities of life. The second premise is that the production of the means to satisfy primary needs leads to new needs. The third premise of historical development is human reproduction; hence the existence of the family. The fourth premise is that the production of life, both in the sense of producing the necessaries of life and of reproduction, is not only a relationship of humans to nature but a social relationship as well.[82] Consequently,

> There exists a materialistic connection of men with one another, which is determined by their needs and their mode of production, and which is as old as men themselves. This connection is ever taking on new forms, and thus presents a 'history'.[83]

79 *The German Ideology* was co-authored by Friedrich Engels.
80 K. Marx, 'The German Ideology', in *The Marx-Engels Reader*, p. 149.
81 Ibid., p. 150.
82 Ibid., pp. 155–157.
83 Ibid., p. 157.

For Marx, consciousness is a social product.[84] A given organization of society gives rise to a certain form of consciousness. With the increase of productivity, the increase of needs and the increase of population there develops a division of labour, which becomes greater with the division of material and mental labour.[85] The end of the division of labour and of the inequality it entails can come about only in communist society,

> where nobody has one exclusive sphere of activity but each can become accomplished in any branch he wishes, society regulates the general production and thus makes it possible for me to do one thing today and another tomorrow, to hunt in the morning, fish in the afternoon, rear cattle in the evening, criticise after dinner, just as I have a mind, without ever becoming hunter, fisherman, shepherd or critic.[86]

However, Marx argues, until communism arrives, there will be a conflict between the different classes. And in all class societies legal and political institutions as well as ideas come to reflect and legitimize class relations. As he puts it:

> The ideas of the ruling class are in every epoch the ruling ideas; i.e., the class which is the ruling *material* force of society, is at the same time its ruling *intellectual* force.[87]

In Marx, therefore, 'ideology' has negative connotations; it consists of this set of ideas that the dominant class has managed to impose on the rest of society and which serves its interests. Thus, there can be no universal morality and, from the Marxist point of view, liberals are wrong when they claim the universality of liberal values and ideas such as 'natural' or human rights. Rather the values preached by the 'American Declaration of Independence' (1776) as well as those that emerged out of the French Revolution (1789) were, so Marxists claim, the values and ideas of the emergent 'bourgeoisie'. In the nineteenth century the bourgeois, having become the major economic force, also established the social and political institutions appropriate to

84 Ibid., p. 158.
85 Ibid., pp. 158–159.
86 Ibid., p. 160.
87 Ibid., p. 172.

capitalist society, which (institutions) were in turn supported by the liberal ideology. As Marx says in the *Communist Manifesto*:

> [...] don't wrangle with us so long as you apply, to our intended abolition of private property, the standard of your bourgeois notions of freedom, culture, law, &c. Your very ideas are but the outgrowth of the conditions of your bourgeois production and bourgeois property, just as your jurisprudence is but the will of your class made into a law for all, a will, whose essential character and direction are determined by the economical conditions of existence of your class.[88]

His Theory of the State

We have seen that in his critique of Hegel's political philosophy Marx had argued that the state was dependent on civil society. But at that stage he had not elaborated on this. This elaboration came later, as Marx developed his view of the state. Accordingly, in the *Communist Manifesto* (first published in 1848) one reads:

> The executive of the modern State is but a committee for managing the common affairs of the whole bourgeoisie.[89]

This is an oft-quoted phrase, but what does it mean? For Marx, all historical societies are characterized by a class struggle.[90] In every historical epoch the dominant class came to oppress the others; so the state has in all ages been the instrument of the ruling class. What is distinctive in the modern era is that the class struggle has been simplified; there are fewer classes in modern capitalist society than in earlier societies. Whereas in ancient Rome there were patricians, knights, plebeians and slaves, and in mediaeval times feudal lords, vassals, guild-masters, journeymen, apprentices and serfs, for

88 Marx, 'Manifesto of the Communist Party', p. 487.
89 Ibid., p. 475.
90 Ibid., p. 473.

example, in modern capitalist society there are two classes, the bourgeoisie and the proletariat.[91] And as the dominant class the bourgeoisie also has political power;[92] in other words, it controls the state, it uses it for its own purposes. It is in this sense that civil society is the basis of the state, for Marx. The modern liberal state is dependent on the division of labour of capitalist society. Thus, civil society or the economic sphere is – in Marxist terminology – the *base*, while the state is the *superstructure*; part of the *superstructure* are also forms of social consciousness such as religion, philosophy and art.[93]

Now one has to be careful because this can lead, and has led, to an over-simplification of Marxism. Clearly, what Marx was concerned to show is that there is a correspondence between the economy and the political organization of society to the effect that the political state proper is adapted to the prevailing economic circumstances. Therefore, the modern liberal state is appropriate to the capitalist economy and in this sense it was created by it; Marx says that feudal relations gave way to free competition, which was 'accompanied by a social and political constitution adapted to it, and by the economical and political sway of the bourgeois class'.[94] However, there is a crucial difference between saying that there is a *correspondence* between base and superstructure and saying that the base *conditions* or *determines* the political superstructure – 'conditions' is less strong than 'determines', for that matter. There has been a tendency to see in Marx's theory a simple *economic determinism*, to the effect that the economic base determines the form of the state. There are at least two reasons why this oversimplification has occurred. For one thing, Marx is partly responsible for this, for, in his attempt to emphasize the significance of the nature of the economy (the 'mode of production' as he calls it), he over-stressed it. At a more philosophical level, one can see how Marx's attempt to differentiate himself from Hegel made him lay emphasis on civil society. For

91 Ibid., p. 474.
92 Ibid., p. 475.
93 On 'basis' and 'superstructure' see Marx, 'The German Ideology', p. 163.
94 Marx, 'Manifesto of the Communist Party', p. 478.

another, Marx's theory was used both in his lifetime and after his death for revolutionary purposes and, as a result, was simplified. However, as it has been noted, Marx's terminology in describing the relationship between the economy and the state is flexible; he sometimes used the verb 'condition', sometimes the verb 'determine' and sometimes 'correspond to'.[95]

Given that, according to Marx, 'Political power [...] is merely the organised power of one class for oppressing another', in a communist society where all class divisions will have disappeared, 'the public power will lose its political character'[96] – that is to say, the state will also disappear. This means that Marx conceived of the state as a transitory phenomenon. In communism

> In place of the old bourgeois society, with its classes and class antagonisms, we shall have an association, in which the free development of each is the condition for the free development of all.[97]

95 McLellan, *Marx*, p. 41.
96 Marx, 'Manifesto of the Communist Party', p. 490.
97 Ibid., p. 491.

Bibliography

Works which discuss several political thinkers

Hampsher-Monk, I., *A History of Modern Political Thought: Major Political Thinkers from Hobbes to Marx* (Oxford & Cambridge, Massachusetts: Blackwell, 1992).
Jones, T., *Modern Political Thinkers and Ideas: An Historical Introduction* (London: Routledge, 2002).
Lively, J. and Reeve, A. (eds), *Modern Political Theory From Hobbes to Marx: Key Debates* (London & New York: Routledge, 1989).
Muschamp, D. (ed.), *Political Thinkers* (Basingstoke: Macmillan, 1986).
Plamenatz, J., *Man & Society: Political and Social Theories From Machiavelli to Marx*, a new edition revised by M. E. Plamenatz and R. Wokler (London & New York: Longman, 1992) – Vol. I: *From the Middle Ages to Locke*, Vol. II: *From Montesquieu to the Early Socialists*, Vol. III: *Hegel, Marx and Engels, and the Idea of Progress.*
Thompson, D. (ed.), *Political Ideas* (Harmondsworth: Penguin, 1969).

Discussion of the writings of major political thinkers from a feminist perspective

Coole, D. H., *Women in Political Theory: From Ancient Misogyny to Contemporary Feminism*, 2nd edition (Hemel Hempstead: Harvester-Wheatsheaf, 1993).

General

D. Miller et al. (eds), *The Blackwell Encyclopedia of Political Thought* (Oxford: Blackwell, 1991).

1. Thomas Hobbes

Primary Text

T. Hobbes, *Leviathan*, R. Tuck (ed.) (Cambridge: Cambridge University Press, 1992, c. 1991).

Secondary Literature

Brown, K. (ed.), *Hobbes Studies* (Oxford: Blackwell, 1965).

Dietz, M. G. (ed.), *Thomas Hobbes and Political Theory* (Lawrence, Kansas & London: University of Kansas, 1990).

Forsyth, M., 'Thomas Hobbes: *Leviathan*', in M. Forsyth & M. Keens-Soper (eds), *The Political Classics: A Guide to the Essential Texts From Plato to Rousseau* (Oxford & New York: Oxford University Press, 1992).

Goldsmith, M. M., *Hobbes's Science of Politics* (London: Columbia University Press, 1966).

Hampton, J., *Hobbes and the Social Contract Tradition* (Cambridge: Cambridge University Press, 1986).

Kramer, M. H., *Hobbes and the Paradoxes of Political Origins* (London: Macmillan, 1997).

Leyden, W. von, *Hobbes and Locke: The Politics of Freedom and Obligation* (London: Macmillan, 1982).

Macpherson, C. B., *The Political Theory of Possessive Individualism: Hobbes to Locke* (Oxford: Clarendon Press, 1962).

——, *Democratic Theory: Essays in Retrieval* (Oxford: Clarendon Press, 1973), Chapter XIV: 'Hobbes' Bourgeois Man'.

Miller, D., 'The Macpherson Version', *Political Studies* (1982).

Morris, C. W., *The Social Contract Theorists: Critical Essays on Hobbes, Locke and Rousseau* (Lanham, Maryland: Rowman & Littlefield Publishers, 1999).

Raphael, D. D., *Hobbes, Morals and Politics* (London: Allen & Unwin, 1977).

Riley, P., 'Will and Legitimacy in the Philosophy of Hobbes', *Political Studies* (1973).

——, *Will and Political Legitimacy: A Critical Exposition of Social Contract Theory in Hobbes, Locke, Rousseau, Kant and Hegel* (Cambridge, Mass.: Harvard University Press, 1982).

Rogers, G. A. J. (ed.), *Leviathan: Contemporary Responses to the Political Theory of Thomas Hobbes* (Bristol: Thoemmes, 1995).

Skinner, Q., *Visions of Politics*, Vol. 3: *Hobbes and Civil Science* (Cambridge: Cambridge University Press, 2002).

Slomp, G., *Thomas Hobbes and the Political Philosophy of Glory* (London: Macmillan, 2000).

Strauss, L., *The Political Philosophy of Hobbes: Its Basis and Its Genesis*, trans. Elsa M. Sinclair (Chicago: University of Chicago Press, 1963).
Trainor, B., 'Hobbes' Sovereign and the Right of Self-Defence', *Political Studies*, Vol. 32, No. 2 (1984).
Tuck, R., *Hobbes* (Oxford: Oxford University Press, 1989).
Warrender, H., *The Political Philosophy of Hobbes: His Theory of Obligation* (Oxford: Clarendon Press, 1957).
Zvesper, J., 'Hobbes' Individualistic Analysis of the Family', *Politics*, Vol. 5, No. 2 (1985).

2. John Locke

Primary Text

J. Locke, *Two Treatises of Government*, ed. P. Laslett (Cambridge: Cambridge University Press, 1992, c. 1988).

Secondary Literature

Berlin, I., 'Hobbes, Locke and Professor Macpherson', *Political Quarterly* (1964).
Cohen, J., 'Structure, Choice and Hospitality: Locke's Theory of the State', *Philosophy and Public Affairs*, Vol. 15, No. 4 (1986).
Coleman, J., *John Locke's Moral Philosophy* (Edinburgh: Edinburgh University Press, 1983).
Day, J. P., 'Locke on Property', *Philosophical Quarterly*, Vol. 16 (1966).
Dunn, J., 'Justice and Locke's Political Theory', *Political Studies*, Vol. 16, No. 1 (1968).
——, *The Political Thought of John Locke: An Historical Account of the Argument of the 'Two Treatises of Government'* (Cambridge: Cambridge University Press, 1969).
——, *Locke* (Oxford: Oxford University Press, 1984).
Gough, J. W., *John Locke's Political Philosophy* (Oxford: Clarendon Press, 1973).
Harpham, E. J. (ed.), *John Locke's 'Two Treatises of Government': New Interpretations* (Lawrence, Kan.: University Press of Kansas, 1992).
Hughes, C., 'John Locke: *The Second Treatise of Government*', in M. Forsyth & M. Keens-Soper (eds), *The Political Classics: A Guide to the Essential Texts From Plato to Rousseau* (Oxford & New York: Oxford University Press, 1992).
Leyden, W. von, *Hobbes and Locke: The Politics of Freedom and Obligation* (London: Macmillan, 1982).

Macpherson, C. B., *The Political Theory of Possessive Individualism: Hobbes to Locke* (Oxford: Clarendon Press, 1962).
——, *Democratic Theory: Essays in Retrieval* (Oxford: Clarendon Press, 1973), Chapter XIII: 'Natural Rights in Hobbes and Locke'.
Milton, J. R. (ed.), *Locke's Moral, Political and Legal Philosophy* (Brookfield, Vt.: Ashgate, 1999).
Morris, C. W., *The Social Contract Theorists: Critical Essays on Hobbes, Locke and Rousseau* (Lanham, Maryland: Rowman & Littlefield Publishers, 1999).
Parry, G., *John Locke* (London: Allen & Unwin, 1978).
Riley, P., *Will and Political Legitimacy: A Critical Exposition of Social Contract Theory in Hobbes, Locke, Rousseau, Kant and Hegel* (Cambridge, Mass.: Harvard University Press, 1982).
Ryan, A., 'Locke and the Dictatorship of the Bourgeoisie', *Political Studies*, Vol. 13, No. 2 (1965).
Selinger, M., *The Liberal Politics of John Locke* (London: Allen & Unwin, 1968).
Simmons, A., 'Locke's State of Nature', *Political Theory* (1989).
Tully, J., *A Discourse on Property: John Locke and his Adversaries* (Cambridge: Cambridge University Press, 1982).
Waldron, J., *God, Locke, and Equality: Christian Foundations in Locke's Political Thought* (Cambridge: Cambridge University Press, 2002).
Zvesper, J., 'The Utility of Consent in John Locke's Political Philosophy', *Political Studies*, Vol. 32, No. 1 (1984).

3. Jeremy Bentham

Primary Texts

J. Bentham, *An Introduction to the Principles of Morals and Legislation*, edited by J. H. Burns and H. L. A. Hart, with a new introduction by F. Rosen (New York: Oxford University Press, 1996).
Bentham's Political Thought, ed. B. Parekh (London: Croom Helm, 1973).

Secondary Literature

Crimmins, J., 'Bentham's Political Radicalism Re-examined', *Journal of the History of Ideas*, Vol. 55, No. 2 (1994).
Dinwiddy, J., 'Bentham's Transition to Political Radicalism, 1809–10', *Journal of the History of Ideas*, Vol. 36 (1975).
——, *Bentham* (Oxford: Oxford University Press, 1989).
Halévy, E., *The Growth of Philosophic Radicalism* (London: Faber & Faber, 1928).
Harrison, R., *Bentham* (London: Routledge & Kegan Paul, 1983).
Kelly, P., *Utilitarianism and Distributive Justice: Jeremy Bentham and the Civil Law* (Oxford: Clarendon Press, 1990).
Lyons, D., *In the Interest of the Governed*, revised edition (Oxford: Clarendon Press, 1991).
Manning, D. J., *The Mind of Jeremy Bentham* (London: Longmans, 1968).
Parekh, B. (ed.), *Jeremy Bentham: Critical Assessments*, 4 vols (London & New York: Routledge, 1993).
Plamenatz, J., *The English Utilitarians*, 2nd revised edition (Oxford: Basil Blackwell, 1958).
Postema, G. J., *Bentham and the Common Law Tradition* (Oxford: Clarendon Press, 1986).
Rosen, F., *Jeremy Bentham and Representative Democracy: A Study of the Constitutional Code* (Oxford: Clarendon Press, 1983).
Rosenblum, *Bentham's Theory of the Modern State* (Cambridge, Mass. & London: Harvard University Press, 1978).
Steintrager, J., *Bentham* (London: Allen & Unwin, 1977).
Waldron, J., *Nonsense Upon Stilts: Bentham, Burke and Marx on the Rights of Man* (London: Methuen, 1987).
Woodard, C., *Utilitarian Legislation: An Examination of the Difficulties Involved in Moving From Individual to Public Utility* (Coventry: Department of Politics and International Studies, University of Warwick, 1992).

4. John Stuart Mill

Primary Texts

J. S. Mill, 'Autobiography', in J. S. Mill and T. Carlyle, *Autobiography etc. Essays and Address*, ed. C. W. Eliot, The Harvard Classics (Norwalk, Connecticut: The Easton Press, 1993).
——, *Principles of Political Economy*, edited with an introduction by Sir William Ashley (Fairfield, N.J.: Augustus M. Kelley, 1987).

——, 'Essay on Bentham' and 'Utilitarianism', in *Utilitarianism*, edited with an introduction by M. Warnock (London: Collins, 1962).
——, 'On Liberty', 'Utilitarianism' and 'The Subjection of Women', in *On Liberty and Other Essays*, edited with and introduction by J. Gray (Oxford & New York: Oxford University Press, 1991).
——, 'On Liberty', 'The Subjection of Women' and 'Chapters on Socialism', in *On Liberty and Other Writings*, ed. S. Collini (Cambridge: Cambridge University Press, 1989).

Secondary Literature

Anderson, B., 'Mill on Bentham: From Ideology to Humanised Utilitarianism', *History of Political Thought* (1983).
Annas, J., 'Mill and the Subjection of Women', *Philosophy* (1977).
Berger, F. R., *Happiness, Justice and Freedom: The Moral and Political Philosophy of John Stuart Mill* (Berkeley: University of California Press, 1984).
Berlin, I., 'John Stuart Mill and the Ends of Life' in his *Four Essays on Liberty* (Oxford: Oxford University Press, 1969).
Boralevi, L. C., 'Utilitarianism and Feminism', in E. Kennedy and S. Mendus (eds), *Women in Western Political Philosophy: Kant to Nietzsche* (Brighton: Wheatsheaf Books, 1987).
Brittan, S., *Towards a Humane Individualism* (London: John Stuart Mill Institute, 1998).
Brown, D., 'Mill on Harm to Others' Interests', *Political Studies*, Vol. 26 (1978).
Coole, D. H., *Women in Political Theory: From Ancient Misogyny to Contemporary Feminism*, 2nd edition (Hemel Hempstead: Harvester-Wheatsheaf, 1993).
Cowling, M., *Mill and Liberalism* (Cambridge: Cambridge University Press, 1963).
Crisp, R., *Routledge Philosophy Guidebook to Mill on Utilitarianism* (London & New York: Routledge, 1997).
Donner, W., *The Liberal Self: John Stuart Mill's Moral and Political Philosophy* (Ithaca, New York: Cornell University Press, 1991).
——, 'John Stuart Mill's Liberal Feminism', *Philosophical Studies*, Vol. 69 nos. 2–3 (1993).
Duncan, G., *Marx and Mill: Two Views of Social Conflict and Social Harmony* (Cambridge: Cambridge University Press, 1973).
Eisenach, E. J. (ed.), *Mill and the Moral Character of Liberalism* (University Park, Pa.: Pennsylvania State University Press, 1998).
Friedman, R. B., 'A New Exploration of Mill's Essay on Liberty', *Political Studies* (1966).
Goldstein, L., 'Mill, Marx and Women's Liberation', *Journal of the History of Philosophy*, Vol. 18 (1980).
Gray, J., *Mill on Liberty. A Defence*, 2nd edition (London: Routledge, 1996).
Halliday, R. J., *John Stuart Mill* (London: Allen & Unwin, 1976).

Hamburger, J., *Intellectuals in Politics: John Stuart Mill and the Philosophical Radicals* (New Haven & London: Yale University Press, 1965).

——, *John Stuart Mill on Liberty and Control* (Princeton, N.J.: Princeton University Press, 1999).

Harris, A. L., 'John Stuart Mill's Theory of Progress', *Ethics* (1956).

Hughes, P., 'The Reality vs. The Ideal: J. S. Mill's Treatment of Women, Workers and Private Property', *Canadian Journal of Political Science*, Vol. 12 (1979).

Lipkes, J., *Politics, Religion and Classical Political Economy in Britain: John Stuart Mill and his Followers* (New York: St. Martin's Press, 1998).

Lyons, D. (ed.), *Mill's Utilitarianism: Critical Essays* (Lanham, Md.: Rowman & Littlefield Publishers, 1997).

Okin, S. M., *Women in Western Political Thought* (Princeton, New Jersey: Princeton University Press, 1979), Part IV.

O'Rourke, K. C., *John Stuart Mill and Freedom of Expression: The Genesis of A Theory* (London: Routledge, 2001).

Radcliff, P. (ed.), *The Limits of Liberty: Studies of Mill's on Liberty* (Belmont, Ca.: Wadsworth, 1966).

Rees, J., 'Was Mill for Liberty?', *Political Studies*, Vol. 14 (1966).

——, *John Stuart Mill's 'On Liberty'* (Oxford: Clarendon Press, 1985).

Riley, J., *Liberal Utilitarianism: Social Choice Theory and J. S. Mill's Philosophy* (Cambridge: Cambridge University Press, 1988).

——, *Mill on Liberty* (London & New York: Routledge, 1998).

——, *Mill's Radical Liberalism: an Essay in Retrieval* (London: Routledge, 2000).

Robson, J. M., *The Improvement of Mankind: The Social and Political Thought of John Stuart Mill* (London: Routledge & Kegan Paul; Toronto: University of Toronto Press, 1968).

Rosen, F., 'Bentham and Mill on Liberty and Justice' in G. Fever and F. Rosen (eds), *Lives, Liberties and the Public Good* (Basingstoke: Macmillan in association with the London School of Economics and Political Science, 1987).

Ryan, A., *The Philosophy of John Stuart Mill* (London: Macmillan, 1970).

——, *J. S. Mill* (London: Routledge & Kegan Paul, 1974).

Schneewind, J. B. (ed.), *Mill. A Collection of Critical Essays* (London: University of Notre Dame Press, 1968).

Schwartz, P., *The New Political Economy of J. S. Mill* (London: Weidenfeld & Nicolson for the London School of Economics and Political Science, 1972).

Semmell, B., *J. S. Mill and the Pursuit of Virtue* (New Haven: Yale University Press, 1984).

Shanley, M., 'Marital Slavery and Friendship: John Stuart Mill's *The Subjection of Women*', *Political Theory*, Vol. 9, No. 2 (1981).

Smart, P., *Mill and Marx: Individual Liberty and the Roads to Freedom* (Manchester: Manchester University Press, 1990).

Stafford, W., *John Stuart Mill* (London: Macmillan, 1998).

Ten, C. L., *Mill on Liberty* (Oxford: Clarendon Press, 1980).

——, *Mill's Moral, Political and Legal Philosophy* (Aldershot & Brookfield, Vt.: Ashgate/Darmouth, 1999).

Thomas, W., *The Philosophic Radicals: Nine Studies in Theory and Practice, 1817–1841* (Oxford: Clarendon Press, 1979).

Thornton, N., *The Problem of Liberalism in the Thought of J. S. Mill* (New York & London: Garland, 1987).

Tulloch, G., *Mill and Sexual Equality* (Hemel Hempstead: Wheatsheaf, 1989, c. 1988).

Urbinary, N., 'John Stuart Mill on Androgyny and Ideal Marriage', *Political Theory* (1991).

Waldron, J., 'Mill and the Value of Moral Distress', *Political Studies*, Vol. 35 (1987).

Williams, G., 'Mill's Principle of Liberty', *Political Studies*, Vol. 24 (1976).

Wollheim, P., 'John Stuart Mill and Isaiah Berlin: The Ends of Life and the Preliminaries of Morality' in A. Ryan (ed.), *The Idea of Freedom: Essays in Honour of Isaiah Berlin* (Oxford: Oxford University Press, 1979).

Wollheim, R., 'J. S. Mill and the Limits of State Action', *Social Research*, Vol. 40 (1973).

Wood, J. C. (ed.), *John Stuart Mill. Critical Assessments* (London: Croom Helm, 1986, c. 1987).

5. Jean-Jacques Rousseau

Primary Texts

The Political Writings of Jean Jacques Rousseau, edited from the original manuscripts and authentic editions with introduction and notes by C. E. Vaughan, 2 vols (Cambridge: Cambridge University Press, 1915; reprinted Oxford: Basil Blackwell, 1962).

J.-J. Rousseau, *A Discourse on Inequality*, translated with an introduction and notes by M. Cranston (Harmondsworth: Penguin, 1984).

——, *The Social Contract*, translated and introduced by M. Cranston (Harmondsworth: Penguin, 1968).

Secondary Literature

Barnard, F. M., 'Will and Political Rationality in Rousseau', *Political Studies*, Vol. 32, No. 3 (1984).

Berman, M., *The Politics of Authenticity: Radical Individualism and the Emergence of Modern Society* (London: Allen & Unwin, 1971).

Cameron, D., *The Social Thought of Rousseau and Burke: A Comparative Study* (London: Weidenfeld and Nicolson for the London School of Economics and Political Science, 1973).

Canovan, M., 'Rousseau's Two Concepts of Citizenship', in E. Kennedy and S. Mendus (eds), *Women in Western Political Philosophy: Kant to Nietzsche* (Brighton: Wheatsheaf Books, 1987).

Charvet, J., *The Social Problem in the Philosophy of Rousseau* (London: Cambridge University Press, 1974).

Cobban, A., *Rousseau and the Idea of the Modern State* (London: Allen & Unwin, 1974).

Colletti, L., 'Rousseau as Critic of Civil Society', in his *From Rousseau to Lenin: Studies in Ideology and Society* (New York: Monthly Review Press, 1972).

Cullen, D. E., *Freedom in Rousseau's Political Philosophy* (De Kalb: Northern Illinois University Press, 1993).

Dent, N. J. H., *Rousseau: An Introduction to his Psychological, Social and Political Theory* (Oxford: Basil Blackwell, 1988).

Ellenbury, S., *Rousseau's Political Philosophy: An Interpretation From Within* (Ithaca & London: Cornell University Press, 1976).

Fralin, R., *Rousseau and Representation: A Study of the Development of his Concept of Political Institutions* (New York: Columbia University Press, 1978).

Gildin, H., *Rousseau's Social Contract: The Design of the Argument* (Chicago & London: University of Chicago Press, 1983).

Hall, J. C., *Rousseau: An Introduction to his Political Philosophy* (London: Macmillan, 1973).

Hampson, N., *Will and Circumstance: Montesquieu, Rousseau and the French Revolution* (London: Duckworth; Norman, University of Oklahoma Press, 1983).

Keens-Soper, M., 'Jean-Jacques Rousseau: *The Social Contract*', in M. Forsyth and M. Keens-Soper (eds), *The Political Classics: A Guide to the Essential Texts From Plato to Rousseau* (Oxford & New York: Oxford University Press, 1992).

Lemas, R., 'Rousseau's Animadversions on Representative Democracy', *Social Theory and Practice*, Vol. 3, No. 3 (1975).

Levin, A., *The General Will: Rousseau, Marx, Communism* (Cambridge: Cambridge University Press, 1993).

MacAdam, J. I., 'The Discourse on Inequality and the Social Contract', *Philosophy*, Vol. 47 (1972).

Masters, R. D., *The Political Philosophy of Rousseau* (Princeton, N.J.: Princeton University Press, 1968).

Miller, J., *Rousseau: Dreamer of Democracy* (New Haven: Yale University Press, 1984).

Morris, C. W., *The Social Contract Theorists: Critical Essays on Hobbes, Locke and Rousseau* (Lanham, Maryland: Rowman & Littlefield Publishers, 1999).

Riley, P., *Will and Political Legitimacy: A Critical Exposition of Social Contract Theory in Hobbes, Locke, Rousseau, Kant and Hegel* (Cambridge, Mass.: Harvard University Press, 1982).

——, 'Rousseau's General Will: Freedom of a Particular Kind', *Political Studies*, Vol. 39, No. 1 (1991).
Roche, K., *Rousseau: Stoic and Romantic* (London: Methuen, 1974).
Rosenblatt, H., *Rousseau and Geneva: From the 'First Discourse' to the 'Social Contract', 1749–1762* (Cambridge: Cambridge University Press, 1997).
Schwartzberg, M., 'Rousseau on Fundamental Law', *Political Studies*, Vol. 51, No. 2 (2003).
Shklar, J. N., *Men and Citizens: A Study of Rousseau's Social Theory* (London: Cambridge University Press, 1969).
Talmon, J. L., *The Rise of Totalitarian Democracy* (Boston: Beacon Press, 1952).
Thompson, D., 'Rousseau and the General Will' in D. Thompson (ed.), *Political Ideas* (Harmondsworth: Penguin, 1969).
Viroli, M., 'The Concept of *Ordre* and the Language of Classical Republicanism in Jean-Jacques Rousseau', in A. Pagden (ed.), *The Languages of Political Theory in Early-Modern Europe* (Cambridge: Cambridge University Press, 1987).
Wokler, R., 'Rousseau's Two Concepts of Liberty' in G. Feaver and F. Rosen (eds), *Lives, Liberties and the Public Good* (Basingstoke: Macmillan in association with the London School of Economics and Political Science, 1987).
——, *The Social Thought of J. J. Rousseau* (New York: Carland Pub., 1987).
——, *Rousseau* (Oxford & New York: Oxford University Press, 1995).
——(ed.), *Rousseau and Liberty* (Manchester & New York: Manchester University Press; Distributed in the USA and Canada by St. Martin's Press, 1995).

6. Edmund Burke

Primary Texts

E. Burke, *Correspondence*, edited by C. William, Earl Fitzwilliam and Sir R. Bourke, 4 volumes (London: Francis & John Rivington, 1844).
——, *Reflections on the Revolution in France*, edited with an introduction by L. G. Mitchell (Oxford: Oxford University Press, 1993).

Secondary Literature

Cameron, D., *The Social Thought of Rousseau and Burke: A Comparative Study* (London: Weidenfeld and Nicolson for the London School of Economics and Political Science, 1973).

Canavan, F. F., *The Political Reason of Edmund Burke* (Durham, N.C.: Published by the Lilly Endowment Research Program in Christianity and Politics by the Duke University Press, 1960).

Cobban, A., *Edmund Burke and the Revolt Against the Eighteenth Century* (London: Allen & Unwin, 1973).

Conniff, J., *The Useful Cobbler: Edmund Burke and the Politics of Progress* (New York: State University of New York Press, 1994).

Dreyer, F., *Burke's Politics: A Study in Whig Orthodoxy* (Waterloo, Ont.: Wilfrid Laurier University Press, 1979).

Freeman, M., 'Edmund Burke and the Theory of Revolution', *Political Theory*, Vol. 6 (1978).

——, *Edmund Burke and the Critique of Political Radicalism* (Oxford: Blackwell, 1980).

Gurr, T. R., 'Burke and the Modern Theory of Revolution', *Political Theory*, Vol. 6 (1978).

Hindson, P., *Burke's Dramatic Theory of Politics* (Aldershot: Avebury, 1988).

Lock, F. P., *Burke's Reflections on the Revolution in France* (London: Allen & Unwin, 1985).

Macpherson, C. B., *Burke* (Oxford: Oxford University Press, 1980).

O'Gorman, F., *Edmund Burke. His Political Philosophy* (London: Allen & Unwin, 1973).

Parkin, C., *The Moral Basis of Burke's Political Thought: An Essay* (Cambridge: Cambridge University Press, 1956).

Stanlis, P., *Edmund Burke: The Enlightenment and Revolution* (New Brunswick, N. J.: Transaction, 1991).

Vaughan, C. E., *Studies in the History of Political Philosophy Before and After Rousseau* (Manchester: Manchester University Press, 1925), Vol. II: *From Burke to Mazzini.*

Waldron, J., *Nonsense Upon Stilts: Bentham, Burke and Marx on the Rights of Man* (London: Methuen, 1987).

Wilkins, B. T., *The Problem of Burke's Political Philosophy* (Oxford: Clarendon Press, 1967).

7. G. W. F. Hegel

Primary Texts

G. W. F. Hegel, *Phenomenology of Spirit*, trans. A. V. Miller (Oxford: Oxford University Press, 1977).

——, *Philosophy of Right*, translated with notes by T. M. Knox (Oxford: Oxford University Press, 1967).

Works by Other Authors

I. Kant, *Foundations of the Metaphysics of Morals*, 2nd revised edition, translated with an introduction by L. W. Beck, Library of Liberal Arts (New York: Macmillan, 1990).

Secondary Literature

Avineri, S., *Hegel's Theory of the Modern State* (Cambridge: Cambridge University Press, 1972).

Buchwalter, A., 'Hegel's Concept of Virtue', *Political Theory*, Vol. 16, No. 1 (1992).

Cristi, F. R., 'The *Hegelsche Mitte* and Hegel's Monarch', *Political Theory*, Vol. 11, No. 4 (1983).

Cullen, B., *Hegel's Social and Political Thought: An Introduction* (Dublin & New York: Gill & Macmillan, 1979).

Fackenheim, E. L., 'On the Actuality of the Rational and the Rationality of the Actual', *Review of Metaphysics*, Vol. 23, No. 4 (1970).

Fine, R., *After the Revolution: The Politics of Hegel, Marx and Arendt* (London: UCL, 2000).

——, *Political Investigations: Hegel, Marx, Arendt* (New York: Routledge, 2001).

Fraser, I., *Hegel and Marx: The Concept of Need* (Edinburgh: Edinburgh University Press, 1998).

Hardimon, M., 'The Project of Reconciliation: Hegel's Social Philosophy', *Philosophy and Public Affairs*, Vol. 21, No. 2 (1992).

Hodge, J., 'Women and the Hegelian State', in E. Kennedy and S. Mendus (eds), *Women in Western Political Philosophy: Kant to Nietzsche* (Brighton: Wheatsheaf Books, 1987).

Hyppolite, J., *Studies on Marx and Hegel* (London: Heinemann Educational, 1969).

Kaufmann, W. (ed.), *Hegel's Political Philosophy* (New York: Atherton Press, 1970).

Kelly, G. A., *Hegel's Retreat from Eleusis: Studies in Political Thought* (Princeton, Guildford: Princeton University Press, 1978).
Kierans, K., 'The Concept of Ethical Life in Hegel's Philosophy of Right', *History of Political Thought*, Vol. 13, No. 3 (1992).
Knowles, D., *Hegel and the Philosophy of Right* (London & New York: Routledge, 2002).
MacIntyre, A. (ed.), *Hegel: A Collection of Critical Essays* (Notre Dame: University of Notre Dame Press, 1972).
Matetz, D. J., 'Hegel on Right as Actualized Will', *Political Theory*, Vol. 17, No. 1 (1989).
Neuhouser, F., *Foundations of Hegel's Social Theory: Actualizing Freedom* (Cambridge, Massachusetts & London: Harvard University Press, 2000).
Pelczynski, Z., *Hegel's Political Philosophy: Problems and Perspectives* (Cambridge: Cambridge University Press, 1971).
——, *The State and Civil Society: Studies in Hegel's Political Philosophy* (Cambridge: Cambridge University Press, 1984).
Peperzak, A. T., *Philosophy and Politics: A Commentary on the Preface to Hegel's Philosophy of Right* (Dordrecht: Nijhoff, 1987).
Pinkard, T., 'Freedom and Social Categories in Hegel's Ethics', *Philosophy and Phenomenological Research*, Vol. 47, No. 2 (1986).
Pippin, R., 'Hegel's Political Argument and the Problem of *Verwicklichung*', *Political Theory*, Vol. 9 (1981).
Planinc, Z., 'Family and Civil Society in Hegel's "Philosophy of Right"', *History of Political Thought*, Vol. 12, No. 2 (1991).
Plant, R., *Hegel: An Introduction*, 2nd edition (Oxford: Basil Blackwell, 1983).
Ritter, J., *Hegel and the French Revolution: Essays on the Philosophy of Right* (Cambridge, Mass.: MIT Press, 1982).
Schmidt, J., 'A Paideia for the '*Burger als Bourgeois*': The Concept of Civil Society in Hegel's Political Thought', *History of Political Thought*, Vol. 2, No. 3 (1981).
Seeburger, W., 'The Political Significance of Hegel's Concept of History', *Monist*, Vol. 48, No. 1 (1964).
Singer, P., *Hegel* (Oxford: Oxford University Press, 1983).
Smith, S. B., *Hegel's Critique of Liberalism: Rights in Context* (Chicago & London: The University of Chicago Press, 1989).
——, 'What is 'Right' in Hegel's *Philosophy of Right?*', *American Political Science Review*, Vol. 83 (1989).
Stillman, P., 'Hegel's Critique of Liberal Theories of Right', *American Political Science Review*, Vol. 68 (1974).
——, 'Property, Freedom and Individuality in Hegel's and Marx's Political Thought', *Nomos*, Vol. 22 (1980).
Taylor, C., *Hegel* (Cambridge: Cambridge University Press, 1975).
——, *Hegel and Modern Society* (Cambridge: Cambridge University Press, 1979).

Tunick, M., 'Hegel's Justification of Hereditary Monarchy', *History of Political Thought*, Vol. 12, No. 3 (1991).
Verene, D. P. (ed.), *Hegel's Social and Political Thought: The Philosophy of Objective Spirit* (Atlantic Highlands, N. J.: Humanities Press, 1978).
Williams, R. R., *Hegel's Ethics of Recognition* (Berkeley, Los Angeles & London: University of California Press, 1997), Part II: 'Recognition in the *Philosophy of Right*'.
Williams, R. (ed.), *Beyond Liberalism and Communitarianism: Studies on Hegel's 'Philosophy of Right'* (Albany: State University of New York Press, 2001).
Wood, A., *Hegel's Ethical Thought* (Cambridge: Cambridge University Press, 1990).
Yack, B., 'The Rationality of Hegel's Concept of Monarchy', *American Political Science Review*, Vol. 74 (1980).

8. Karl Marx

Primary Texts

The Marx-Engels Reader, 2nd edition, ed. R. C. Tucker (New York & London: W. W. Norton Co., 1978).
K. Marx and F. Engels, *The German Ideology*, Part One with selections from Parts Two and Three, together with Marx's 'Introduction to a Critique of Political Economy', edited and introduced by C. J. Arthur, 2nd edition (London: Lawrence & Wishart, 1974).
——, *The Communist Manifesto*, with an introduction and notes by A. J. P. Taylor (Harmondsworth: Penguin, 1985).

Secondary Literature

Althusser, L., *For Marx*, trans. B. Brewster (London: Verso, 1979).
Avineri, S., *The Social and Political Thought of Karl Marx* (Cambridge: Cambridge University Press, 1968).
Buchanan, A., *Marx and Justice. The Radical Critique of Liberalism* (London: Methuen, 1982).
Burns, T. and Fraser, I., *The Hegel-Marx Connection* (Basingstoke: Macmillan, 2000).
Carter, A., *Marx: A Radical Critique* (Brighton: Wheatsheaf, 1988).
Carver, T., *Marx's Social Theory* (Oxford: Oxford University Press, 1982).

Cohen, G. A., *Karl Marx's Theory of History: A Defence* (Oxford: Clarendon Press, 1978).
——, *History, Labour and Freedom: Themes from Marx* (Oxford: Clarendon Press, 1988).
Draper, H., 'The Death of the State in Marx and Engels', *Socialist Register* (1970).
Duncan, G., *Marx and Mill: Two Views of Social Conflict and Social Harmony* (Cambridge: Cambridge University Press, 1973).
Evans, M., *Karl Marx* (London: Unwin & Allen, 1975).
Fine, R., *After the Revolution: The Politics of Hegel, Marx and Arendt* (London: UCL, 2000).
——, *Political Investigations: Hegel, Marx, Arendt* (New York: Routledge, 2001).
Francis, W., *Karl Marx* (London: Fourth Estate, 1999).
Fraser, I., *Hegel and Marx: The Concept of Need* (Edinburgh: Edinburgh University Press, 1998).
Fromm, E., *Marx's Concept of Man* (New York: Ungar, 1966).
Hook, S., *From Hegel to Marx: Studies in the Intellectual Development of Karl Marx* (University of Michigan Press, 1962).
Hunt, G., 'Development of the Concept of Civil Society in Marx', *History of Political Thought*, Vol. 8 (1987).
Husami, Z., 'Marx on Distributive Justice', *Philosophy and Public Affairs*, Vol. 8, No. 1 (1978).
Hyppolite, J., *Studies on Marx and Hegel* (London: Heinemann Educational, 1969).
Kocis, R., 'An Unresolved Tension in Marx's Critique of Justice and Rights', *Political Studies*, Vol. 34, No. 3 (1986).
Laclau, E., 'The Specificity of the Political: The Poulantzas-Miliband Debate', *Economy and Society*, Vol. 5, No. 11 (1975).
Lee, W. L., *On Marx* (Belmont: Wadsworth/Thomson Learning, 2002).
Lefevre, H., *The Sociology of Marx* (Harmondsworth: Penguin, 1972).
Levin, A., *The General Will: Rousseau, Marx, Communism* (Cambridge: Cambridge University Press, 1993).
Lukes, S., *Marxism and Morality* (Oxford: Clarendon Press, 1985).
McLellan, D., *The Thought of Karl Marx: An Introduction* (London: Macmillan, 1971).
——, *Marx Before Marxism* (Harmondsworth: Penguin, 1972).
——, *Karl Marx. His Life and Thought* (London: Macmillan, 1973).
——, *Marx* (London: Fontana, 1975).
Miliband, R., 'Poulantzas and the Capitalist State', *New Left Review*, Vol. 82 (1973).
——, 'Marx and the State', *Socialist Register* (1975).
Ollman, B., *Alienation: Marx's Concept of Man in Capitalist Society* (Cambridge: Cambridge University Press, 1976).
Plamenatz, J., *Karl Marx's Philosophy of Man* (Oxford: Clarendon Press, 1975).
Poulantzas, N., 'The Capitalist State: A Reply to Miliband and Laclau', *New Left Review*, Vol. 95 (1976).
Rader, M., *Marx's Interpretation of History* (New York: Oxford University Press, 1979).
Sanderson, J., 'Marx and Engels on the State', *Western Political Quarterly* (1973).

Singer, P., *Marx: A Very Short Introduction* (Oxford & New York: Oxford University Press, 2000).

Smart, P., *Mill and Marx: Individual Liberty and the Roads to Freedom* (Manchester: Manchester University Press, 1990).

Smith, C., *Marx at the Millenium* (London & East Haven, CT.: Pluto Press, 1996).

Stillman, P., 'Property, Freedom and Individuality in Hegel's and Marx's Political Thought', *Nomos*, Vol. 22 (1980).

Waldron, J., *Nonsense Upon Stilts: Bentham, Burke and Marx on the Rights of Man* (London: Methuen, 1987).

Walker, D. M., *Marx, Methodology and Science: Marx's Science of Politics* (Aldershot: Ashgate, 2001).

White, J. D., *Karl Marx and the Intellectual Origins of Dialectical Materialism* (Basingstoke: Macmillan, 1996).

Wood, A., 'The Marxist Critique of Justice', *Philosophy and Public Affairs*, Vol. 1, No. 3 (1972).

——, 'Marx on Right and Justice. A Reply to Husami', *Philosophy and Public Affairs*, Vol. 8, No. 3 (1979).

——, *Karl Marx* (London: Routledge & Kegan Paul, 1981).

Index